European cities towards 2000

European cities towards 2000

Profiles, policies and prospects

edited by
Alan Harding, Jon Dawson,
Richard Evans and Michael Parkinson

MANCHESTER UNIVERSITY PRESS

MANCHESTER and NEW YORK

distributed exclusively in the USA and Canada by ST. MARTIN'S PRESS, New York

Published by Manchester University Press
Oxford Road, Manchester M13 9NR, UK
and Room 400, 175 Fifth Avenue,
New York, NY 10010, USA

Distributed exclusively in the USA and Canada
by St. Martin's Press, Inc.,
175 Fifth Avenue, New York, NY 10010, USA

British Library Cataloguing-in-Publication Data
A catalogue record for this book is available from the British Library

Library of Congress Cataloging-in-Publication Data applied for
        European cities towards 2000 : profiles, policies and prospects /
        edited by Alan Harding ... [et al.].
            p.   cm.
        ISBN 0-7190-4166-X
        1. Cities and towns–Europe–Case studies. 2. Urban economics–
        Case studies.   I. Harding, Alan.
    HT131.E92 1994
    307.76'094—dc20   93-27981
                                                                 CIP

ISBN 0 7190 4166 X hardback

Typeset in Joanna
by Koinonia Limited, Manchester
Printed in Great Britain
by Biddles Limited, Guildford and King's Lynn

Contents

Foreword

This book grew out of a project entitled 'Urbanisation and the Functions of Cities in the European Community', commissioned 1990 by the Directorate-General for Regional Policy (DGXVI) of the European Commission. The study was co-ordinated and managed by the European Institute for Urban Affairs at Liverpool John Moores University. Project research was undertaken by the Institute and seven other teams based in France, Spain, Germany and Greece. The research generated detailed case study reports of twenty-four major cities in the European Community plus six thematic reports dealing with cross-national issues. A report of the project was published, under the same title, in DGXVI's series on *Regional Development Studies* in 1993. The wide-ranging nature of the report meant that city case study material necessarily appeared only in very abbreviated form.

As co-authors of the DGXVI report, we felt the city case studies were sufficiently new and important to deserve a wide readership in their own right. This volume therefore contains a selection of the city case studies along with further development of the major themes raised in the DGXVI study. We did not ask contributors to rewrite their case studies. The original studies were empirically based, interpretative essays written to a common format and we felt that, suitably edited, they were ideal for a comparative volume of this type. For those cities where we felt events had moved on considerably in the period since the research was completed, however, we asked contributors to provide updated material.

The choice of case studies to include in this volume was not an easy one. We would like to record our gratitude to all of the contributors to the DGXVI study whose efforts could not be included here but whose work has been invaluable to us: Edmond Preteceille (Centre du Sociologie Urbaine, Paris), Soledad Garcia Carbeza (Department of Economic and Managerial Studies, University of Barcelona), Harry Cocossis and Aurora Markopoulou (Ellconsult-EKEM consultancy team, Athens), Michael Wegener and Jutta Brosza (Institute für Raumplanung, University of Dortmund), Jens Dangschat (Centre for Comparative Urban Research, University of Hamburg) and Constanza Tobio (Humanities Department, University Carlos III, Madrid).

Alan Harding
Jon Dawson
Richard Evans
Michael Parkinson

Liverpool, January 1994

A note on contributors

Alan Harding, Jon Dawson and Richard Evans are all Senior Research Fellows at the European Institute for Urban Affairs, Liverpool John Moores University.

Professor Michael Parkinson is the Director of the Institute.

Franco Bianchini is a Reader in the School of Arts at DeMontford University in Leicester.

André Donzel is a member of the Centre National de la Recherche Scientifique and is based at the Centre de Recherche et Ecologie Sociale in Marseille.

Klaus Kunzmann is a Professor at the Institute für Raumplanung, University of Dortmund.

Markus Lang is a Research Assistant at the Institute für Raumplanung, University of Dortmund.

Patrick le Galès is a member of the Centre National de la Recherche Scientifique and is based at the Centre de Recherches Administrative et Politique, University of Rennes.

Abbreviations

Alderly.	Association pour le Développement de la Région Lyonnaise.
BHL.	Birmingham Heartlands Limited.
BSA.	Bilanco Sociale di Area (area Social Accounting).
CCI.	Chamber of Commerce and Industry.
CEAM.	Concerted European Action on Magnets.
CHDDA.	Custom House Docks Development Authority.
Courly.	Communauté Urbane de Lyon.
CSF.	Community Support Framework.
ERDF.	European Regional Development Fund.
ESF.	European Social Fund.
ICC.	International Convention Centre
IDA.	Industrial Development Authority.
IDO.	Integrated Development Operation.
IFSC	International Financial Services Centre.
LCC.	Lyon City Council.
LRT.	Light Rapid Transport.
MILAN.	Motor Industries Local Authority Network.
MMA.	Milan Metropolitan Area.
MOPU.	(Spanish) Ministry of Public Works.
MTTC.	Ministry of Transport, Tourism and Communications.
NEC.	National Exhibition Centre.
NIA.	National Indoor Arena.
NPCIM.	National Programme of Community Interest for Motorways.
PDS.	(Italian) Democratic Party of the Left.
PIM.	Integrated Mediterranean Programme.
PSDI.	(Italian) Social Democratic Party.
PSI.	(Italian) Socialist Party.
RENFE.	(Spanish) National Railway Company.
RPR.	Raison Parti Républicain.
SME.	Small and Medium-sized Enterprise.
STIB.	Brussels Intercommunal Transport Company
TGV.	Train Grand Vitesse (High-speed Train).
UDG.	Urban Development Grant.

Introduction

Changing cities in a changing world

In a rapidly changing economic and institutional environment, cities are once again high on the European agenda. Historically cities have been the source of much of the creativity as well as of tension in Europe and have generated much of its economic, social and cultural dynamism. However, after a long period of post-war growth, during the 1970s economic and population decline and growing social problems in many large European cities raised serious questions about their long-term futures or even viability. But during the 1980s the trend changed once again as cities re-emerged on the European agenda, not only as a source of problems or as recipients of substantial public assistance but as important economic and political actors in an emerging European-wide urban economic system.

The re-emergence of cities was driven by a variety of factors: the impact of global economic restructuring; political and administrative decentralisation within many nation states; the failure of traditional government regional policies; growing awareness of economic competition between cities in an increasingly integrated Europe and changing cultural attitudes which led to a renaissance in urban living (Parkinson et al. 1992). However, the world that European urban leaders face in the 1990s is a changing one. In some respects they face a more stable environment than that of earlier decades. Many of the factors which drove urban change in Europe in the post-war period have slowed down in recent years. The transition from manufacturing to service sector based urban economies has in the main been achieved. The scale of migration from the periphery of Europe to its core areas, and from rural to urban areas in peripheral regions, has slowed down and in some cases has been reversed. Fertility rates have declined dramatically in southern and peripheral countries and ageing populations are a more typical feature of northern European cities. The rapid growth of smaller and medium-sized cities, and the equally rapid decline of larger cities, also slowed down during the 1980s.

Despite those apparent sources of stability, new challenges are also emerging. The service sector economy itself is not necessarily stable as many cities which boomed on financial services in the 1980s have already found in the international recession of the early 1990s. Other factors still cause change – the replacing of traditional skills, long-term suburbanisation, the ageing of the population, changing household structures, intense stresses on the physical and social environment caused by growth. More threateningly, although traditional migration patterns have changed, the uncertain but large numbers of legal and illegal migrants entering western Europe from the former communist countries in the east through Germany and from the countries of the Maghreb into southern Spain and France, who flow on into major European cities, present an increasingly serious challenge. This will compound the problems of many city leaders who already face problems of successfully integrating ethnic minorities, migrants and their families into their cities' economic and social mainstream.

The experience of minorities and migrant groups underlines a wider trend. Throughout the 1980s the spatial impact of economic change was highly uneven. In many cities there was growing economic, social and political dynamism which did create increased prosperity. In others there was continuing economic decline. But neither prosperity nor poverty was equally distributed as different parts of cities and different groups within them were affected differently by change. Some benefited; others clearly did less well. As a result, in many European cities there is a continuing process of economic marginalisation, social exclusion and physical segregation of vulnerable and marginal groups.

Despite some signs of convergence between cities and regions, urban Europe remains enormously heterogeneous. The different historical, institutional, economic, social and environmental experiences of cities in different nation states still generates diversity. Equally, despite an increasingly integrated international and European economy, which transcends national boundaries, geography and location still affect the overall shape of the European urban system. The economic, social and environmental characteristics of cities in the peripheral areas of Europe, for example, still differentiate them from cities nearer to the economic centre of Europe and present them with particular challenges. Nevertheless, a more economically and institutionally integrated European urban system has been emerging in recent years. New economic and institutional relationships, alliances and networks have been formed as cities seek new functions and niches in a dynamic European-wide system of economic and political hierarchies. Two contradictory trends are apparent as cities seek to define their role. At one level there is a pattern of increasing political and institutional collaboration between cities as they seek common solutions to common problems. But there is also an economic logic which encourages cities to compete with each other to attract increasingly scarce, mobile international capital. In particular, the conflict between the economic and social logic became more, not less, marked throughout the 1980s. This competitive search for economic growth and increased international weight has generated substantial costs as well as benefits, losers as well as winners.

Markets, politics and cities in a global economy

The most important factor affecting Europe's cities during the past decade has clearly been the process of economic transformation. The profound changes that have taken place in the global economy over the last two decades have affected major urban areas directly and indirectly. The direct effects are the result of a progressive shift to an information or post-industrial economy (Castells 1989; Savitch 1988) which is increasingly organised on a global rather than national basis (Sassen 1991). This has had important consequences for business locational choices, patterns of sectoral change and the nature of urban labour markets. Rapid economic change in urban Europe has been triggered by two interrelated processes: economic globalisation and technological innovation. Globalisation is a product of the ever-growing importance of international – as against domestic – trade, the liberalisation of global capital movements, the industrialisation of previously underdeveloped regions of the world and the continued expansion and influence of multinational corporations. As the global competition for trade has grown, the comparative strength of Europe as a base for the production of goods and services has been challenged not just by traditional competitors such as the United States and Japan but increasingly by the newly-industrialising regions of the Pacific Rim and Latin America.

But European businesses have no necessary attachment to place.

Large corporations owe their allegiance to shareholders, not to the localities or countries where they were founded. They have been instrumental in creating a new international division of labour which has both benefits and costs for Europe (Knox and Agnew 1989). European-owned corporations have actively globalised, for example, by shifting basic production to areas outside Europe which offer cheaper labour and favourable financial regimes. On the other hand, foreign-owned corporations have increasingly become active in Europe and now depend to a significant degree on the buoyancy of the huge European market. As a result, the relationship between decision-making in the corporate sector and national economic interests has become increasingly tenuous.

Increased global competition has triggered a search for new ways of ensuring corporate profitability. Europe is broadly unable or unwilling to compete with newly-industrialising areas on the basis of labour costs and financial incentives. The major corporations have therefore relied on the development and application of new technologies and working practices in their attempts to increase productivity and promote innovation. Some commentators argue that recent changes in the way production is organised have produced a strikingly new system of flexible specialisation (Scott 1988). Others stress the continuities between old and new production methods (Lovering 1990). Whatever their differences, both sides agree that corporations in Europe and elsewhere have effectively sought to compete at the global scale by utilising comparative advantages in the knowledge industries. The technological revolution has had different implications for the main sectors of the European economy. Broadly speaking, the sectors which have fared worst are the primary and heavy industries and those producing standardised consumer goods for the mass market. Global competition has been most intense in these industries and European producers have been able to survive only through intense capital restructuring, rationalisation and job-shedding. Other manufacturing sectors have fared better. They include advanced assembly industries and those which are either research and development-intensive or produce specialist, designer goods for affluent consumers in niche markets.

Change within the manufacturing sector has meant that traditional semi-skilled and unskilled manual jobs have disappeared in huge numbers. Even if we discount the substantial proportion of service jobs in modern manufacturing – white-collar professional, managerial and technical occupations – service employment now dominates urban labour markets. The service sector increasingly accounts for more than seventy per cent of all city employment. Within the service sector, the most spectacular growth has been in financial and business services: precisely those sectors which enable production and distribution to be organised on a global scale. Consumer and personal services have also grown, though more slowly, reflecting the rise in real incomes and leisure time of those in work. In contrast, the re-evaluation of national welfare state strategies since the late 1970s has generally seen stagnation in public sector employment which had hitherto been the fastest-growing segment of services.

The spatial implications of economic change

Changing business locational factors and the recent experience of sectoral change have produced very complex patterns of spatial change. Standard textbook analyses of the balance of regional economic power in Europe have traditionally been framed in terms of core and periphery (Hull, Jones and Kenny 1988). Definitions of the European core have varied, but they generally point to the existence of golden triangles – for example those linking London, Paris and the Ruhr or Birmingham, Milan and Hamburg – which define areas where the bulk of production and control and command functions are concentrated. The areas beyond the core, the peripheral regions, are invariably judged to have less economic potential and fewer links to the global economic system.

Core-periphery definitions provide a reasonable guide to the historical pattern of industrialisation in Europe but their relevance to the geography of post-industrial development has increasingly been questioned. In the 1980s two processes – economic decentralisation and reconcentration – affected patterns of regional and urban development in complex ways which can not easily be captured by the traditional distinction between core and periphery. Economic decentralisation was consistent with the argument that established industrial metropolitan areas were no longer the strongest magnets for economic growth and were losing out to smaller towns and cities and areas on the metropolitan fringe. This debate was essentially trying to come to terms with a process of economic decentralisation which saw rapid development in European urban areas that had traditionally been less industrialised. These areas also offered modern locational advantages: local strengths in higher education, good residential and cultural facilities, clean environments and less congested communications infrastructures.

Much attention was focused on spectacular growth rates within the Alpine and Mediterranean regions, remote from the traditional European core. This led to speculation whether the economic gravity of Europe was shifting inexorably southward to the smaller, expanding urban centres of southern Germany, southern France, northern Italy and even north-eastern Spain. Closer examination of the process of change, along with the experience of the later 1980s, tempered such speculation for three principal reasons. First, it became apparent that the smaller urban areas of southern Europe were not the only beneficiaries of economic decentralisation. Whilst Grenoble, Sophia Antipolis and the districts of the third Italy, for example, undoubtedly experienced a surge in economic activity, so did some of the more established urban centres in the same broad region, for example Frankfurt, Milan, Munich, Barcelona. Overall changes in the levels of economic activity in the larger cities did not match those of their smaller neighbours. But this was primarily because they started from a much larger economic base and were also adjusting to the restructuring of mature industrial sectors.

Second, the development of new industrial districts was by no means confined to the Alpine-Mediterranean belt. Small, independent cities in northern Europe, which could offer many of the locational advantages of the south and had little or no legacy of heavy industry, also experienced considerable growth. Some of these also lay beyond the traditional European core, for example Rennes in France. Third, and most important to the concerns of this book, there was a process of economic reconcentration which revived the fortunes of some of the older metropolitan centres.

From the mid-1980s it became apparent that much of the growth in high-level private services, particularly in financial and business services, was concentrated in Europe's largest and most powerful cities. There was no sign that senior decision-makers in the control and command sectors of the European economy were willing to use the potential of new telecommunications technologies to transfer their operations to more peripheral locations. Quite the reverse. Major metropolitan areas, situated at the centre of communications networks and offering easy access to national and international institutions, the arts, cultural and media industries, if anything became more attractive to international finance houses, corporate headquarters and producer service companies.

By the end of the 1980s, it was possible to refine the traditional core-periphery analysis and identify three broad economic areas in Europe. The **old core** covered the older industrial areas of northern Europe which had been subject to much industrial restructuring but retained its pre-eminence in the command and control functions which underpin the process of economic globalisation. A **new core** covered the historically less industrialised Alpine and Mediterranean areas which had benefited from recent growth in modern industrial sectors. The new core did not supplant the old core. Rather, these two areas together formed an expanded European core.

The European **periphery** embraced Greece, Portugal, southern Italy, southern and western Spain, Sardinia, Corsica, western France, the Republic of Ireland and northern Scotland. This area was characterised by poor infrastructure, a reliance on technologically undeveloped and vulnerable indigenous enterprises and limited inward investment, often based on branch plants performing routine assembly functions. Location within one of these areas continued to be important to the prospects for urban development; but it did not automatically imply success or failure. As we shall argue, cities are not simply passive victims or fortunate beneficiaries of impersonal economic forces. Decisions taken within cities can and do play a role in shaping the way these forces work.

Metropolitan resurgence?

One indicator of the change brought about by economic and institutional change is the growth in population of many of Europe's major cities in the later 1980s. Cities have experienced a demographic transition in recent decades. Higher income levels and better social and health provision produced a general decline in mortality rates, soon followed by reductions in fertility rates. A broad balance between births and deaths now means that indigenous national populations are not growing quickly as they did in the post-war period. This trend occurred first in those old core cities which industrialised earliest. It emerged more recently in peripheral cities which, generally, have higher, if declining birth rates.

Despite the growing pressure for migration to EC countries from eastern Europe and the Maghreb, the influx of foreign workers has also slowed considerably. The end of the economic boom heralded a big reduction in the scale of international immigration as employment opportunities dwindled and national governments imposed stricter immigration controls. The declining scale of international and rural–urban migration, and the convergence in national mortality and fertility rates mean that urban population sizes are a reasonably good guide to the pattern of metropolitan economic development.

Several trends both reflect and explain the pattern of urbanisation in Europe since the war. Whilst different cities grew or declined at different times, there is a clear cycle of urban change – urbanisation, suburbanisation, deurbanisation and reurbanisation. In the urbanisation phase cities grow rapidly. In the suburbanisation phase, the central cities decline whilst the wider metropolitan population grows. In the deurbanisation phase the entire metropolitan area loses population. With reurbanisation the population of the cities grows once again. The 1950s were an era of urban growth, with large-scale movement of people from rural to urban areas throughout Europe, especially to the larger cities. By the end of the 1960s, this phase of the urban cycle had ceased in many countries. But it continued in the peripheral countries of Spain, Portugal, Greece and Ireland. Suburbanisation and deurbanisation were prevalent in the 1970s as larger old core cities, especially their centres, lost population and smaller cities grew. Peripheral cities have increasingly followed this trend. Despite an important time-lag, cities throughout Europe have converged in their patterns of urban development.

During the 1980s a pattern of reurbanisation emerged in some European cities. This process had two elements. First, the growth rate of smaller cities slowed down. Second, larger cities which had steadily declined throughout the 1960s, 1970s and early 1980s began to grow again in the second part of the 1980s. Reurbanisation was particularly marked in the former West Germany, reflecting immigration from the former East Germany and eastern Europe. However, this trend was not confined to Germany. It has also emerged in cities in France, the Netherlands and Britain. Between 1980 and 1985, only Seville in the periphery and Lyon in the new core of the cities studied in this book increased in population. But the position changed dramatically between 1985 and 1990. The old

Table 1 Population change (%) in selected city cores and rings, 1980-90, with indication trends*

	1980-85			1985-90		
	CORE	**RING**	**TREND**	**CORE**	**RING**	**TREND**
W. Berlin	-0.49	0	S	2.52	0	R
Frankfurt	**-1.01**	**-0.4**	**D**	**1.62**	**0.06**	**R**
Paris	-1.02	0.66	S	1.01	2.06	R
Seville	**0.16**	**1.19**	**U**	**0.75**	**0.52**	**U**
Valencia	-0.41	1.26	S	0.6	0.48	R
London	-0.38	-0.6	D	0.56	-0.32	R
Dortmund	-1.15	-0.56	D	0.54	0.37	R
Amsterdam	**-1.18**	**0.57**	**S**	**0.34**	**0.47**	**R**
Madrid	-0.63	3.16	S	0.28	0.07	R
Hamburg	-0.77	0.06	S	0.24	0.06	R
Rotterdam	**-0.28**	**0.56**	**S**	**0.22**	**0.28**	**R**
Lyon	**0.07**	**-0.04**	**R**	**0.07**	**1.21**	**R**
Barcelona	-0.58	0.71	S	0.04	-0.04	R
Brussels	**-0.95**	**0.02**	**S**	**-0.17**	**0.04**	**S**
Birmingham	**-0.33**	**0**	**D**	**-0.37**	**0.06**	**S**
Copenhagen	-0.59	-0.12	D	-0.72	0.14	S
Milan	**-2.02**	**0.6**	**S**	**-1.03**	**0.35**	**S**
Marseilles	-1.1	1.57	S	-1.1	2.84	S
Glasgow	-1.06	-0.17	D	-1.41	-0.32	D

* **U = Urbanising, S = Suburbanising, D = Deurbanising, R = Reurbanising.**

Source: Drewett *et al.* 1992

core cities of Amsterdam and Rotterdam, the new core cities of Frankfurt and Lyon and the peripheral city of Seville increased in population. Moreover, the rate of population decline slowed significantly in Brussels and Milan.

Table 1 shows that reurbanisation, though not universal, has been a marked trend in cities across Europe since the mid-1980s, often reversing decades of suburbanisation or absolute population decline. It is a feature of many of the case study cities examined in this book – those in bold type in the table.

Reurbanisation is a complex mixture of economic, social and demographic trends and has a variety of social, economic and environmental consequences. The most important factor in reurbanisation is almost certainly the successful restructuring of metropolitan economies and the rapid development of higher-order service-sector activities in the centres of many large cities. Economic resurgence has been paralleled by cultural changes which have seen older and younger households – often child-free with above average incomes – move back to take service-sector jobs or enjoy the cultural and lifestyle advantages of urban living. It has also been encouraged by city governments undertaking initiatives to revitalise their city centres. The revival of urban cultural activities, lengthening travel-to-work times, and public and private sector investment in prestigious urban regeneration schemes have also made living within cities more attractive. In some cities, evidence suggests that higher birth rates amongst ethnic communities is fuelling population growth.

The process of selective reurbanisation has further contributed to the image of cities as economic assets rather than social liabilities and has created renewed political interest in their role and future. However, reurbanisation brings social costs as well as economic benefits. Low-income residents and low value-added economic activities can get displaced from city centres or squeezed into less desirable areas with fewer facilities as gentrification occurs. Despite such problems the trend seems likely to continue in many cities. Indeed, the late 1980s and early 1990s could be a watershed for cities in Europe and mark the beginning of their demographic and economic renaissance.

Towards the divided city

The recent process of economic change might suggest that major metropolitan centres have become much more dynamic in recent years. It must be remembered, though, that improved urban fortunes are not necessarily shared equally by all groups within a city's population. Examinations of the general processes of economic change often imply that growth is good and decline is bad. The latter part of this statement is almost always true. But the former is much more problematic once we recognise the realities of contemporary occupational structures. In truth, growth is good for some but not for all. Modern labour markets bear little resemblance to those of the post-war boom period when employment opportunities were broadly shared between groups (of males) possessing different levels of skill. The labour shake-out in manufacturing meant the disappearance of huge numbers of manual jobs, whereas such growth as there was in manufacturing employment tended to draw on specialised, highly-qualified, non-manual labour.

In the service sector, employment has grown at both ends of the skill spectrum. The growing supply of knowledge-intensive professional, managerial and technical jobs has meant that good salaries and conditions have increasingly become available to well-qualified, largely indigenous male, middle-class workers. The expansion in consumer and personal services, on the other hand, has largely drawn on female and ethnic minority workers and provides jobs that are often insecure, part-time and poorly paid. The net effect of occupational changes in manufacturing and services has been a strong polarisation in incomes, employment standards and job security between different groups within the urban work-force.

The creation of a dual labour market, caused by the progressive erosion of intermediate occupations, has been a major factor in the recent development of divided cities (Fainstein, Gordon and Harloe 1992). Even in those cities that are generally argued to be booming, there has been a heavy price to pay for those groups whose access to the more secure, better-paid service-sector jobs is limited. Structural unemployment is no longer simply a feature of traditionally depressed areas. Many potential workers in the most successful cities, be they young labour-market entrants or older workers displaced from declining sectors, lack the skills needed in modern services.

As incomes have become more polarised, so social segregation has widened. Households able to command reasonable salaries have found that their standards of living have grown whilst those excluded from the economic mainstream have suffered in absolute and relative terms. The latter have become concentrated in the poorest-standard accommodation in the public and private sectors. The growing trend toward inner city gentrification, whilst it brings more affluent groups back into the city, has been paralleled by the growing geographical and economic marginalisation of the most dependent social groups at a time when social welfare provision has often been cut back. This process is particularly apparent amongst the growing ethnic minority communities in urban Europe who often face discrimination in the housing and labour markets as well as the problems caused by language barriers. The continuing process of family reunification and higher fertility rates amongst ethnic minorities threatens to depress their marginal status still further unless better ways can be found of integrating ethnic minority communities into the economic mainstream.

The national context

National policies are an important part of the context in which cities have to respond to economic change. The institutional, financial, planning and legislative frameworks still vary enormously amongst European countries. Nevertheless, three trends which transcend national boundaries are worth noting. The first is that throughout the 1980s the balance between national, regional and local responsibilities and powers has been changing in many European countries. In particular, there has been a growing pattern of decentralisation of powers and responsibilities to lower levels of government. Traditionally decentralised countries like Germany and the Netherlands have continued that process. But even more traditionally centralised countries like Belgium, France, Spain and Italy have been creating or increasing the authority of regional and urban institutions throughout the 1980s.

National motives varied. Sometimes the changes were in response to regional demands for greater territorial autonomy. Sometimes governments were anxious to dismantle centralised decision-making systems created in the post-war period. Sometimes national leaders were anxious to shift responsibility for difficult problems of urban economic restructuring down to local level. The degree of national fiscal support given to regional and urban institutions to face their new responsibilities varied and brought with them differing degrees of financial difficulties. Nevertheless, the important point is that decentralisation created greater autonomy and political space at the lower levels of decision-making, which many of Europe's most dynamic urban and regional leaders exploited to develop new political roles for themselves and new economic strategies for their areas. By contrast, where countries did less to decentralise, as in Portugal, Greece, Ireland and Britain, cities have fewer powers and perhaps less capacity to generate local responses to economic restructuring.

A second general trend in the 1980s was the emergence of more explicit national urban strategies in many European countries. The countries which urbanised first and hence experienced urban decline first – Britain, France and Germany – were the first to develop systematic urban policies. The process which began during the late 1960s increased in the 1980s. But the trend emerged in many other countries during the 1980s. The scale and sophistication of national strategies still varies and they remain relatively undeveloped in some countries, but national recognition of the importance of cities and their problems strengthened throughout the 1980s and should continue through the 1990s.

Paradoxically, a third trend was growing; recognition of the economic opportunities for cities, which was encouraged by increased awareness of the importance of economic competition between nations and cities during the 1980s and the potentially increased pace of that process after the creation of the Single European Market. Urban leaders became more aware of the need to avoid falling behind the already successful European cities and sought to identify new economic niches in the European economy. But national leaders also became conscious of the potential contribution of cities to national economic competitiveness and performance. In particular, in many countries the contribution of capital and larger cities was acknowledged and the governmental restrictions that had been placed upon their growth by redistributive regional and planning policies in the 1970s were frequently relaxed during the 1980s. This encouraged the economic and population resurgence of many cities, but it also encouraged the growth of economic competition amongst European cities. In these three ways, national strategies guarantee that cities will remain high on both domestic and European agendas during the 1990s. This will no doubt be encouraged by the growing interest of supranational bodies like the European Commission in urban problems and opportunities, which also led to an increased and sharper policy focus upon urban issues during the late 1980s, and which is expected to continue.

The case-studies

This book focuses upon the way in which these wider economic, social and institutional changes have been played out in a number of major urban areas in Europe. Case-studies present in-depth examination of the major themes identified in this introduction. The choice of case-studies reflects a number of key variables which are important to understanding the nature and effects of European urban change. First, in order to strengthen the book's comparative focus, we have chosen areas which together illustrate the heterogeneity of urban Europe. The case-studies therefore focus upon the experience of cities in each of the three broad areas of Europe – the old core, the new core and the periphery – and provide an indication of the diversity and variety that can be found in urban Europe.

Second, we wish to explore the role of strategic decision-making in the process of urban change. In so doing, we do not underestimate the structural economic and social forces which constrain the freedom of decision-making choice. But we do insist that politics as much as economics help to shape relationships within and amongst European cities. It is therefore important to ask what decision-makers have done to help cities adapt to and exploit these wider forces. The case-studies examine the parts that decision-makers at various levels of the public sector, along with private and community sector leaders, played in urban change over the last decade. They describe the patterns of institutional restructuring and the mobilisation of resources for urban development and examine the factors that helped, or hindered, the development of strategic responses. They look at the different kinds of economic strategies they have adapted to confront the consequences of economic change.

Third, we are concerned with the distributive consequences that flow from economic and political change. The case-studies ask whether there has been a clear pattern of costs and benefits – of losers as well as winners – in those cities where there has been a highly competitive search for economic growth and increased international weight during the last decade. They also examine the pattern of costs and benefits in those cities where there has been less commitment to competition. Finally, they assess whether there has been conflict, or a broad balance, between economic and social logic and assess the implications these relations have for achieving social cohesion within cities.

The case-studies cover the following cities: in the old core of Europe the experiences of Birmingham, Brussels, Amsterdam and Rotterdam are examined, the last two being combined in a single chapter; in the new core, Frankfurt, Lyon, Milan and Montpellier are discussed; Dublin and Seville illustrate the experience of cities in the periphery of Europe. With the exception of Montpellier, they are all major metropolitan areas with central city populations of 500,000 or more set within wider conurbations of over one million. Montpellier is included because we considered it essential that at least one of the smaller, dynamic cities of the new core should be examined. All of the cities are commonly perceived to have a growing European profile and to have developed significantly during the last decade.

The experience of the case-study cities and the broader lessons they suggest are brought together in the concluding chapter. This looks at the characteristics of urban economic competitiveness and assesses the extent to which key urban decision-makers have been able to change or affect them. It asks whether the experience of the case-studies suggests that we are witnessing the emergence of an entrepreneurial European city and the implications such a trend might have in the years to 2000. Finally it identifies the main sources of potential instability and change both within and amongst cities and outlines the main implications for decision-makers who will shape urban development policies in the coming years.

References

Castells, M. (1989), *The Informational City* (Oxford: Blackwell).

Drewett, R. *et al.* (1992), *The Future of European Cities: The role of science and technology*, Prospective Dossier No. 4, FAST Monitor Programme (Brussels: European Commission) European Commission 1991: The Regions in the 1990s (Brussels: European Commission).

Fainstein, S.S., Gordon, I. and Harloe, M. (eds) (1992), *Divided Cities: New York and London in the contemporary world* (Oxford: Blackwell).

Hull, A., Jones, T. and Kenny, S. (1988), *Geographical Issues in Western Europe* (Harlow: Longman).

Knox, P. and Agnew, J. (1989), *The Geography of the World Economy* (London: Edward Arnold).

Lovering, J. (1990), 'Fordism's unknown successor: a comment on Scott's theory of flexible accumulation and the re-emergence of regional economies', *International Journal of Urban and Regional Research* 14 (1), 159-74.

Parkinson, M., Bianchini, F., Dawson, J., Evans, R. and Harding, A. (1992), *Urbanisation and the Functions of Cities in the European Community* (Brussels: European Commission).

Sassen, S. (1991), *The Global City* (Princeton, NJ: Princeton University Press).

Savitch, H.V. (1988), *Post-Industrial Cities* (Princeton, NJ: Princeton University Press).

Scott, A.J. (1988), "Flexible production systems and regional development: The rise of new industrial spaces in North America and Western Europe", *International Journal of Urban and Regional Research* 12 (2), 171-86.

Part I Old core cities

1

Amsterdam and Rotterdam

Alan Harding

Amsterdam and Rotterdam, the two largest cities in the Netherlands, lie within the country's western core region, the Randstad; literally, the 'rim city'. The Randstad covers a quarter of Dutch territory and exerts more influence within the Netherlands than do the Paris and London regions within France and the United Kingdom. Forty-five per cent of the Dutch population is there, along with fifty per cent of the country's employment, seventy per cent of domestic head offices, sixty-five per cent of research and development and high tech companies, ninety-three per cent of foreign services and eighty per cent of foreign commercial enterprises (van der Cammen, *et al*, 1988). In contrast to the unified 'global city' model, the Randstad is a complex polynuclear urban agglomeration within which separate cities perform independent though sometimes overlapping regional, national and international functions.

Because of their common regional location and similar experiences of national and regional economic, political and administrative conditions, this chapter compares these two cities. But such similarities cannot mask substantial differences between the two in historical, functional and cultural terms and in their respective urban forms. Relations between the two cities are based more on independence and rivalry than on functional integration and complementarity within the Randstad region. This situation shows every sign of deepening in the competitive economic environment of the 1990s.

Amsterdam is the capital city of the Netherlands, and its financial and cultural centre, though not the Government and administrative centre, which is found in the Hague. Rotterdam is dominated by trade, distribution and allied commerce and industry. Between them, the two cities form the largest and most advanced international trading and distribution complex in western Europe. They encompass two ports; the world's largest by tonnage shipped (Rotterdam) and the fifth largest in Europe (Amsterdam), plus two airports, one of which is of major international importance.

The key 'gateway' role which the two cities perform means they are linked into a vast regional, national and international goods and passenger transportation network, encompassing road, rail, waterway, pipeline and air links. Schiphol airport serves 207 destinations in ninety-one countries and ranks fourth and fifth respectively amongst European airports in freight and passenger trade. International trade flows to and from the cities are further served by a dense network of motorways, trains and waterways which provide southern links to Belgium and into France and southern Europe, eastern and south-eastern routes to Germany which lead to northern, central and eastern Europe, and western links to the main inter-continental shipping routes. The waterway system links both cities to the North Sea. Both cities also have river or canal links to the continent's busiest internal waterway – the 1320 km stretch of the River Rhine serving Germany and beyond – and, via the Rhine–Marne Canal and the River Meuse, to Belgium and France. The completion of the Rhine–Main–Danube canal will make much of eastern Europe accessible by waterway too.

The train system links the two central cities, plus Schiphol airport and the port areas to the national and European network. The two cities tap into the national motorway system, which serves all Dutch cities before linking into the networks of neighbouring countries via their respective city ringways. Most of the motorway and railway system is jointly used by goods and passenger traffic. The resulting congestion has been the subject of much debate in Randstad in recent years. Amsterdam is linked by pipeline to North Sea oilfields, whilst Rotterdam is connected to other parts of the Netherlands, Belgium and Germany by pipelines for oil and chemical products.

Historical development

The early origins of Amsterdam and Rotterdam were as fishing ports which developed trading and transhipment functions when their rivers, the Amstel and the Rotte, were dammed in the thirteenth century. This was but one stage in what has become an ongoing artificial adaptation of the environment by dam-building, reclamation and navigation projects; key characteristics of Dutch economic and urban development.

The two cities grew rapidly in the late sixteenth and seventeenth centuries, initially as a result of an influx of artisans and merchants fleeing the Spanish during the Eighty Years War, and later on the basis of the riches generated by Dutch colonialism. The second major urban expansion period, after the war-torn stagnation of the next 150 years or so, came in the later nineteenth and early twentieth centuries. Initially the impetus was external rather than the result of growing domestic industrial production. Both cities benefited from the increased trade which followed rapid industrialisation in the Ruhr area, the liberalisation of trade associated with laissez-faire capitalism, and developments in transport technology. Far-sighted local entrepeneurship helped to intensify the trading and commercial functions of the two cities by providing greater market access in the form of the North Sea Canal, opened in 1876, and the New Waterway. The latter, opened in 1872, effectively gave the Rhine a new estuary, through Rotterdam and the Hook of Holland, to the North Sea. Given Amsterdam's more difficult access to the Rhine, this began the pattern of water-borne trading advantage over Amsterdam which is readily apparent in the modern Rotterdam.

A late-nineteenth-century crisis in Dutch agriculture saw large-scale migration to both cities, particularly to Rotterdam. There was also an influx of east European immigrants fleeing religious persecution, leading to substantial Jewish settlement in Amsterdam. Rotterdam grew from 110,700 inhabitants in 1850 to 318,500 in 1900. Between 1870 and 1900, Amsterdam grew from 255,000 to 510,000. Expansion followed the social and political patterns common elsewhere in Europe. The municipal boundaries were extended rapidly through annexation of neighbouring territory, and low-standard housing was hastily erected by private speculators to house the growing population. Poor housing and health standards in the cities provided the impetus for proto social-democratic-movements – initially much stronger in Amsterdam than in Rotterdam – promoting social reform and urban planning.

The period also witnessed the first significant wave of Dutch industrialisation. Port cities played an important role, developing dockside processing of raw materials, industries related to large metropolitan markets (apparel, printing) and port-related services (transport and distribution), banking and insurance. Growth in port facilities and related industry spread along the main waterways, spawning new developments in heavy industries. Shipbuilding became a feature of both ports. Rotterdam's first petroleum harbour was opened in 1929, and Shell developed its first refinery there in 1937. Although slowed down by the depression of the 1930s, growth continued in the two cities both physically – aided by annexations and developments in the public transport infrastructure – and in population. By 1945 Amsterdam had 773,000 inhabitants; Rotterdam 610,000.

To this day, the war experience still underpins many of the differences between the two cities. Words can barely convey the scale of devastation suffered in Rotterdam. In one bombing raid in 1940 – which promptly ended official Dutch war resistance – 25,000 homes and nearly 7,000 commercial, industrial and other buildings were destroyed. One thousand, one hundred people were killed and seventy-eight thousand made homeless. Much of the harbour was then obliterated in the final phase of the war. Amsterdam's port and airport were also destroyed by bombing, but the city survived the war with essentially the same urban form it had had in 1939. Rotterdam, on the other hand, emerged with virtually no city centre or harbour. The history of post-war Rotterdam, therefore, is indistinguishable from the history of public policy in the period, such was the volume of state investment needed to re-establish the city. This has made the city's almost continuous post-war redevelopment task more difficult because of its sheer scale. Paradoxically, however, it was less severe than Amsterdam's, since the city did not have to live with the legacy of pre-industrial infrastructure.

The Randstad was the major beneficiary of post-war reconstruction in the Netherlands. The critical international trading roles performed by Amsterdam and Rotterdam ensured that they experienced continued expansion in employment and population, despite the beginnings of suburbanisation and population dispersal. Continued migration to the booming Randstad, plus high Netherlands birth-rates meant that by 1960 Amsterdam's population had reached 869,000 and Rotterdam's 730,000. But the cities were unable to satisfy heavy housing demand. Intra-city suburbs developed to the west, north, south and south-east of pre-war Amsterdam, requiring nominal municipal boundary extensions in 1966 and 1977. The building of the city's ringway, combined with the ever-growing importance of the rebuilt Schiphol airport, gave significant impetus to new housing and non-port-related industrial and commercial development in the southern and south-eastern 'lobes' which straddled the municipal boundary, and in neighbouring authorities like Amstelveen, Haarlemmermeer, and Ouder Amstel. This period saw the start of the shift of economic gravity to south Amsterdam and beyond which characterises the present-day situation.

In Rotterdam, reconstruction of the port and city centre were the immediate post-war priorities. The rebuilt port was continuously extended westward along the southern banks of the New Waterway. The major Botlek and Europort harbour and industrial areas were completed in 1957 and 1968 respectively. In 1962 Rotterdam overtook New York as the largest port in the world by tonnage handled; a position it has retained ever since. In addition to its transhipment, storage and distribution roles, the port provided the foundation for the two pillars of Rotterdam's post-war industrial economy – the massive oil/petrochemicals complex and shipbuilding – as well as for supporting sectors in the 'dry' economy in insurance services, for example. The municipal boundary expanded to include the new harbour areas, giving the municipality of Rotterdam a sort of 'tail' along the waterway. But it could not prevent the effective geographical and psychological break between city and port. The city centre was completely rebuilt on a grid system, in functionalist style, with wide boulevards suitable for heavier car traffic, and almost exclusively for commercial, retail, cultural and public administrative uses. New housing did not appear in the inner city; rather it was developed in districts beyond the inner ring and outside the municipality completely.

Economic development

The populations of Amsterdam and Rotterdam peaked in the mid-1960s at around 870,000 and 730,000 respectively. From then on the selective flight from the cities, which had fuelled steady sub-urbanisation in the previous two decades, intensified considerably. This was intensified in the 1970s by the onset of changes in urban household structures (greater proportions of single-person households) and by greater demands for residential space. Both led to less intensive use of housing space in the cities. Population outflow was fuelled by families unable or unwilling to satisfy their housing needs within the central municipalities. The more affluent were bound for higher-status suburban areas, the poorer for supported housing with better space and amenity standards in one of the growing centres of the periphery. Both cities became characterised by under-representation of children and over-representation of twenty to forty year-olds, with high levels of non-family households.

The 1960s – an era of continued national economic prosperity – also marked the beginning of substantial immigration, the other main characteristic of the modern urban population structure. Immigrants, lured to the country to relieve pressing labour shortages, came first, from the mid-1960s onward, from the Mediterranean – principally Turkish and Moroccan, but also Spanish and Yugoslavian workers. They were joined in the 1970s by others – mainly Dutch passport-holders – from the former Dutch colonies in Surinam and the Antilles. Immigrants became concentrated disproportionately in the older pre-First World War, poor-quality housing areas of the inner cities, progressively abandoned by the more affluent white Dutch.

Urban population decline was quickly followed by employment decline. Economic decentralisation accounted for some of this, but the results of structural economic change particularly in long-established industrial sectors, the recessionary climate of the later 1970s, and higher economic growth rates outside the established core areas were more important. Decline on both fronts continued for fully three-quarters of the period from 1970 to 1990. The change was most dramatic in Rotterdam, where reliance on a few failing or restructuring sectors led to steep and rapid rises in unemployment. The shipbuilding industry collapsed in the face of competition, particularly from the Pacific Rim, and lost some eighty per cent of its work-force during the late 1970s and 1980s before stabilising on the basis of contracts in more specialist markets. Containerisation and other developments in port technology, combined with the downturn in transhipment sparked by the lull in world trade, led to falls both in demand for labour and in labour intensity. The result was a steep decline in traditional port employment. The oil and petrochemical sector too was forced into significant restructuring and employment losses. Unemployment, particularly amongst unskilled and semi-skilled workers and new, under-qualified entrants to the labour market, grew rapidly.

In Amsterdam, where the economy was more diversified, individual

changes were less spectacular but the cumulative effect in terms of
local unemployment were if anything more severe. Unemployment
rose from 20,000 in 1980 to 75,000 in 1985 before falling back to
70,000 in 1988. Losses occurred in the transport, wholesale, construction and retail fields as well as in established industrial sectors
like metals, food, glass and chemicals. Whilst growth in local public
sector employment helped cushion the effect of losses elsewhere for
much of the 1970s, the austere public expenditure climate which
followed the recession caused stagnation in this source of employment too.

From the mid-1980s however, with the revival in world trade,
there were signs of both economic resurgence and reurbanisation in
both cities. From population lows in 1985 of 676,000 in Amsterdam
and 571,000 in Rotterdam – some 200,000 and 150,000 below
their respective mid-1960s peaks – there was a slow recovery.
Although the reasons for this are complex, involving changing
household structures and residential preferences and the effect of
public policies, greater economic health was certainly a contributory
factor. Both cities emerged from the recession with stronger, restructured port and industrial sectors and both benefited from the marked
1980s growth in services.

In Rotterdam, the municipal harbour authority, with state support, invested heavily in port reorganisation and new transport
logistics. Examples can be found in the creation of 'Rotterdam
Distripark', a distribution centre near the main container-handling
points, the new European Combined Terminal for container traffic at
the mouth of the Maas, and in the development of the INTIS
computer network for monitoring cargo flow through the port.
Enormous corporate investment occurred in the petrochemicals
sector too, indicating confidence in the region on the part of key
multinationals. Significant commercial investment occurred in the
1980s as major companies like Unilever, Robeco, Shell and National
Nederlander committed themselves, through new headquarters
buildings, to remaining in a rejuvenated city centre where rents were
more comparable to Mediterranean than to northern European levels.

High-quality commercial space also developed north of the city
near the ring road. A 'Brainpark' catering for small, highly
professionalised companies was developed near a major university
site in the north-east, and a new business park towards Zestienhoven
airport saw considerable investment by distribution companies from

the Pacific Rim looking to enter the European market. Within the service sector, which grew at between six to ten per cent per year in the later 1980s, the highest growth was in business services – up more than thirty per cent between 1985 and 1989 – particularly those related to the port. Moderate growth also occurred in banking and insurance, though other areas within the region and in Amsterdam showed stronger growth. Retail and hotel and catering employment also grew steadily, fuelled by developments in leisure and entertainments such as those in the riverside-city centre 'Waterstad' area.

In Amsterdam the pattern of modern development – involving a heavier shift towards an information/service-led economy – intensified the southward shift of economic gravity towards the highly accessible ring road and the booming Schiphol airport. The southern axis now links major employment centres. Amsterdam south, the area lying between the older city and Schiphol, is the base for around 60,000 jobs and the highest-status residential and shopping areas in the city. It includes concentrations of the fashion and design industry, research organisations and audio-visual companies as well as the World Trade Centre and the highly successful Exhibition and Congress Centre. The 25,000 jobs in Amsterdam south-east are mainly commerce-related, including concentrations in the financial and medical fields. Beyond the municipal boundary, the Schiphol area itself has 50,000 jobs related to aviation and distribution. The clear loser in this process was Amsterdam city centre. Despite maintaining its pre-eminence in the fields of culture, leisure and public administration, the core area declined in employment terms from 150,000 to 80,000 in the 1980s.

Foreign investment was an important factor in Amsterdam's economic development. The largest recent growth was amongst Japanese firms establishing headquarters to manage their European trading operations, although similar US firms still outnumbered others, providing more than half of all Amsterdam-based headquarters of foreign companies. There was significant presence too from other Pacific Rim countries and from Scandinavia. The key attractions offered by Amsterdam are its location, its distributional infrastructure, the presence of Schiphol and the multilingual Dutch work-force. The 'software' infrastructure – telecommunications, the density of business services like banking, law, accountancy and the availability of international schools, high-income housing and cultural attractions –

were also important. Nissan's decision to establish its European headquarters between Schiphol and the teleport was a clear reflection of Amsterdam's attraction as a base in the run-up to the Single European Market.

In neither city did vigorous economic development translate into revitalised urban labour markets. One reason was that much investment, particularly in port and related sectors, was capital-intensive, resulting in 'jobless growth'. Where employment-creation occurred, the skill demands of the new jobs meant that suburban commuters, rather than city-centre residents, benefited most. Unemployment levels in both cities, though below their mid-1980s peaks, remained alarmingly high in 1990 – twenty-four per cent in Amsterdam, twenty per cent in Rotterdam. These figures mask wide variations amongst groups, with the low-skilled, under-qualified and disabled faring worst. However, there are higher than average concentrations of unemployed graduates in Amsterdam, because many students stay in the city on completion of their degrees.

Inevitably too, those areas where marginal groups are concentrated suffer unemployment levels far higher than the city average. The late nineteenth-/early twentieth-century housing areas exhibit the highest degrees of joblessness in both cities, although in Amsterdam the Bijlmermeer area – a massive 1960s high-rise development in the south-east periphery, which contains a high proportion of Surinamese – exhibits very high rates too. Ethnic minorities suffer disproportionately in the labour market. In Rotterdam over thirty per cent of the registered unemployed are from Surinam, the Antilles or the Mediterranean countries, whereas foreigners – including this group and other nationalities – account for only 11.8 per cent of the total population. In Amsterdam foreigners account for twenty-four per cent of the population but thirty per cent of the registered unemployed. The Amsterdam figures underplay the true nature of ethnic minority labour market disadvantage. Estimates suggest that there may be 35-40,000 illegal immigrants in the city living on insecure, marginal jobs in the informal sector. Long-term unemployment is a particular problem across all communities, especially in the 25-44 age-group. In 1990 over half of the unemployed in Rotterdam had been without work for more than two years (van Lier 1990).

Immigrants and their families seem set to constitute a growing percentage of the urban disadvantaged. Whilst new immigration has slowed, there is a continual process of family unification which increases ethnic minority populations, and family sizes amongst these groups remain larger than amongst their white Dutch counterparts. In 1990 thirty-five per cent of under-15s in Amsterdam were from ethnic minorities and they represented forty per cent of 0-4 year-olds and thirty per cent of primary school children in Rotterdam. Current projections indicate that half of the 0-4 year-old group will be from ethnic minorities in the year 2000. In both cities there are a substantial number of schools with high ethnic minority concentrations (over seventy per cent). Eighteen per cent of Rotterdam schools fall into this category. The link between education and employment is a cause of great concern. There are high drop-out rates from the education system, making access to jobs for the unqualified young very difficult. There are also high functional illiteracy rates, compounded by language difficulties amongst first-generation immigrants. Rotterdam under-performs further up the educational scale too. Only thirteen per cent of city residents have degrees compared to the national average of seventeen per cent and Amsterdam's twenty-four per cent.

The new jobs are disproportionately biased towards the more affluent areas beyond the city boundaries, with average incomes within the cities falling relative to the national average over the last twenty years whilst they have grown in the commuting ring areas. One result is rapid growth in commuting. With the exception of the south Amsterdam municipalities and outlying port areas to the west of Rotterdam, development outside the city boundaries since the 1960s was heavily weighted towards housing and local services rather than regional, national or internationally-oriented industry and commerce.

Finally, compared to cities in other European countries, the central municipalities have not experienced fiscal crises as a direct result of the impoverishment of a growing section of their resident populations. This reflects the intergovernmental financing system in the Netherlands where around ninety per cent of municipal expenditure comes from specific and general Government grants. This does not mean that crises have not occurred. The two core municipalities are prevented from facing the difficult choice of arresting any erosion in services by compensating for lost income via local taxes. In practice, welfare and social service demands from Amsterdam and Rotterdam residents increased in the 1980s but central Governments cut back on budgets and instituted stricter entitlement rules in the same period. Social housing investments and subsidies have not suffered greatly from fiscal austerity, as they have in some other European countries, but cuts in other service areas are an important factor in the widening gap between rich and poor (Oude Engberink 1990).

Development strategies

The institutional context is vital to the development strategies which affect the two cities. The planning system plays an extremely important role in the Netherlands, possibly more than in any other European country (Davies 1988). Planning responsibilities are divided between three, and occasionally four levels of government – national, regional, provincial and municipal. The most problematic element in the system has long been the regional level. The provinces have found it difficult to arbitrate effectively on inter-municipal conflicts, particularly between large core cities and their suburban municipalities. This reflects the balance of power within the system which lies overwhelmingly with the lowest tier. City interests have long been accustomed to exercising control over local development affairs. The largest cities in particular wield great influence over development not only through planning legislation but through large-scale land ownership.

The national and regional context for city planning in Amsterdam and Rotterdam has been provided by interrelated national physical planning policies and regional/industrial policies. These can roughly be divided into two periods. Those characterised by national economic difficulties – the post-war period and more recent recessionary times – saw the Randstad regarded as the key national asset for encouraging economic growth. In the more prosperous intervening period the Randstad was seen as potentially over-crowded, economically 'overheated' and a threat to development in the peripheral areas of the Netherlands.

Immediate post-war development in the two cities was heavily underwritten by the state. A powerful alliance between spending ministries and city municipalities was created which stimulated rapid urban growth – fed by high birth-rates and rural depopulation – and economic reconstruction. The success of this approach meant that by the late 1950s there were fears about the costs of such growth to the Randstad and the more peripheral areas. The dominant analysis suggested strict control over further urbanisation in the Randstad. This was to be achieved by retaining the distinctiveness of the various urban centres through the designation of intervening buffer zones, and by safeguarding the agricultural zone within the urbanised rim – the Green Heart – for non-urban uses. This has been the mainstay of policy for the Randstad ever since. The national policy review also saw the beginnings of regional policy – a system of investment incentives designed to encourage relocation and/or establishment of businesses in the periphery. The first National Physical Planning statement in1960 followed this line by suggesting that the Randstad become the preferred location only for key international functions whilst for the rest, particularly in the case of manufacturing industry, attention should be directed towards peripheral locations.

The 1960s saw higher economic growth beyond the Randstad, though it is questionable whether public policy was the decisive factor. Nevertheless, the Randstad continued to expand during the 1960s, triggering both city and suburban growth. A second Physical Planning statement in 1966, fearing continued *ad hoc* suburban development which might threaten the Green Heart, proposed a 'clustered decentralisation' away from the cities. Growth centres were designated on the outer fringes of the Randstad to attract city migrants and develop independent economic functions thus reducing commuting.

In practice, the power of independent municipalities and the greater attraction of Green Heart fringe areas as business locations limited the impact of this policy. Whilst the big cities rapidly lost population, the growth centres failed to achieve their population and economic development targets. Most residential development for commuters was realised in other municipalities and, together with commercial development, led to *ad hoc* incursions into the Green Heart (van Weesep 1985).

This experience, plus the crisis faced by the cities in the 1970s, led to the third Physical Planning statement which responded to calls within the cities for bigger housing renewal programmes but persisted with the growth centre policy, arguing that city housing redevelopment would lead to lower residential densities and that provision for population overspill would, therefore, still be needed.

The high level of investment in growth centres also made it politically difficult to discontinue the policy. It was only with the publication of the 1984 Structure Sketch for the Urban Areas, in the context of falling city populations and the economic crisis, that the Government began to favour the core cities again. Population targets for the growth centres were substantially reduced and there was a switch towards encouraging greater intensity of city land use and strengthening the international competitiveness of Randstad cities. The stage was therefore set for a full reversion to the immediate post-war analysis of the Randstad in the later 1980s.

Local planning

Planning by the Rotterdam and Amsterdam authorities had to be conducted in the context of national policies which positively discouraged growth in the two cities for much of the post-war period, and in a difficult climate of inter-municipal relations occasioned by the 'stealing' – at least in the city authorities' view – of some of the fruits of city development by highly autonomous neighbouring authorities. Immediate post-war planning concentrated on economic reconstruction – particularly the rebuilding of the port and city centre in Rotterdam – and in providing additional housing for rapidly expanding populations. The housing programme sacrificed quality to quantity, reflecting the urgency and the level of demand, and had a high social housing component. It was also achieved at the price of neglect of the pre-war neighbourhoods. In both cities there was a high degree of co-operation between municipal and private sectors on the broad direction of development. The first post-war crisis in city planning came towards the end of the 1960s. To understand the reasons for this, some understanding of the political climate is needed.

By the late 1960s, both cities had undergone two decades of almost continuous population and economic expansion which made future prosperity seem almost inevitable. However, in the older neighbourhoods, increasingly the base for new immigration, conditions had steadily deteriorated since the war. Both city authorities, in the context of Government policies to encourage population and economic decentralisation, had developed strategies to strengthen the economic base of the central cities and facilitate greater access to them by public and private transport from areas of population growth. The principal proposed means for achieving these ends were the bulldozing of inner-city housing quarters and the relocation of residents to peripheral areas, followed by the utilisation of space thereby created for central business district expansion, extensive car parks, inner-city motorway building and the development of underground transport systems. These plans aroused massive opposition which took a decisive but different form in the two cities.

Late 1960s Amsterdam was the centre of alternative cultural and political movements growing from environmental and ecological concerns, anti-consumerism, feminism and democratisation, with students a key group. These groups coalesced around a conception of the city which favoured the extension of residential and cultural quarters and the creation of lively public space rather than commercial development. This broad collection of interests, which began to have an impact on the composition of the city's dominant Labour Party (PvdA) from the late sixties onward, led opposition to the municipality's comprehensive inner-city renewal programme, in loose association with civic societies, and motivated by a desire to preserve historic quarters of the city. Groups of residents, who resisted the idea of relocation, and squatters were also active in the older neighbourhood areas.

Resistance to comprehensive redevelopment proceeded through a number of highly visible campaigns and demonstrations centred on key development projects. Some were successfully resisted. Others, such as the building of Amsterdam's first (and so far only) metro-line, were not. But they were critical in influencing the wider climate of debate. The metro development required the destruction of large residential sections of the historic inner-city Jewish quarter (Joden-hoek) and aroused concerted opposition. This culminated in violent clashes between protesters and police which delayed the opening of the line for more than ten years and provided an enduring focus for opposition groups. The significance of such protest arguably lies in the effect it had on city politics and municipal policies towards urban development. Community and student activists secured a strong foothold within the PvdA during the early 1970s, sufficient to paralyse decision-making during the period from 1974 to 1978. Thereafter the 'new left' wrested control of the council from the old guard. In Rotterdam the fight against inner-city neighbourhood redevelopment took a more pragmatic form. Disquiet over the costs of economic growth centred on the much more tangible pollution problems facing the city. There was also highly visible social unrest – including anti-Turkish riots in the early 1970s – in inner-city housing areas threatened by redevelopment and which had seen no significant investment since the war. Opposition forces in Rotterdam also quickly gained in political importance, dominating the PvdA by the mid-decade.

The 1970s had a number of important implications for urban development. Comprehensive redevelopment was dropped and social priorities assumed centre stage within a programme which emphasised the merits of a 'compact city', rather than one which was the daytime base for commuters from the suburbs and growth centres – a wholly different position from that advanced by central government and the provincial council. Municipal energies were concentrated on housing refurbishment and redevelopment within the older neighbourhoods for reuse by existing low-income residents. Once this priority attracted Government support, large-scale housing renewal projects were undertaken which remained extremely important throughout the 1980s and improved social housing conditions immeasurably. The new social orientation also had a less positive side. The 1970s had a strong anti-business flavour; urban housing renewal was an entirely public programme. Commercial redevelopment virtually ceased and many small traders were swept aside by redevelopment. In Amsterdam it was common for offices to be redesignated for housing development, speeding the process of employment decline in the city centre. In Rotterdam, disused harbour sites in central locations, which could have been used for commercial development, were appropriated for social housing.

Municipal policy, 1980s style

With the recession of the early 1980s and the disastrous rise in unemployment, a fundamental policy review was carried out in both cities. It became clear that urban renewal, despite its success in raising housing standards, was only a partial solution to the cities' problems and new economic activity required greater municipal sophistication in dealing with the market. Better public–private cooperation was also needed if private investment was not to become exclusively a suburban phenomenon. In both cities the earlier social orientation therefore shifted to a concern with housing and economic renewal.

Rotterdam

In Rotterdam early initiatives focused on support programmes for small businesses, particularly in urban renewal districts, retraining schemes for the unemployed and massive investment in the port's transport and communications infrastructure. There also developed a commitment to broaden the economic base of the city, initially on an indiscriminate basis. This approach was summed up in a 1984 document, proclaiming "Rotterdam – Good for All Markets". Underpinning these various elements was an attempt to use the municipality's limited powers to encourage dynamic development in the private sector. The municipality was helped considerably by the fact that even allowing for a cut-back in Government funding – generally for welfare programmes – it was able to use its many sources of income, from land-leasing, municipal utility companies and the port, to support economic development programmes, including pump-priming investment and joint ventures.

From the early 1980s and with the benefit of a pick-up in the property market, the municipality began to engage in a number of specific public–private development deals. These led to office developments which have transformed the appearance of the Weena area of the city centre, and tourism, leisure and entertainments schemes, particularly in the newly designated Waterstad area. The last formed part of the efforts made to attract tourists, visitors and residents back to a lack-lustre city centre.

Rotterdam lacks high-income housing. Ninety per cent of the housing stock is rented, giving the city a very blue-collar image, and Rotterdam's high-income workers live in areas as far afield as south Amsterdam and the coastal areas to the north of The Hague. This was seen as a weakness in attracting higher-order services and a factor in limiting the development of city-centre retail, cultural and entertainments industries. It was felt that at least a part of the commuter market, young professional people who felt a strong affinity to the city, could be tempted back if the right housing were available. Thus the heavy bias towards social housing development was changed, in

a 'renewal of urban renewal', and bigger proportions of private
housing – up to sixty per cent in some cases – built into housing
development plans. The success of one scheme – three multi-storey
apartment blocks close to the waterfront area near the city centre –
suggests that high-income housing demand is indeed high.

City-wide planning for economic development received a significant boost in the mid-1980s with the appointment of a new
Planning Director from private practice. The reinvigoration of planning which has since occurred, with strong political support, has
produced two massive redevelopment schemes which will dominate
the municipality's efforts in the 1990s – the Kop van Zuid, a "New
Manhattan" on the south bank of the Maas immediately opposite the
city centre, and the Noordrand area near Zestienhoven airport. These
are the largest in a huge range of projects in offices, retail, housing,
tourism and industrial development.

The municipality's approach to economic strategy became more
selective in the later 1980s. The rapid growth in services related to
the port, for example in the opening of the Rotterdam Energy
Futures Exchange in 1989, underlined the fact that Rotterdam's 'wet'
economy had many spin-offs for the 'dry' sector too. Whilst
retaining the emphasis on the enlivenment of the city centre, efforts
in the commercial field have focused on attracting companies which
support the logistic functions of the port, for example in legal and
insurance services and information technology. In the industrial
sector, priority is being placed on food, heavy metals and electrical
engineering.

The changed policy climate of the 1980s has led to better relations
with the private sector. Various attempts have been made to involve
financial institutions and developers at an early stage of the planning
process. Relations with the Chamber of Commerce are also much
better. A key symbol of the new co-operative spirit was the
formation, in 1989, of ROTOR, a municipality/Chamber of Com-
merce-funded organisation established, as one result of a city
commission on social and economic renewal, as the engine to propel
the process of modernisation (Albreda Advisory Commission 1988).
Whilst ROTOR's work became dominated, in practice, by the issue
of regional co-operation, it has been involved in building bridges
between public and private sectors and generating ideas for collaboration, particularly in social renewal schemes.

Amsterdam

In comparison with Rotterdam, the municipal authority in Amsterdam had a much lower profile in 1980s economic development programmes. The policy shifts in the city none-the-less followed the broad pattern seen in Rotterdam. As a result of the recession and the political maturity of the leading group within the PvdA, the compact city approach utilised for urban renewal has slowly been extended to the economic sphere. The arguments which underpinned planning in the 1980s centred on reversing the decline of urban facilities caused by earlier population loss, particularly in the city centre, through intensifying the use of city land for residential, commercial and industrial purposes. There remains a large housing component in the municipality's approach but, as in Rotterdam, a shift can be seen away from the prioritisation of social housing. The later 1980s have seen more higher-income housing, with greater private-sector involvement, in parallel with the continuing process of urban renewal.

The economic development problem facing the authority remains the massive drawing power of the southern axis. This continues to generate a somewhat schizophrenic policy approach. On the one hand planners attempt to counteract the decline of the city centre, ostensibly helping at the same time to prevent pressure for further encroachment into the Green Heart. On the other hand, those sections of the authority pursuing potential investors, often with considerable success, are helping to deepen market trends since the south is the area to which most new firms are attracted. Indeed the Economic Affairs Department, which co-ordinates the municipality's investment acquisition and marketing strategy, does not operate to a spatial remit. Rather it has concentrated on selling the city's competitive advantages and international ambience to companies in the fields of logistics, distribution and finance, particularly those in the Pacific Rim and the United States looking to make their first entry into the European market. It is also involved in attempts to capture more of the business convention market, in which Amsterdam is far ahead of Rotterdam and the Hague, and to 'buy' international public organisations.

The municipality has tried to square this circle in three ways. The north-western Sloterdijk area has been developed as a teleport in association with the Netherlands national telecommunications firm.

The resulting space for offices, high-tech companies, supporting services and housing has been utilised quickly, helping to siphon off some development pressure from the southern belt. Attempts have also been made to strengthen city-centre functions. Amsterdam city centre retains an advantage over Rotterdam since its population has actually grown in the last decade as a result of urban renewal and gentrification, resulting in a stronger base for services. To promote additional economic development orientated to regional, national or international markets, however, the municipality has developed a series of measures including the creation of underground car-parks, improvement of public spaces, the attraction of specialised offices, the development of cultural industries, including new museums, and the development of high-quality retail stores.

The final and potentially most important element is the planned development along the IJ axis. This waterway linking IJsselmeer to the east and the North Sea Canal to the west runs through the city centre immediately north of the main railway station and takes in abandoned port areas ripe for redevelopment once the necessary infrastructure is in place. The IJ axis is Amsterdam's key 1990s project and its success will largely determine whether the southern domination of development trends will continue unchallenged. There are also important signs of greater self-determination within the corporate sector in Amsterdam. One example is the Amsterdam International Financial Centre foundation – an umbrella group for key institutional interests – which has developed a broad-based plan aimed at maintaining and enhancing the city's international position in the face of stiff European competition. Such sectoral groupings will increasingly be needed if the city is to be successful in its attempts to attract international banks and other prestigious institutions.

Development debates in the two cities

There are two strands to the current debate about the two cities, on which local and national government are much closer than they have been since the early post-war period. The main issue is internationalisation and the desire to reinforce the critical gateway and commercial roles performed by Amsterdam and Rotterdam. The second is social renewal, which expresses a concern that economic success can too easily lead to a 'two-track' society. The issue of internationalisation is dominated by a concern with the Randstad's position in post-1992 Europe.

At central government level there is clear support once again for viewing the Randstad as the motor for national economic development. The general Government approach is to continue restrictions on development in the Green Heart, thus creating greater scarcity value in the cities and strengthening urban locational attractiveness, whilst dropping most disincentives to investment in the Randstad. Three issues on the national government agenda are of greatest local relevance: support for key national projects aimed at creating ' top international centres' in critical Randstad locations; infrastructural improvements to upgrade trading corridors and tackle traffic bottlenecks whilst reducing commuter flows, and facilitating regional co-operation.

Key national projects

The Kop van Zuid and IJ axis projects have both been designated as key national projects. This means that subject to satisfactory levels of involvement by private investors, which has to be organised by the municipalities, Government support will be offered through the absorption of infrastructural costs and prioritisation as locations for internationally-orientated cultural and educational institutions. Inter-departmental collaboration is also invoked to ensure co-ordinated Government decision-making to support the area-based approach. The two projects show a number of similarities. Both are based in areas left vacant by the westward shift of port activity and lie on the 'wrong' side of their respective cities; the IJ development area in the declining central northern city centre of Amsterdam and the Kop van Zuid on the south bank of the Maas, close to the city centre but not linked particularly well in either infrastructural or functional terms. Both involve high-quality office development plans which, to be successful, need to reverse current market trends towards locating nearer the Green Heart. They are phased for development from the early 1990s with the IJ project having a much more ambitious time-table for completion; seven to eight years as opposed to the Kop van Zuid's fifteen to twenty.

The Kop van Zuid development is expected to involve around

400,000 square metres of office space, 80,000 of industrial space
and 5,000 dwellings split equally between the social rented and
private sectors, the latter comprising high- and low-rise apartments.
Hotels, shops, restaurants, leisure shipping berths and tourist and
leisure facilities are also planned, with public access provided by
means of a new tube station and re-routing of tram-lines. The IJ axis
project has a similar mix to the Kop van Zuid. It plans for 350,000 to
400,000 square metres of top quality office space, 340,000 square
metres of residential space, split equally between social rented and
upper-income private tenures, with proposals for luxury hotels,
conference centres, theatres/concert hall, a shopping centre, an
extension of the existing maritime museum, a science centre and a
museum for modern art plus waterside attractions.

Infrastructural improvements

National infrastructural investments are critical to the key development projects and a number of transport developments are planned
or under discussion. New tunnels are already in construction to
strengthen the two cities' congested ring-road systems, along with
further road improvements, such as a western peripheral link
between Schiphol and the port in Amsterdam. The key debate in the
Randstad is about how to improve the flow of goods and reduce
commuter traffic, since the combination of the two is responsible for
most traffic problems. Enhancement of the public transport system is
the most important means of reducing commuter traffic and is an
important national issue. Both cities will have completed, by the end
of the 1990s, an orbital light rail system which will link up with
existing or new radial metro lines. In Amsterdam the system will
serve all of the major employment centres. An accessibility plan has
been agreed with Randstad municipalities which means that new
concentrations of employment activity will only be permitted in
areas with good access to the public transport network. Both cities
will also be linked to the TGV network. Business leaders and senior
policy makers see this having massive commercial and symbolic
value.

Regional co-operation

Central and local government increasingly recognise the need for decision-making structures which can operate on a spatial scale that reflects current economic realities rather than municipal boundaries which make little economic sense. The powerful city municipalities have realised, if reluctantly, that not all of the problems which their areas face are soluble within the city boundaries, and that the compact city approach will not automatically be accepted by neighbouring municipalities which have grown in importance in recent decades. It is clear to central government that inter-municipal competition for, or resistance to, investment can generate suboptimal outcomes which will directly affect the international competitiveness of the Randstad. It is therefore encouraging the formation of voluntary metropolitan tiers of government with a view to giving them statutory force and a range of decentralised responsibilities in the 1990s. Negotiations on this issue in both regions suggest that a common view is emerging over the problems to be faced. At the practical level, though, there is still a strong anti-urban feeling outside the cities and intense suspicion of the core municipalities.

After internationalisation, the second major issue is social renewal. Here Rotterdam is by far the more advanced in its thinking. The social renewal debate in Rotterdam arose at a time when the city was giving heavy public relations emphasis to its "New Rotterdam" economic renewal programme, and new office developments – planned many years earlier – were simultaneously materialising in the city centre. A combination of the two provoked a backlash in the city from critics who questioned the benefit of new policies, which seemed to favour the higher-qualified, for the victims of earlier redundancy and economic marginalisation. The municipal authority responded with plans for a social renewal programme whose main theme could be characterised as 'workfare, not welfare'.

In Rotterdam, the programme has developed through an *ad hoc* process, with a new social renewal team, other municipal departments and external bodies offering ideas for potential projects. These include a number of ideas for linking economic and social benefits. Examples are found in the development of a Rotterdam 'Compact' scheme, which links school pupils, their parents, school authorities and employers and offers employment opportunities to disadvantaged youngsters subject to certain standards of achievement; a 'job pool' of older long-term unemployed, members of which are offered work placements by employers and continue to receive their welfare payments; positive action programmes in the recruitment of ethnic minorities, initially by Gemeente Rotterdam with the hope that private employers will follow; and exploration of ways of achieving a social return from major redevelopment projects. The last has proceeded furthest on the Kop van Zuid scheme which is near some of the most deprived districts of the city. Here the municipality is developing schemes to safeguard and develop local small businesses, to train the local unemployed, to improve the quality of public space and to use the bargaining structures developed for the urban renewal programme to encourage dialogue between residents and the other parties involved in the Kop van Zuid development.

Future scenarios

Because of their key international trading and transhipment roles and the small size of Dutch domestic markets, the future prosperity of Amsterdam and Rotterdam is heavily dependent on European and world trade conditions. The economic shocks of the later 1970s and early 1980s saw worries expressed within both cities about the Netherlands' place within new trading patterns. However, there is now considerably more optimism about the twin 'threats' which earlier caused most concern: the growing volume of trade handled in Pacific Rim countries and an apparent southward shift of European economic gravity from the older, northern industrial areas which provide much of the Randstad's trading business to southern France, northern Italy and southern Germany.

High economic growth rates and the expansion of trade in Pacific Rim countries are no longer seen as threatening the two cities directly if the European economy continues to grow. There is an appreciation in Rotterdam, for example, that the port of Singapore, for all its recent spectacular growth, is not a rival in any direct sense, because it cannot threaten Rotterdam's trading base. Much more important would be growth of European competitors as a result of the changing geography of European production and consumption. Two factors have helped virtually to eradicate such fears. First, the north–south shift of economic gravity in Europe has proved less decisive than appeared likely in the early 1980s. Northern Germany in particular has undergone the sort of economic resurgence which suggests that the writing off of the older industrialised north was very premature. More recently the changes in eastern Europe hold out the promise, in the medium term, of the development of new markets and productive capacity in countries which will refocus their economic orientation to the west, rather than to the former East European trading block. Both trends will increase trade flows through the Randstad and reinforce the trading and distributive sectors of the two cities' economies.

Local fears about the international competitiveness of the Randstad are subsiding further as the national government increasingly puts its weight behind initiatives aiming to build up the core (Randstad) rather than the periphery of the country. With growing confidence that both market development and government policies will tend to favour the Randstad in the medium-term future, the internationalist debate within the two cities is becoming more focused and sophisticated. Economic analyses increasingly revolve around particular sectors or sub-sectors of the city economies. There is a recognition that growing international competition in the 1990s and beyond will take a different form for each sector, depending on the cities' current strengths and the level – international, national, regional – at which the cities perform a particular economic specialism.

In Rotterdam, strong trade growth through the port is expected into the next century even in the worst-case scenario. However, there is some worry that under current trends the benefit of having the world's largest port, by tonnage of goods handled, will accrue more to foreign traders than to the local economy. There is now widespread recognition that for the port to have a bigger local knock-on effect, particularly in employment terms, it needs to develop greater added values. The volume of goods which are simply transhipped should be reduced and more local processing or partial assembly of goods should take place. The port authorities, having recognised the better performance of competitors like Antwerp and Hamburg, are already reacting to this problem, making it likely that this will be a key policy issue throughout the 1990s.

For the large, mainly multinational companies in Rotterdam, the most dramatic restructuring period seems to be over and many such enterprises, particularly in the petrochemicals sector, have committed themselves to the city region through massive investment programmes. Pollution problems related to this sector will continue to be high on the public policy agenda, however. The most common critical observation made about the capital intensive corporate sector is that its employment levels, stable from the later 1980s onward, are unlikely to grow, although some employment growth will take place amongst corporate suppliers. The greatest employment growth in the future, as in the 1980s, is likely to take place in small businesses. In Rotterdam's case, the small business sector is generally regarded as weak and vulnerable to increased competition, making it essential that programmes to support small business growth continue to be developed.

In Amsterdam, there are fears that Schiphol airport, again due to the small Dutch domestic market and the consequent reliance on passenger transfers and goods transhipment, may struggle to hold its place in the league table of European aviation hubs in the liberalised climate after 1992. Schiphol's reaction has been to put forward large-scale expansion plans and to concentrate more on intercontinental trade. It is hoped that the TGV link and the proposed joint venture with Gemeente Rotterdam over Zestienhoven Airport will enable some of Schiphol's expanding intra-European trade to be siphoned off.

There is less concern in Amsterdam than in Rotterdam over the levels of competitiveness within small businesses, although technical modernisation within the sector is again viewed as very important. The sectors which experienced greatest problems in the early 1980s, as in Rotterdam, are now generally robust and stable in employment terms, although once more unlikely to grow significantly. The biggest change which could take place in Amsterdam over the next fifteen years or so rests on the success of the IJ development. However, it is inconceivable that the thriving southern belt, barring a catastrophic loss of status by Schiphol, will lose its appeal to investors. Nor, despite Gemeente Amsterdam's planning commitment to guide development to the north, is the municipal authority likely to do anything to threaten future development in the south if this were to mean that the city would lose out overall.

In each city, both optimistic and pessimistic scenarios see some expansion of population and employment as national and local government support for compact, internationally competitive cities begin to affect private investment patterns. The hoped-for increase in private house building in the cities will depend on the economic and political situation. Given the historically high degree of state intervention in the Dutch housing market, the power of private house builders is quite weak. If investor confidence in the private housing market is low, there is likely to be a switch from private to social housing in the two cities' planned developments since the latter, with its more reliable source of income generation (rents rather than sale), tends to be seen as a better investment in less buoyant times.

The extent to which this proves to be the case in Rotterdam and Amsterdam obviously depends on developments in the private housing market. It also depends on national policy shifts and the extent to which social housing funds, which remained at a high level during the 1980s but are seen as more vulnerable to expenditure cuts in the 1990s, continue to be provided by the Government. Both factors clearly depend on general national economic growth rates. Whatever the state of the national private housing market, Amsterdam will continue to be more attractive in this regard than Rotterdam. The change in the tenure split in Rotterdam, and hence the image of the city for higher-income residents and the house builders who can cater for their needs, can happen only very slowly, such is the legacy of social housing development in the city. Compared to Amsterdam, the city will therefore continue to have a much more blue-collar image for a long time to come.

In neither city is it easy to be optimistic about unemployment. Even allowing for reasonable economic growth and expansion of small business development and labour-market initiatives, unemployment is likely to remain high throughout the nineties. There are growing fears about the emergence of an underclass, with ethnic minorities heavily represented, which is permanently excluded from the socio-economic mainstream. The performance of the education system will be critical in determining how far such a scenario develops – making education a key national political issue in the 1990s. The social renewal programme, which is likely to face intense pressure for much higher expenditure levels, has a daunting task, particularly in establishing dialogue and joint action with private businesses. Thus far it has shown limited signs of assuming some responsibility for the plight of deprived sections of the urban community. The greatest danger for the social renewal programme is that it will quickly become seen as tokenistic, a mere symbol of political concern which cannot attract the resources, supporters or innovative ideas which will be needed.

References

Albreda Advisory Commission on Social-Economic Renewal in Rotterdam (1988), *New Rotterdam* (Gemeente Rotterdam Information and Publicity Department).

Davies, H. W. E. (1988), 'The control of development in The Netherlands', *Town Planning Review*, 59, 2.

Oude Engberink, G. (1990), 'The re-emergence of poverty'. Paper to the conference on *Segretatie in Rotterdam: Feiten en beleid*, August (Gemeente Rotterdam: Bureau Sociale Vernieuwing).

van der Cammen, H., Groenweg, R. and van de Hoef, G. (1988), 'Randstad Holland: Growth and planning of a ring of cities' in van der Cammen (ed.), *Four Metropolises in Western Europe* (Assen: Van Gorcum), 119-75.

van Lier, J. M. (1990), 'Segregation in Rotterdam: Facts and policy in education'. Paper to the conference on *Segregatie in Rotterdam: Feiten en beleid*, August (Gemeente Rotterdam: Bureau Sociale Vernieuwing).

van Weesep, J. (1985), 'Regional and urban development in The Netherlands: The retreat of government', *Geography*, 73, 2.

2

Brussels

Richard Evans

In the past two decades Brussels has become a classic international city. Its development and future are intimately connected to its role as host for major international organisations and functions. Apart from housing the headquarters of the EC, including the Commission of the European Communities, the Economic and Social Committee and the Secretariat of the Council of Ministers, it is also the base for NATO and other international organisations, many multinational corporations and banking interests, a major conference and exhibition centre and an important financial centre. However, Brussels' transformation into a leading international service city has produced a complicated balance sheet of benefits and disadvantages. This chapter examines the pattern of winners and losers in the city as a result of the dramatic changes of the last thirty years.

Historical development

Visitors arriving at Brussels Airport at Zaventem are confronted by a large poster describing the city as the crossroads of Europe. Fundamentally, the city owes its significance to its strategic position. What was originally a village and fortification on an island on the river Senne belonging to a local tenth-century duke grew in size primarily because it became a crossing point for a major trade route linking England and Flanders to the fertile lands of the Rhine and Meuse rivers.

Key historic events can be pinpointed which still exert a crucial influence upon contemporary life in the city. Prior to the end of the eighteenth century, the majority the inhabitants of Brussels spoke Flemish. But following the French annexation of the Austrian

Netherlands of which the city was part in 1794, a systematic policy of Frenchification was implemented and French became the official language of civil servants, intellectuals and the professions. Dutch was looked upon disdainfully as the local vernacular. Notwithstanding the defeat of the French at Waterloo, subsequent Dutch control and the creation of an independent Belgian state in 1830 with Brussels as its capital, French continued to be the official language. Immigration of French-speakers into Brussels from Wallonia to the south and even from France was encouraged because insufficient numbers of the native population could speak the language.

In the nineteenth century independence, rapid industrialisation and growing prosperity suppressed linguistic tensions between a largely Dutch-speaking north (Flanders) containing Brussels and the largely French-speaking south (Wallonia). In the twentieth century, though, tensions have steadily grown between these two main linguistic communities. These have been fuelled by different attitudes to German occupation in both world wars, the divisiveness of the language laws of 1962 and 1963, the post-war growth in the economic and political influence of Flanders, the industrial decline and depopulation of Wallonia and consequent debates about the spatial allocation of economic development programmes. They led to the division of each of the three traditional political parties – the Catholic Christian Democrats, the Socialists and the Liberals – along linguistic lines and also to the appearance of federalist/linguistic parties. Francophone Brussels, containing most government functions in what was until recently a highly centralised state, pointedly demonstrated these linguistic problems as it became a potent symbol of Frenchification in what was a Flemish part of the country (De Ridder & Fraga 1986). Linguistic and territorial issues eventually led to the recognition of both languages in the city and to profound reform of the structure of governance.

The physical growth of Brussels

Throughout the nineteenth century Brussels grew extremely rapidly with the population tripling in the latter half of the century. Recent development has occurred outside the nineteen communes which constitute the Brussels metropolitan region. Urbanisation of the region, as in Belgium as a whole, has been very dispersed (Vandermotten

1991). This reflects Belgian preferences for single-family dwellings in rural locations, subsidies for those travelling to work by rail, a highly developed rail and road network orientated towards commuter needs, and parts of the Belgian town-planning system and housing policies. Deindustrialisation of the urban core has resulted from displacement by offices and transportation schemes, lack of space, rising land values, lower overheads and a greener environment on the periphery. National and regional government provision of modern industrial estates has further reinforced the exodus of population and economic activity from the city (Merenne-Schoumaker 1977).

Local politics has also played its part in this skewed physical development of the city. The nineteen communes of Brussels are surrounded by six Flemish communes which have consistently resisted the outward spread of the capital because of the threat of Frenchification. However, the boundary between Flanders and Wallonia which also separates Flemish and French as official tongues, runs east–west just a few miles to the south of Brussels. Many Francophone couples working in Brussels have moved into Namur province for linguistic and cultural reasons.

Brussels in its regional and national context

Approximately 270,000 of Brussels' 640,000 employees commute daily from outside its administrative boundaries. This makes it difficult to define the true extent of the urban region. Many commentators suggests that its true extent embraces seventeen peripheral communes in addition to the official nineteen, boosting its area from 170 sq km to 318 sq km and its population to 1.2 million. The mismatch between administrative and functional boundaries generates important political questions about resource distribution. Given Belgium's small size – essentially the country is a rectangle approximately 200 x 80 km – and the excellence and density of its road, rail and canal communication networks, the entire country may be described as a single urban system with Brussels at the hub. The most important cities in Belgium perform complementary functions. Brussels contains most of Belgium's political institutions and a concentration of tertiary rather than manufacturing activities, with a particularly strong international representation. Antwerp and other northern cities are more important manufacturing and trade centres. Flows of goods and services are strongest along the Brussels–Antwerp axis. However, Brussels' pivotal position within the road and rail system and its role as supplier of higher-order office employment and business services means it has strong links with most provincial cities.

Population trends

Since the war, Brussels has suffered a steady loss of population. Between 1970 and 1988 its population declined from 1.075 million to 0.97 million (INBEL 1990). In some respects, Brussels' problems are similar to those of the country as a whole – a low rate of natural increase and an ageing population. Between 1961 and 1981, numbers of children in the capital initially rose in the 1960s and then fell dramatically in the 1970s, whilst those aged over sixty-five have grown in number. Demographic decline has been accentuated by suburbanisation, deindustrialisation and decentralisation of economic activity to other parts of the surrounding Brabant province. By 1987, nearly four times as many people left the city as arrived there.

The decline would have been much greater but for substantial immigration and the higher birth-rate of ethnic groups. Between 1970 and 1988, for example, the foreign population of the Brussels region increased from 173,000 to 264,000, over a quarter of the total population. Of these, 120,000 came from other EC countries, especially Italy, Spain and France, 58,000 from Morocco and 23,000 from the Far East. Other parts of Brabant have gained population at Brussels' expense, particularly among younger age groups. This has posed increased fiscal problems for the nineteen Brussels communes whose revenue relies heavily upon the taxation of the resident working population. Since many immigrants from developing countries have inferior qualifications to the native population and tend to be either low-income earners or unemployed, in financial terms they do not compensate for the departure of a more affluent population. However, Brussels' rate of population loss has considerably slowed from around one per cent per annum in the late 1970s to about 0.3 per cent in the late 1980s. In 1989 the net loss was only marginal, though this apparent stabilisation was due in part to a heavy influx of foreigners.

Economic performance

Although Brussels contains only ten per cent of the Belgian population, it provides twenty per cent of national employment. The city's economy has become increasingly dominated by service rather than manufacturing activities. In 1977 the proportion of firms engaged in secondary activities was 25.5 per cent. By 1988 it was only twenty per cent. Manufacturing employment shrunk to sixteen per cent per cent of total employment in the same period. In the period from 1980 to 1987, service sector employment declined only slightly as growth in credit and assurance was offset by decline in transport and communications. Manufacturing and construction activities, on the other hand, suffered heavy job losses and their share of total employment slipped from 16.8 per cent to 12.8 per cent whilst services' share rose from 79.6 per cent to 84.2 per cent.

Today, Brussels' most important sectors are banking, assurance and credit institutions, transport and communications, public services, and other business services such as conferences, exhibitions and tourism. The presence of many international organisations and multinational corporations in these sectors is the crucial motor in the economy. Brussels contains fifty-two per cent of national employment in credit and assurance, twenty-three per cent of retailing jobs, twenty-one per cent of restaurant, cafe and hotel staff and twenty-one per cent of national employment in public services and education. It was the only European financial centre to increase its market share during the 1980s and it is currently the seventh biggest financial centre in the world, particularly predominant in ECU transactions. Seventy per cent of all foreign or foreign-owned banks with interests in Belgium are based in Brussels.

As was true of the Belgian economy as a whole, the economy of Brussels enjoyed rapid growth in the latter part of the 1980s in contrast to the stagnation of the earlier part of the decade. Nationally, impressive increases in corporate investment and private consumption prompted a revival of economic fortunes and led to a reduction of unemployment. Between 1975 and 1985 total employment in Brussels fell from 661,000 to 611,000. However, in the late 1980s employment rose again to 623,000. Whilst the number of firms fell from 21,300 in 1977 to 19,800 in 1983, numbers have since significantly increased to above 1977 levels. The decline in larger firms was more than offset by the growth in small, mainly service sector firms, particularly those with fewer than five employees. The traditional dominance of the Brussels economy by larger companies has disappeared and the proportion of firms in different size categories now broadly reflects the national average. However, Brussels' firm structure continues to differ from the national norm in one key respect – there are few very large firms with more than 500 employees in Brussels mainly because of the lack of space.

The prime characteristic of the local economy is its openness. This is true of the Belgian economy as a whole; exports from the country account for forty-one per cent of total economic output. Brussels has an international economy primarily because of the presence of important European and global political institutions such as the European Commission and NATO, which moved to the city from Paris in 1967. These two institutions are important employers in their own right, employing about 23,000 people each. Their presence has attracted many other ancillary activities to Brussels, notably international press and media interests, lobbyists, lawyers and accountants. These have stimulated the growth of Brussels as a conference and exhibition venue and boosted the hotel, restaurant and entertainment sectors of the economy. Brussels' political signifi-cance, its centrality within one of the most lucrative markets in the world, with 321 million inhabitants, the availability of a well-educated and multilingual labour force and government tax incen-tives explains why so many international organisations have been attracted to Brussels. In 1987, 1,100 international organisations had their corporate headquarters in Brussels and 1,500 foreign com-panies had their head offices there (Brussels Chamber of Commerce and Industry 1990).

Social polarisation

Economic processes, especially the internationalisation of the economy, deindustrialisation and the growth in the importance of service sector jobs have played a crucial role in social change and heightened the debate about distributional issues. They have created polarisation within the city and raise the question of in whose interests Brussels is governed.

The most deep-rooted polarisation is between the Francophone majority and the Flemish-speaking minority. The sensitivity of linguistic issues is evident in many aspects of daily life in a city which has been officially bilingual since 1976. In the underground metro, the destination boards switch from one language to the other every fifteen seconds. Yet many Flemish still feel that the city is 'occupied' and point to the disfigurement of the city as evidence that international factors matter much more than local values and the preservation of the city's culture and heritage. There are, however, some signs that growing Flemish economic and political influence, and the lengthy process of governmental reform which has recognised cultural and territorial differences, have lessened some of these tensions.

The second aspect of polarisation in the capital is much more recent. From the 1960s onward substantial numbers of migrant workers, largely from the Mediterranean basin, moved to the city to work in poorly-paid jobs in the service sector such as hotels and restaurants, public transport, and construction. More recently, many immigrants have become unemployed and found it increasingly difficult to compete in both labour and housing markets. The majority of the city's male unemployed are concentrated in seven inner communes where there are high proportions of migrants and other low-income workers. In Brussels as a whole, at the end of the 1980s, the unemployment rate was relatively high at 17.4 per cent. The number receiving benefit as a proportion of the total work-force insured against unemployment in September 1990 made the region sixth out of the twenty-six administrative regions in Belgium. In part, the problem is due to the increasing demand for employment from an ethnic population which is expanding at a much more rapid rate than the native population. In the late 1980s foreigners accounted for forty-five per cent of all births in the region and only seven per cent of deaths (Gay 1987).

However, there is also a fundamental mismatch between the jobs and skills on offer in the local labour market and the level of education and training of many of the migrants. Although there has been some additional employment creation in the tertiary sector in recent years, many of the jobs are poorly paid and part-time. Deindustrialisation and the shift towards highly qualified service sector jobs has marginalised many migrants who lack qualifications and, in some cases, a command of either French or Flemish. The high quality of the Belgian education system and the vast Brussels labour market area means that many migrants have little likelihood of finding work or being able to improve their job status given the competition from the indigenous population. Despite the fact that Brussels' labour market boomed in the late 1980s a substantial proportion of the unemployed (forty-two per cent) had been inactive for more than two years in September 1990.

The third facet of polarisation reflects the distinction between the interests of the residential population and the increasing numbers of 'outsiders', either commuters or employees and visitors from abroad. Often there is an ambivalent attitude on the part of the native Brussels population towards such groups. Whilst the city is proud of its international profile, there is growing concern at the price that has been paid to achieve it. The infrastructure of the city has become increasingly orientated towards the needs of commuters and the international community. Many of the associated costs have been internalised and the benefits externalised because of the shape of the administrative region and the financing of local government. Many who use the city's services do not contribute towards their upkeep through taxes, since they live outside the city. Many employees of international organisations are in any case exempt from personal taxation. They tend to live in national enclaves and are able to pay rents three times as high as the average Belgian can afford. To make matters worse the authorities' ability to fund services is limited further by the fact that the Brussels buildings of many international agencies are exempt from property taxes.

Housing dilemmas

Housing is a major problem in the city. Whereas the single owner-occupied family house comprises two-thirds of all Belgian housing, in Brussels rented housing constitutes two-thirds of the stock (Kesteloot & Cortie 1991). Private, often absentee, landlords control fifty-eight per cent of all stock, and the non-profit-making social rented sector only eight per cent. Less than ten per cent of a total stock of 450,000 dwellings in the city is publicly owned. No social housing has been constructed in the last decade.

For many Brussels residents, the primary issue is the affordability of housing. The absence, or ineffectiveness, of state rent controls and regulations has meant that rents in the private sector have risen rapidly in recent years, especially in the property boom in the late

1980s. Moreover, the price of owner-occupied housing, coupled with the limited number of state-supported organisations encouraging co-ownership, means that many cannot escape from the rented sector. Housing conditions are often worst in the dilapidated properties in the inner communes, where absentee landlords predominate and where pressure for change of use to offices is greatest. Short-term tenancies prevail and the possibility of change of use not only adds to tenants' feelings of insecurity but also means that owners do not take full advantage of state grants to improve property.

The inner areas are the most overcrowded and contain the highest proportion of unfit properties or those requiring improvement. They also experience concentrations of low-income groups and ethnic minorities experiencing unemployment, low levels of educational attainment, alcoholism, delinquency and poor health. Relatively few housing organisations, with the exception of the Fonds du Logement and Assam-Sorelo, explicitly deal with issues such as ethnic minority needs and social and economic integration of the poor in the way they manage their stock.

Politics in Brussels

During the last thirty years, the Belgian government system has shifted from a unified, centralised system to a federalised, devolved structure. Debates over linguistic rights and territorial conflicts between Flanders and Wallonia over the allocation of national resources were the main impetus for change. The process of structural reform has been long and complicated, especially in Brussels which has suffered from being used like a political football.

The unpopularity of the 1960s language laws and later Flemish discontent with the scale of governmental help for the ailing Wallonian economy made it clear to the Government that extensive reform was necessary. However, the sensitivities involved meant that change had to be gradual. After protracted negotiations the Belgian constitution was revised in 1970 to recognise four linguistic regions – French, Dutch, German and bilingual. An elaborate system of checks and balances was incorporated to ensure that each linguistic group's interests would be adequately represented.

Continued dissatisfaction with government decisions concerning resource allocation between the regions prompted further change in the early 1980s when Flanders and Wallonia were given greater independence and control over resources. However, disagreements between Flemings and Walloons over the fate of Brussels prevented it from gaining full regional status until 1988. Flemings had feared that granting the Brussels region more independence would favour the Francophone majority and had argued for Brussels to become a capital district containing two ethnolinguistic regions. Eventually a compromise solution was found. Substantial powers were granted to each of the three regions in economic policy, scientific research and communications networks. But responsibility for the more sensitive personal services including cultural matters, education, health and advertising on radio and television were devolved to the communities. Central government remained responsible for foreign affairs, defence, justice, social security, macroeconomic and monetary matters.

As a result, Brussels now possesses an extremely complex four-tiered governmental structure with overlapping responsibilities. The nineteen communes and provinces each have their own administrative offices, councillors and mayors and are responsible for planning, parks and gardens and certain aspects of environmental health. The most important organs of government are the regional authority and the community councils. The regional government, established in 1989, comprises a seventy-five-member council responsible for regional matters and defining the policies of the nineteen communes. It also has an executive of five ministers who govern the city on a daily basis, supported by three Secretaries of State. Policies are delivered by seven administrative organisations responsible for environmental management, employment, information, housing, inter-communal transport, regional development and regional investment. The Council has sixty-four Francophone and eleven Flemish councillors. But each linguistic grouping includes politicians from six different parties, which makes life rather complicated!

Community matters are handled by separate Community Councils for the two linguistic groups. Each has a parliament, an executive and an administrative body and is governed by the councillors from the appropriate linguistic group of the Regional Council. Matters of common concern are handled by a Community Commission comprising delegates from both communities, where a majority in each linguistic group is required for the approval of specific measures. Most funding decisions are taken by the national assemblies of either the Flemish or Walloon Community Councils, depending on the linguistic community. Delegates from Brussels serve on these bodies. Funding of the Community councils broadly reflects the size of their population and their sociodemographic characteristics.

As a result governing the city is complicated and the co-ordination of city-wide policies is extremely difficult given the number of interests and overlapping bureaucratic layers. In the past Brussels suffered from national rule and was dominated by schemes in the national interest (Murphy 1988). Brussels also suffers from fundamental problems of fiscal capacity. Although the region has major powers, it has great difficulties fulfilling its new responsibilities since its financial base largely depends upon the amount of income tax raised from its residents. Brussels' income fell much faster than other parts of Brabant in the period from 1978 to 1987 and its share of national income tax receipts (IPP) and the proportion of its net taxable income accounted for by IPP in the region is falling. The city now faces two dilemmas. The first is how to maintain the city's international status without encouraging further depopulation and stimulating reurbanisation without strangling commercial growth. The second is how to attract higher-income groups back into the city without displacing poorer elements of the community, which would prove controversial if additional investment in public housing became necessary, since the poor would have nowhere to go.

The region has also inherited three problems. The fact that Brussels is surrounded by Flemish communes resistant to inclusion in its administrative area has resulted in the exclusion of suburban areas which would have greatly contributed to its tax base. Also, the Government has indicated that the regions will have to play their part in reducing public debt. Third, the region has to deal with the consequences of past public expenditure decisions which were in the national, rather than the city's, interest. This has resulted in unbalanced investment in the capital's infrastructure, especially in public transport and roads.

Although devolution has eased linguistic tensions, further political conflict seems inevitable given difficulties in reducing the public debt burden and disagreements on the form that the final phase of devolution should take. The urban development of Brussels, as of Belgium as a whole, has long been market-led and unregulated. A deep-rooted tradition of liberalism and respect for individual property and development rights produced considerable resistance to planning, and urban form was shaped by the decisions of individual property owners. Public intervention was sectoral and fragmented, rather than deriving from any comprehensive view of how the city should be managed. With the creation of the Brussels region, however, more strategic and integrated policies begin to emerge.

Until the Second World War there was little discussion of the need for either economic or urban planning. After the war, the task of reconstruction, the growing problems of regional economic disparity associated with Wallonia's outmoded industrial structure and congestion problems caused by the rapid growth in car owner-ship, led to more public intervention. But the highly centralised government structure meant that such problems were treated on a sectoral rather than an integrated basis – with profound con-sequences, especially for Brussels. Powerful national public works departments emerged, each geared to meeting particular infra-structural needs in roads, traffic and transport and housing, on a separate basis (Godard 1986). In Brussels, a dispersed urban form was encouraged by the combination of bonuses to individuals to construct or occupy government-built housing, the minimal control of the layout of peripheral industrial and housing estates, and the implementation of ambitious road-building proposals in the late 1950s as American solutions to urban traffic problems were adopted. As the capital, Brussels was also the scene of prestigious, expensive projects such as the metro system and a new road system which included extensive tunnelling. These emphasised the city's pivotal role within the Belgian economy and its newly-acquired interna-tional status as headquarters of the EC. These schemes physically transformed much of the city. Many old buildings were demolished and tree-lined boulevards were lost.

The most pressing environmental problems confronting the city are traffic congestion and pollution. Brussels' centrality in Belgium, coupled with the activities of a heavily centralised public works department in the 1950s and 1960s, have made the city the focus of extensive transportation systems. The extensive road-building and tunnelling programmes which resulted from Brussels hosting the World Fair in 1958, and the impetus that provided the modernisa-tion plans regarded as necessary for the city to aspire to an international role, have proved a mixed blessing. Much of Brussels' heritage was swept away by redevelopment and parts of the city are now dominated by the car at the expense of the pedestrian. Despite a large number of underground car parks, illegal car parking on pavements is common and inadequately controlled, and the ensuing chaos inconveniences pedestrians and causes retailers and offices servicing problems. The scale of commuting and the dominance of the car also leads to increasing noise and air pollution and congestion, particularly on the arterial routes in Brussels. Traffic flows on the outer ring road are increasing constantly because of the coincidence of commuter traffic and the extensive volume of through traffic traversing Belgium.

Brussels, and indeed Belgium as a whole, did not possess a planning regime until 1962. Even then legislation had only a limited effect. Public works departments continued with their technocratic approach and resisted the introduction of planning controls which they suspected might erode their power bases. The new system lacked credibility because there was little fit between planning and economic development instruments, such as those operated by the Regional Development Corporation in the case of Brussels. Nor was it clear that the political will existed to implement a national plan, because of linguistic problems. Furthermore, there was no suitable administrative tier for implementing a regional plan (Albrecht 1982). The period up to 1970 can be summed up as one of segmented public works planning devoid of any cultural, social or economic rationale.

Environmental protection and the emergence of land use planning, 1971–87

Towards the end of the 1960s there was growing concern with the effects of unregulated urban growth and the costs in environmental, historical and human terms of the transformation of the Brussels landscape. Ambitious redevelopment schemes were increasingly resisted by residents' groups opposed to further change of their neighbourhood. Two schemes were particularly controversial; the proposal to extend the Palace of Justice complex by demolishing housing in the Marolles working-class district and the redevelopment of sixty hectares in the Quartier Nord for an International Trade Centre. Both were successfully resisted.

In the 1970s and much of the 1980s there was a shift in emphasis from clearance to more sensitive refurbishment. However, it is difficult to discern the degree to which this has been due to the the new planning system, the urban struggle movement, or the enlightened activities of a few communes, the Fonds du Logement and the Ministry for the Brussels Region, created in 1980. Cost criteria (refurbishment is less expensive) and the collapse of the property market in 1970, which resulted in the bankruptcy of housing companies constructing new middle-income apartment blocks, may have been more influential factors. Despite the good intentions of the sectoral plan, there were many cases when its provisions were breached, especially after the property market began to improve again in the mid-1980s. Equally, negotiations with powerful institutions such as the EC whose property requirements exceeded planners' original expectations, resulted in the incursion of office uses into residential areas. Some municipalities were reluctant to rehouse lower-income groups because of the structure of local government finance and the premium placed upon attracting higher-income uses. Others lacked the finance or the organisational capacity to mount a refurbishment programme.

Despite the sectoral plan, in many respects the situation in the 1970s changed remarkably little from that of the 1950s and 1960s. Whilst the worst excesses of the technocratic approach were avoided, many public sector organisations pursued narrow, sectoral approaches in the absence of any strategy for the development of the city. The metro system continued to be developed with little regard to questions of land use and development. Housing was regarded as a tool of social policy rather than an integral part of town planning. Historic buildings were considered a cultural matter properly dealt with by the community tier of government, again militating against integrated planning. After the passage of the Economic Expansion Laws of 1980 Brussels became entitled to economic aid incentives such as capital grants and interest subsidies, but economic planning remained separate from physical planning (Swyngedouw 1985). The planning system, based on a defensive zoning scheme, was vulnerable to allegations of rigidity and impracticability. It failed to take account of changes in market conditions and to produce a dynamic vision of the city's future development which could reconcile conflicts of interest within the city.

A new era of regional planning after 1988?

Brussels was finally given its own regional tier of government, with substantial financial powers and control of most important local services, in 1988. Whereas city services had been administered by national politicians who were not necessarily based in the city, regional government offered the prospect of locally elected councillors with a commitment to planning service provison in a more co-ordinated fashion. The new minister displayed an awareness of the vital strategic issues facing the region such as reconciling protection and enhancement of its international status with protecting residents' interests, dealing with the growing problems of social polarisation and preserving the historic fabric and distinctive character of the city. Equally importantly, the regional government leadership has displayed considerable tact in uniting the city's different political and linguistic factions. For the first time an integrated land use and transportation plan has been prepared which will eventually form the basis of a new sectoral plan. Particular attention is being devoted to areas of the city where rapid physical change is anticipated such as the EC area, the canal zone and sites which may be affected by the routing of the TGV through the city.

The Brussels Intercommunal Transport Company (STIB), which is responsible for all forms of public transport with the exception of the railways, has been reorganised and there are signs that the integration of most transportation-related functions within a single administration is yielding fruit. Discussions with the Belgian national railways are taking place in an attempt to improve commuter services to relieve road congestion. Re-routing is also occurring so that the network is better integrated and more reflective of customer needs; at present inter-urban services geared to commuter needs are far better than intra-urban services, which require improvement. In housing, attempts are being made to persuade the private sector to become more involved in low-cost refurbishment schemes and municipalities are being encouraged to impose special rent conditions so that housing is accessible to the poor.

The financial constraints under which the region and the municipalities are currently operating suggest limited room for manoeuvre and in some ways are a disincentive to dealing with the problems of the poor. Policies for encouraging urban regeneration remain under-developed, and if redevelopment does occur there is a danger that it will primarily benefit the better-off because the priority for most communes will be to boost their tax base by constructing upper-status dwellings or offices. Formidable problems remain in traffic congestion, the loss of residential accommodation to office use, sometimes by illegal changes of use and the status of and conditions endured by migrant workers.

Despite administrative reform, there are still inherent difficulties with the structure of governance for the capital. The continued subdivision of a small city into nineteen communes, each with their own mayor and substantial planning and other functions, undermines consistent management of the city as a whole. The fact that regional politicians also represent particular communes inevitably produces parochial attitudes. Also, the pressure to maximise local income may well continue to limit the efficacy of city-wide planning controls. Too often, the provisions of the sectoral plan have been breached as a result of deals struck between commune politicians and developers, leading to a loss of public confidence in the planning process.

International policy

The regionalisation of government has created a change in the nature of Brussels' external relations. Before 1988, a coherent foreign policy for the city hardly existed. This was not, however, because of passivity by central government which had been responsible for the most important civic functions. Major initiatives had been taken to consolidate Brussels' functions as a capital and to fulfil its wider ambitions of becoming the capital of Europe. The prestigious metro system was developed. Equally significantly, the development of conference, exhibition, trade, business-related and heritage-based tourist industries was strongly encouraged. Brussels is now the third most important conference centre in the world.

The Government also took steps to preserve the city's financial status. In the late 1970s and early 1980s there was increasing alarm at the diminishing number of multinational companies locating in the city and surrounding region because of high taxation levels and a highly regulated financial sector. The Government introduced a series of measures to protect and enhance its status. In 1983, multinational companies wishing to establish co-ordination centres in the city to carry out financial, auditing, accounting, market research, training or lobbying functions (but not commercial or production activities) were granted a favourable tax regime for a ten-year period. Benefits include calculation of corporate income tax on a favourable cost-plus basis, exemption from withholding, capital registration and real-estate taxes and tax credits and concessions for expatriate personnel. As a result, 250 such centres have since been established. They currently employ about 5,000 people, of whom approximately three quarters are Belgian.

More recently, concern about high levels of withholding tax on interest and dividend income and the consequent outflow of capital to Luxembourg and elsewhere, combined with the fear that the Single Market will see financial services become increasingly concentrated in such major European centres as London and Frankfurt, have prompted further financial measures. The most important have been the reduction of withholding tax, tying the Franc to the Deutschmark and abolition of the twin foreign exchange market. As a result, there have been heavy inflows of capital into Brussels and government economists are optimistic that the city will retain its financial standing, especially with other organisational reforms such as the deregulation of the stock exchange, including brokers' fees and money markets.

Finally, the Government has consistently sought to cater for the property requirements of the EC and other international organisations. For some considerable time the Government has also been lobbying for the European Parliament to be transferred from Strasbourg to Brussels. Currently an International Congress Centre is being constructed alongside the recently expanded Council of Ministers building, and this could readily provide the necessary facilities. Long-standing plans to expand the airport and upgrade visitor reception facilities are under way.

The creation of the Brussels Region has also led to a more coherent set of promotional 'foreign' policies which are more integrated with 'domestic policies'. Attention is not merely being devoted to attracting foreign investment but also to making Brussels a city with no aliens, able to reconcile its international role with a good quality of life for its inhabitants. The approach has three strands. A number of planned projects attempt to improve the hospitality shown to foreign visitors and prospective residents. Whilst visitors will benefit from the new European terminal and concourse at the airport, prospective citizens of Brussels will be offered a multilingual reception service to help them cope with administrative formalities. There are plans to develop a European Culture Centre where each cultural group would be able to express itself. Brussels already encourages cultural interchange by operating 'Europalia' which every two years provides a foreign country with the opportunity to display the best of its art and culture in prominent city locations, attracting nearly a million European visitors in the process.

The second policy is to raise Brussels' international profile by preparing appropriate publicity material promoting, for example, its conference and tourist facilities and arts and cultural heritage, undertaking trade missions and establishing links with other regional capitals such as Washington and Berlin. Traditionally, Brussels has promoted itself much less forcefully than other Belgian cities such as Antwerp.

The third strand is the creation of a Brussels export policy to add to the financial aid and interest-free loans to export companies and support for promotional activities provided in the past by national government. A regionalised Belgian Office of Foreign Trade is seeking to target the incentives according to the region's indigenous strengths and to draw upon the expertise of local companies and academic institutions, particularly in international collaboration in research and development projects.

Despite the development of a more sophisticated foreign policy post-1988 and attempts to reconcile foreign and native interests, a number of caveats need to be made. Many of the projects will only come to fruition if novel public–private partnership mechanisms are devised. Second, many of the projects are in their infancy. Compared with Barcelona and Lyon, for example, the concept of city networking is new to Brussels. The organisational context suggests that progress may be slow. There is no regional administration for foreign affairs and missions abroad are invariably cumbersome affairs as protocol demands the involvement of all three regions and the National Ministry of Foreign Affairs! Many important matters are still handled at national level.

Future scenarios

In assessing Brussels' future prospects as an international city, it is essential not only to comment on the future development of the city's economic and social infrastructure but also to identify potential external threats which might undermine Brussels' niche in various markets.

In general terms, Brussels can be optimistic about the future. Belgium now has a strong economy. Inflation, high unemployment and the large balance of payments deficit of the early 1980s have been reduced and output and corporate investment grew impressively in the late 1980s. Despite some concern at the burden of the social security system and the depressive effect upon earnings of higher-status workers, this has formed part of an enduring post-Second World War social contract between employers and employees whereby wage negotiations have been linked to productivity gains, thereby avoiding major industrial unrest. There is no reason to suppose that labour relations will not continue to be good in the future in the private sector. The multilingual and highly qualified character of the local work-force, coupled with other cost advantages such as lower overheads, will continue to prove attractive to international investors.

Short-term projections, (up to the mid-1990s) by the National Planning Office suggest a slow-down in the rate of economic growth that was achieved in the late 1980s (Ministry of Economic Affairs 1989). They nevertheless predict a comfortable balance of payments surplus, low inflation and GDP growth of about 2.4 per cent per annum, well above that achieved in the period from 1983 to 1988. Brussels' economy is expected to reflect this broader picture. But its highly open nature, coupled with the city's world-wide political significance, means that international developments will exert a particular influence on its future. Given past levels of foreign investment, recent fiscal measures and continued expansion of co-ordination centre activities, Brussels seems well placed to gain a fair share of the 6.4 per cent gain in the EC's GDP which is expected to flow from the Single European Market. The likely expansion of the EC's economic and financial powers should also consolidate Brussel's political significance and ensure that the many related ancillary activities such as legal, lobbying, press and conference organisations will continue to develop. Whilst relocation of the European Parliament would prove a further asset, eighty per cent of the Commission's economic, social and political decisions are already taken in Brussels.

Brussels' infrastructure is also being upgraded to enable the city to fulfil its aspirations. The dated facilities at Zaventem International Airport are being extended and modernised. A new terminal, concourse and underground railway station are being built. Runways are being extended, new courier facilities provided and concessions made to private companies to construct new cargo warehousing alongside the air-freight terminal. The rail system around the airport is to be realigned to permit access from the north and eventually a two-way loop system linking the airport and the city centre is envisaged. As a result of these improvements the airport will be able to handle twenty million passengers a year. Expansion of the freight facilities will enable further growth in freight traffic; tonnage increased from 165,000 in 1980 to 280,000 in 1989. The majority of improvements will be complete by the end of 1992 in anticipation of the arrival of the Single European Market. The area around the airport is already a popular location for high-tech companies and this trend is likely to continue with the expansion of the airport.

The introduction of the TGV high-speed rail network will further consolidate Brussels' pivotal position within Europe. Despite difficulties in clarifying the exact route into the city and arbitrating between three potential locations for the station, there is a strong political will to push the scheme through. Brussels lies at the intersection of the *transmanche* route via Lille to London and there will be further links to Paris, Amsterdam and Cologne. The main question is when rather than whether the scheme will be completed. Despite hopes that the TGV will be operational by June 1993, some believe there could be significant delay due to opposition from residents in Brussels and from farmers in more rural parts of Flanders and Wallonia. Such delays could produce short-term congestion, especially if Brussels is chosen as the site for the European Parliament. More generally, the unification of Germany and the possibility that Norway and Sweden may join the EC will lead to additional rail traffic to and from the north and east.

The moratorium on road-building within the capital, except for some additional tunnelling in the increasingly congested vicinity of the EC headquarters will increase the urgency of upgrading other forms of transport. Unless traffic is switched from roads, further congestion will result from Brussels' central position within Belgium, continued growth of car ownership and the likelihood of further east–west traffic following the opening of the Liege–Cologne road tunnel in 1992. The Brussels region is now investing in public transport in a balanced fashion. However, public expenditure restrictions will probably hinder progress and result in additional congestion problems for much of the 1990s.

There are fewer problems with the city's built infrastructure. Since 1985, the local property market has been extremely buoyant. Office construction averaged about 250,000 sq m per annum during that period. Rents doubled from 3,500 to 7,000 BF per sq m per annum and yields fell from 7.25 per cent to six per cent in the late 1980s and early 1990s in anticipation of 1993. A further 600,000 sq m of floor space was expected to come on stream in 1991. While the industrial and retail market is not so buoyant due to deindustrialisation and over-provision, provision of hotel and conference facilities continues apace. Most of these trends are expected to continue in view of the city's international appeal.

Brussels is geographically and economically well placed for continued prosperity in view of its location. The city is at the centre of a 'europolygon' of capitals whose corners are London, Amsterdam, Bonn, Luxembourg and Paris. Its role as a political centre and meeting-place means that it has carved a distinctive niche from which it will not easily be dislodged. Maintaining Brussels' international role will, however, prove difficult to reconcile with local interests, especially as high value functions such as offices continue to displace lower-value uses such as residential areas and industry. Problems caused by the lack of affordable housing and suitable jobs have been further exacerbated by the inability of the city to expand for cultural and linguistic reasons. The growing dominance of the tertiary sector and its preference for highly trained white-collar labour has meant that unqualified labourers, particularly those belonging to ethnic minorities, are increasingly excluded from both labour and housing markets.

Besides having to deal with such social problems, the regional administration is struggling with other legacies. The absence of planning gain and other linkage mechanisms means there is no automatic link between international investment in the city and community benefit. Similarly, urban regeneration mechanisms urgently need to be developed to counter the effects of past anti-urban policies such as transport subsidies which have resulted in depopulation and erosion of the local fiscal base. The traditional lack of integrated land use and transportation planning on a conurbation-wide basis which has exacerbated congestion problems will also take time to correct.

But because the city's new administration is excessively fragmented and underfunded, it will probably find these challenges
impossible to overcome unless there is further structural and financial reform. Remedying the past under-investment in public housing
and providing affordable housing, countering growing traffic congestion and reinvesting in infrastructure will impose a considerable
local tax burden. As matters stand, the inadequate resource base,
coupled with declining transfer payments from central to local
government following decentralisation, could jeopardise standards of
local service delivery and quality of life in the capital and ultimately
deter future investment.

Predicting what path reform might take is, however, difficult
given the uncertainties concerning the future of the nation state. The
increasing popularity of both Flemish and Wallonian separatist
movements could mean that Brussels will become increasingly
isolated given its peculiar geographical position as an enclave within
Flanders. It remains to be seen whether the uneasy coalition of
interests governing the capital will remain intact. If the Belgian state
unravels into two camps, it may be that the movement for an
autonomous Brussels could gather force in an attempt to stave off the
possibility of loss of influence and subservience to a Flemish state.

References

Albrecht, L. (1982), 'Organisational structure versus the emergence of plans as applied to
    Belgian planning', Planning Outlook, 24, 2.
Brussels Chamber of Commerce and Industry (1990), 'Brussels – Heart of Current Events',
    Entreprendre 116, 10.
De Ridder, M. & Fraga, L.R. (1986), 'The Brussels issue in Belgian politics', West European
    Politics, 7, 3, 376–92.
Gay, F.J. (1987), 'Benelux', in H.D. Clout (ed.), Regional Development in Western Europe, David
    Fulton Publishers.
Godard, M. (1986), 'A Remission of Fifteen Years', A+91 Journal.
INBEL (Belgian Instutute of Information and Documentation) (1990), Belgium: A Statistical
    Survey, Brussels.
Kesteloot, C. & Cortie, C. (1991), Political System and the Formation of Urban Regions: Amsterdam and
    Brussels.
Merenne-Schoumaker, B. (1977), New Industrial Estates in Belgium, Working Paper, Institute
    of Geography, Reims, 31–32, 5–31.
Ministry of Economic Affairs (1989), The Belgian Economy. Facts and Figures 1988-89, Brussels.
Murphy, A.B. (1988), The Regional Dynamics of Language Differentiation in Belgium. A Study in Cultural-
    Political Geography, University of Chicago Research Paper 227.

Swyngedouw, E. (1985), *Contradictions between Economic and Physical Planning in Belgium*, Working Paper 3, Villeneuve d'Ascq: Johns Hopkins European Centre for Regional Planning & Research (1985), section 1.

Vandermotten, C. (1991), 'Brussels – The morphological town: delimitation and population', *Comparative Atlas of European Towns*.

3

Birmingham

Richard Evans

Birmingham is Britain's leading provincial city not only because of its population of almost a million but because of its growing range of economic and social functions. Its traditional strength in manufacturing remains today, although in a streamlined form after a traumatic period of restructuring in the early 1980s. This has been supplemented by a range of service industries including financial services and business-related tourism. The visitor to Birmingham is immediately impressed with the volume of development activity. Britain's first purpose-built convention centre has recently been completed in the city centre and a million square feet of offices are under construction. A new terminal is being built at the airport and nearby the highly successful National Exhibition Centre is being expanded.

In many ways, the city is an important barometer of urban change in Europe. Birmingham is well placed to benefit from increasing interaction with other European countries because of its central location and excellent communications with the rest of the United Kingdom. In addition, the city council has made consistent efforts to ensure that Birmingham becomes an important European city. The degree to which the Channel Tunnel and other pan-European developments prove to be advantageous to Birmingham will indicate how far Britain can cope with the problems of being on the periphery of Europe.

Birmingham's future is, of course, complicated by a number of local considerations. Its proximity to London and lack of regional sovereignty may check its aspirations to become an increasingly important European centre for business services. The city's relatively poor physical image may prove a constraint. It has little inherent aesthetic appeal, situated as it is in a flat landscape punctuated only by unremarkable monuments to its industrial past. The city centre possesses few landmarks, is characterised by the bland architecture typical of 1960s redevelopment and is dominated by the motor car.

There are also important distributional questions facing the city and the wider sub-region. If regional economic growth continues, to what extent will it benefit Birmingham? In the latter part of the 1980s the city moved to the 'right' side of the north–south regional divide. However, there is an acute shortage of quality industrial land in the city and there are growing signs of a divide within the West Midlands between the prosperous south, where growth industries are locating adjacent to the developing motorway network, and more northerly districts, especially inner-city Birmingham, Wolverhampton and the Black Country, where high unemployment levels persist. Within Birmingham itself, there remains the question whether new economic activity will mainly benefit the growing number of commuters into the city or whether ways can be found to enable its substantial core of long-term unemployed and significant ethnic population to gain their share of the new jobs and prosperity.

But the city does have one institutional advantage. Many British cities are characterised by difficult relations between central and local government, traditionally poor relations between public and private sectors and weak local agencies with limited executive and administrative capacity. Birmingham is different because it possesses a powerful and entrepreneurial local government bureaucracy and a tradition of good, pragmatic relations between local and national government and the private sector (Commission of the Bishop's Council of the Diocese of Birmingham 1988).

Historical development

To understand Birmingham's evolution, it is necessary to sketch briefly the emergence of the surrounding West Midlands region as the industrial heartland of England (Spencer et al. 1988). Extensive and easily workable deposits of coal, ironstone and limestone in south Staffordshire, Warwickshire and Shropshire have supported mining and metal crafts since medieval times. However, in the late eighteenth and nineteenth centuries, a combination of technical innovations such as the application of coal to the smelting of iron and the invention of the steam engine, burgeoning demand for coal

and iron from the development of new industrial processes and the
opening of new markets arising from the development of the canal
system led to a growth and diversification of activity.

In the first half of the nineteenth century principal manufactures
included jewellery, guns, buttons, buckles and brassware, to which
were added various iron hardware goods such as fasteners, and then
in the late nineteenth century and early twentieth century, light and
medium engineering industries such as cycles, motor vehicles and
electrical goods. However, rapid industrialisation had unfortunate
social consequences. The city's population grew from 71,000 in
1801 to 401,000 in 1881 and then to a staggering 1,000,000 by
1931, resulting in overcrowding and unhealthy living conditions,
particularly in the poorer districts close to the town centre.

Population decentralisation and economic concentration

The inter-war years saw a dispersal of the population from the city.
Demographic movements were reinforced by restructuring in the
manufacturing sector. Production in the inter-war period became
concentrated in a relatively small number of growth industries such
as motor vehicles, engineering and metal goods, within increasingly
large production units which were able to reap the advantages of
mass production and economies of scale. Many of these assembly
plants preferred to locate on spacious greenfield sites. From the
1950s to the 1970s, regional planning policies and national industrial policy accelerated the process of decentralisation. Birmingham
and the West Midlands' most pressing problems were seen to be
congestion and environmental degradation and it was thought that
these would be best dealt with by a combination of comprehensive
redevelopment of the city centre, improvement of the transportation
system, reclamation of the older industrial areas and the dispersal of
housing and jobs to new towns such as Redditch and Telford and
other peripheral areas. Between 1956 and 1966 the core area lost
forty-two per cent of its factories as firms either folded or moved out
into more peripheral areas.

In the 1970s and 1980s, the status of Birmingham and the West
Midlands as Britain's prime manufacturing zone was severely eroded
as the region experienced unprecedented rates of job loss, particu-

larly in the recessionary period of 1978-82 when nearly a quarter of local jobs – 250,000 – disappeared. Traditionally, the unemployment rate in the region had been very low by national standards – rarely above one per cent between 1948 and 1966. But by 1986 it had climbed to 18.3 per cent. In the early 1980s, output in the region fell more rapidly than in any other UK region. The region had come to rely on a narrow range of manufacturing sectors dominated by a few large firms and a network of component suppliers. Persistent under-investment in capital and training, removal of protected commonwealth markets, and stop–go trade policies adversely affected the performance and competitiveness of such sectors. Combined with increased competition from the EC, US and Far East they sent the regional economy into a tailspin as falling orders and closures had severe knock-on effects within a highly integrated manufacturing economy. Since the 1980s efforts have been made not only to retain a viable, streamlined manufacturing base but to encourage new forms of economic activity. Conscious attempts to regenerate the local economy and attract new inward investment have augmented more long-standing policies to regenerate the conurbation's decaying physical infrastructure and stem the continued decentralisation of population (Birmingham City Council 1989a).

Birmingham has a variety of locational advantages. It is the heart of the West Midlands conurbation, and is centrally located in the United Kingdom with good transportation links with most other important cities. Traditionally, Birmingham has been well placed within the canal and railway system. Electrification of the rail link between London and the north-west in the 1970s further improved inter-city travel times. More significantly, the city became the hub of the national motorway system during the same decade epitomised by 'spaghetti junction', which remains the most extensive motorway interchange (M5–M6 junction) in the country. Significant further additions to the motorway and trunk road network, particularly with the prosperous south, will consolidate the conurbation's locational advantages. Intra-regional transportation is even more dominated by road rather than rail movement. This has, however, created congestion problems especially on the approaches to the city centre.

Compared with the dark days of the 1979-82 recession, most economic analysts agree that the city-region's current economic prospects are brighter and that its dependence on manufacturing has been lessened by the creation of 250,000 jobs in the service sector between 1983 and 1988 (West Midlands Enterprise Board 1990). The crucial question on both counts is by how much and what is Birmingham's position within the wider region? Services now account for fifty-nine per cent of jobs in the West Midlands region compared with forty-five per cent before the recession. This is, however, still ten per cent lower than the national average. Within Birmingham the proportion of jobs in the service sector is closer to the national average, but the sector has not grown as quickly as in the region as a whole. While the number of manufacturing jobs in the city declined by twenty-four per cent in the period from 1981 to 1987 to 167,000 jobs, 36 per cent of total employment, the service sector grew by only 4 per cent to 296,000 jobs, 63 per cent of total jobs. This failed to compensate for the decline in the manufacturing base which between 1971 and 1986 resulted in the disappearance of almost a third (170,000) of the city's jobs. The construction sector accounts for about 25,000 jobs in the city.

Since 1986 the economy has shown signs of improvement. Business and financial services such as law and accountancy firms and British and foreign banking concerns have generated 50,000 additional jobs in the city (Birmingham City Council 1989a). The unemployment rate fell from 20.6 per cent in August 1985 to 10.3 per cent in August 1990. Property prices and rentals, company profits and skill shortages have shown an upward trend. The city centre is becoming a strong growth pole for business services and tourist activity, stimulated by council initiatives such as the International Convention Centre and hotel and leisure schemes. There is a growing presence of small but innovative and rapidly growing high-tech firms on Aston Science Park on the periphery of the city centre near Aston University. Fifty-six companies employ nearly 1,000 people and further expansion is under way. Despite these promising developments there are restraints upon recovery. The city economy remains heavily dependent upon the manufacturing base. Thirty-five per cent of the West Midlands GDP stems from manufacturing activity compared with twenty-five per cent nationally (West Midlands Enterprise Board 1990). Many local service firms are either directly or indirectly dependent on manufacturing. In addition, growth of business services is constrained by the proximity and continued dominance of London's corporate finance sector.

The recent record of manufacturing industry is mixed. The rate of job loss within the city's manufacturing firms slowed to about two per cent per annum within Birmingham (Birmingham City Council 1989a). Within the region as a whole it stabilised. Key manufacturing firms such as Rover, IMI, Lucas, GKN and Cadbury/Schweppes, upon which the network of smaller engineering supply firms depend, are enjoying renewed prosperity. Many have sold off non-core activities and diversified into overseas markets. There has been a partial reversal of decades of under-investment in new production technology, and outlying parts of the region have recently benefited from inward investment particularly from Japan and West Germany. Overseas companies invested £2.5 bn and created 18,000 jobs in the region, and in the late 1980s a quarter of total foreign investment in the UK went to the West Midlands.

The danger is that improvement may have been caused by the boom conditions of the late 1980s rather than long-term structural change and improved competitiveness. Capital investment per employee is still below the UK average and the level of investment in micro-electronics production, product development and manpower training is poor by national standards and vastly inferior to Britain's major international competitors. Despite recent improvements in performance, the city's automotive industries, which account for a third of all manufacturing jobs, are entering a period of extreme turbulence, given excess productive capacity within Europe and fierce competition between local and overseas component firms to supply parts for the new Japanese car plants within the region and elsewhere in the UK.

Whilst Birmingham's economic fortunes have fluctuated over the last ten years, social conditions have followed a more consistent trend. Those living in relatively poor inner areas and outer council estates have become much poorer whilst the position of those living in the more affluent suburbs and beyond has improved. Although unemployment rates fell throughout the city in the latter part of the 1980s, the inner core of the city still has rates nearly double the city average and three times the national average. The inner city also contains a preponderance of low-paid workers employed in hotels, catering and retail work and as home-workers in the clothing industry. At the end of the 1980s about half the Birmingham work-force earned less than the Council of Europe decency thresholds (Birmingham City Council 1989b). Unemployment is also concentrated amongst specific groups in the population. Unemployment rates are highest amongst the young, but the city's severe long-term unemployment problem affects older age-groups worst. Inner-city Asian and Afro-Caribbean communities particularly suffer disproportionately despite possessing qualifications better than the average of the unemployed. In the mid-1980s the average unemployment rate amongst blacks was thirty-two per cent compared to thirteen per cent for whites.

Housing conditions are another problem. Birmingham has a stock of 400,000 dwellings. Of these, 240,000 are privately owned, 35,000 are Housing Association dwellings, and 125,000 are council-owned, making the city council the second largest public landlord in Europe. Despite the range of housing and substantial quality accommodation, the city is facing a crisis. Cutbacks in central government grant in the 1980s have added to the backlog of repairs. Of the private dwellings, 70,000 are either unfit, lacking in amenities or in need of renovation costing more than £3,000 per dwelling. This, along with changes in the social security and housing benefit system, has led to more homelessness and a growing council housing waiting list. Ethnic minorities' housing choices have traditionally been constrained. Birmingham has the largest ethnic minority population (twenty per cent) of any city in the country. Some inner areas contain over fifty per cent ethnic minorities. Afro-Caribbeans, Indians and Pakistanis have become increasingly disadvantaged in the labour and housing markets and endure multiple forms of deprivation. Social polarisation and race have contributed to the largest single concentration of deprivation anywhere in the country. Riots in the inner city in 1985 dramatically highlighted the dangers of this situation.

Quality of life

Birmingham experiences severe environmental problems associated with industrial dereliction, the 'concrete jungle' created by city-centre redevelopment in the 1960s and the priority then given to cars over pedestrians. Nevertheless, it does have assets – more miles of canal than Venice and more parkland than any other Western European city. Its growing range of tourist, arts and leisure facilities make the city attractive to visitors. For suburbanites there is a substantial amount of green space, good shopping and leisure facilities. They can also use new city-centre attractions like the Birmingham Symphony Orchestra's new concert hall, the National Arena, Sadlers Wells Royal Ballet and D'Oyly Carte. The outstanding challenge is to ensure that residents of more deprived areas benefit from this new investment.

Key urban actors

In the late nineteenth century Birmingham was seen not only as a successful manufacturing city but as the best governed city in the world. The Conservative mayor in the 1870s, Joseph Chamberlain, later prime minister, established a tradition of municipal enterprise and interest in economic affairs which has continued to the present day. There has always been good co-operation between middle- and working-class groups and municipal interests. The multitude of small business interests and high social mobility within the city prevented class confrontation (Commission of the Bishop's Council of the Diocese of Birmingham 1988). The political process has consistently been consensual and pragmatic and has given continuity to policy making, despite changes in political control.

Birmingham City Council is the most powerful local authority in the country, with a budget of over £750 million and substantial land holdings. However, its influence is increasingly being checked by a combination of socio-economic change and reductions in central government financial support. Population loss, particularly of wealthier residents, has reduced the city's resource base. This has been exacerbated by the failure to attract new inward investment and new rate income into the city. The city council none the less plays a leading role in promoting the economic and physical regeneration of the city. Good relations continue between the council and the business community, represented principally by the Chamber of Commerce and Industry.

Local development strategies

Since the Second World War there have been three main phases of urban and regional planning and economic development policy. The policy arena has become characterised by a growing number of agencies pursuing increasingly diverse initiatives. For thirty years after the Second World War, Birmingham's development was greatly influenced by regional planning policies which assumed continuing growth of the local population and its economy. National governments viewed the West Midlands as a prosperous area whose growth should be held back in favour of depressed regions.

'Time for action', 1975–84

The deepening industrial crisis in the late 1970s and early 1980s prompted increased interventionism on the part of central and local government. The loss of population and industry from Britain's inner cities in the early 1970s resulted in a fundamental shift in post-war planning policies. Comprehensive redevelopment and dispersal policies gave way to urban regeneration. In Birmingham, an Inner City Partnership scheme was launched in 1978 involving Birmingham City Council, West Midlands County Council, the Birmingham area health authorities and central government in the preparation of urban regeneration programmes.

A change in political control of the city council from Conservative to Labour in 1984 saw the approach of county and city to economic development converge. The city council's earlier approach had been conventional. In the 1970s the city attempted to retain industry through marketing measures, infrastructural work, and encouraging high-tech firms through developing a Science Park at Aston University and three other technology and product development facilities. Economic development functions were given a clearer focus in the early 1980s with the creation of an Economic Development Unit whose strategy mirrored the county's concern with training, business development and community enterprises in addition to conventional land and property initiatives. A key innovation was the West Midlands Enterprise Board (WMEB), established by the county council in 1982 to provide long-term equity and loan finance to small and medium-sized enterprises, primarily in manufacturing.

The late 1980s also witnessed novel policies and projects. The city council made a sustained effort to implement its economic development strategy. The private sector played an increasingly prominent part in a variety of local initiatives, encouraged by reviving economic fortunes and central government exhortations. Finally, an increase in the amount of external aid channelled into the region gave an additional boost to local investment projects. Following the West Midlands region's designation as an assisted area in 1984, after a long campaign, the region became eligible for assistance from the European Social and Regional Development Funds.

The city council played a major part in helping the city out of the economic crisis of the early 1980s. With a total budget of over £0.75 bn, a work-force of 54,000 and a £30 m budget for economic development, it was a powerful economic influence. It consistently emphasised the importance of prestige flagship projects to maximise leverage from other sources, in the belief that the council's role was to create the conditions in which private investment could occur. The council's long-term aim is the creation of a dynamic, wealth-creating economy (Birmingham City Council 1989a). Highest priority is placed upon supporting lead sectors of the economy such as manufacturing, business and tourist services and higher education, which export a high proportion of output. The city council also has a more people-centred approach, involving the promotion of equal opportunities, the elimination of disadvantage, and emphasis upon the adoption of good working conditions and employment practices.

The city's strategy has seven strands: the business development programme incorporates financial assistance to small businesses and managed workshops; the technology programme includes an innovation centre and development of the Science Park at Aston University; the land and buildings programme deals with commercial property needs and industrial improvement areas; a training programme delivers government schemes to meet local training needs; a tourist and environment programme involves the development of major facilities such as the NEC and the ICC plus environmental improvements at key locations such as city approaches and canals; a marketing and promotion programme aims to attract inward investment and provide advisory services. Finally there is a community initiatives programme.

Two initiatives epitomised the harmonious relationship between the city council and the private sector. The Birmingham Heartlands initiative was a public–private partnership venture to regenerate 2,500 acres of derelict, under-used and largely industrial land to the north-east of the city centre. With government backing, a consortium of interests including the city council, five construction companies and the Birmingham Chamber of Commerce formed and took shares in Birmingham Heartlands Limited (BHL) with the task of overseeing the redevelopment of the area (Roger Tym & Partners 1988). Subsequently the government has redefined the initiative by transforming BHL into an Urban Development Corporation to ensure the necessary public funding for infrastructural works.

Many of the key elements of the development strategy are in place. The centre-piece of the project will be a £⅓ bn commercial centre comprising 3.5 m sq ft of floor space. Three other developments involving a mix of industrial, retailing, residential, leisure and community uses are also planned. BHL successfully lobbied the Department of Transport for a £117 m spine road to open up the area. The city council is financing road improvements through the Transport Policy and Programme and has made good progress with land acquisition and clearance. The Heartlands initiative will cost over £1 bn and take 10 to 15 years to complete. It will generate an estimated 5.2 m sq ft of new business space and 20,000 new jobs. Six hundred and fifty new houses will be constructed and 2,000 others refurbished. The main outstanding challenges confronting BHL are to deliver recruitment training programmes for local residents on a sufficient scale to ensure they benefit from job creation, to involve the local community and to address difficulties in compulsorily purchasing land for the Midland Metro rapid transit system which is due to be routed through the area.

The second example of close collaboration between the city council, private sector and community interests is the Highbury Initiative. In 1988 the city council set up a symposium of public and private bodies with interests in the city centre and invited a group of international experts in urban design and economic development to discuss how it might be improved. It had become apparent that the city had to change its poor image if it was to attain its ambition to become a successful international city with a high quality of life. The improvement in the appearance and layout of an unattractive city centre was a key part of the task. The results of symposia held in 1988 and 1989 made a major contribution to the development of the city-centre strategy, originally drawn up in 1986 as an informal guide to investors (DEGW Partnership 1988, 1989). Many of the first symposium's recommendations were adopted by the city council despite their frequent critical comment. The importance of downgrading the ring road and diverting through traffic on to the middle ring road, maintaining accessibility to the city centre, raising urban design standards, giving pedestrians greater priority and reinforcing the character of distinctive quarters of the city centre were recognised and incorporated in subsequent plans. This responsiveness reinforced the strong consensus between city council and business interests.

The impact of local development strategies

The city council's market orientated approach has had an important leverage effect upon investment trends, particularly in the city centre. By concentrating on the development of prestigious 'flagship' schemes and provision of basic infrastructure which encourages further investment by other organisations, the impact of council expenditure was magnified. The new International Convention Centre (ICC) is an important example. It built on the success of the National Exhibition Centre (NEC) which has an annual turnover of over £200m and supports about 11,000 full-time jobs (Peat Marwick & McLintock 1989). There are plans to double its capacity to around 200,000 sq m by the year 2004. The city council and the Chamber of Commerce who jointly run the NEC complemented it by jointly developing the first multi-purpose international conference centre in Britain in the city centre. This £160 m scheme opened in 1991. It has eleven main halls with seating capacities ranging from 120 to 3,000 and is expected to attract half a million visitors per annum.

The ICC acted as a catalyst in stimulating other city-centre investments such as a five star Hyatt Hotel, a £250 m leisure and retailing complex incorporating a £50 m National Indoor Arena (NIA) for national and international sporting events, a National Aquarium, cinemas, shops, a hotel and offices. The city council estimate that the ICC, NIA and associated office and hotel schemes generate nearly 2,000 jobs. This could increase to 7,600 if further plans are realised. A range of office and retailing schemes elsewhere in the city centre also followed the ICC. Pump-priming investment and a construction boom in the late 1980s combined to produce a large-scale investment in the city centre. Birmingham's status as a commercial centre was enhanced with prime office space commanding rentals of £20 per sq ft. The total stock is set to overtake Manchester and make Birmingham the country's largest provincial centre. Moreover, the city's retail status showed a recovery in the late

1980s with the completion of the Pavilions Shopping Mall (250,000 sq ft) and the City Plaza (81,500 sq ft) and the planned redevelopment of the Bull Ring (£400 m, 0.6 m sq ft) and Brindley Place.

The council's opportunism and concentrated action in specific locations has enabled it to make the most of Birmingham's assets. The traditional under-representation of high-tech companies was reduced by exploitation of the technical and scientific research resources of two universities and a polytechnic. The growing Aston Science Park, developed jointly by the city council, Aston University and Lloyds Bank, contains start-up units, business support services and an advanced manufacturing centre. A university research institute was also launched in collaboration with Birminghan University and a microsystem centre established at Birmingham Polytechnic. Considerable expenditure has been devoted to improving the canal network – one of the city centre's few environmental assets – which flows through key redevelopment areas like Heartlands and the Convention Centre site and plays an important role in the regeneration process.

The city council has been able to generate a neighbourhood effect by concentrating investment in particular areas and promoting investment by the private sector. Judicial packaging of various grant programmes such as Urban Development Grant (UDG), Derelict Land Grant, Urban Programme and money for Industrial Improvement Areas revived the fortunes of the Jewellery Quarter of the city. Birmingham made more use of UDG than any other city. Over £10 m was obtained for just two schemes, the Holford Industrial Park and a major commercial and hotel development near the city centre. In housing, Birmingham was the first authority to experiment with 'enveloping' schemes which entailed comprehensive external improvements to whole blocks of housing. As a consequence, confidence in particular areas was enhanced and the scale of internal improvements increased.

Despite these success stories and the considerable entrepreneurialism of the public and private sectors, much of the city continues to face profound problems because of insufficient investment in physical infrastructure, the underperformance of the local economy and the persistent disadvantage suffered by the poorer sections of the community, especially ethnic minorities. In housing, despite the introduction of innovative housing measures like enveloping, Estate Action, design improvements, and joint ventures with the private sector and housing associations, the overall scale of government and private sector capital programmes cannot keep pace with the growing obsolescence of the older stock and with design faults in more recent council housing. Half of the city's 400 multi-storey blocks are in need of extensive repair.

In an attempt to redress economic disadvantage, the city council and the government's City Action Team gave increased emphasis to training and enterprise and linked major developments such as the Copthorne Hotel with local pre-recruitment training programmes. They also encouraged enterprise, particularly amongst ethnic minorities, by launching a venture capital fund for black businesses and an Asian Business Institute. The disadvantage suffered by these rapidly growing elements in the local population is none the less proving difficult to eradicate.

Worries also persist about whether the city centre can be adapted quickly enough and, given the predominance of road over rail and the growing congestion of arterial routes into the city centre, whether the traditionally high level of accessibility can be maintained.

Local foreign policy

Birmingham has a well-developed international strategy with a particular focus on Europe. Birmingham became eligible for EC structural funds in the mid-1980s and the city council geared up very quickly to maximise those resources. Unlike many other UK cities, it has broadened its perspective beyond 'grantsmanship' to consider how the city should position itself to deal with the advantages and threats associated with growing European economic and social integration. The city council rapidly took advantage of EC resources. It was the first authority to submit a programme under article 15 of the ERDF – a package of measures entitled The Business and Technology Support Programme. More significantly, the authority and the UK government were successful in having the first Integrated Development Operation (IDO) approved in 1988. This was due to strong local political and administrative leadership, the size of Birmingham and its capital programme and extensive governmental involvement in the city.

The chief executive of the council from 1982 was responsible for much of the early impetus. Having successfully lobbied for EC funding status he made sure that Birmingham reaped the maximum benefit. An early success was securing £13 m of ERDF for phase 1 of the ICC. Between 1984 and 1988 the city council itself was awarded over £60 m of EC monies. The city received £75 m of ERDF grants in the period 1984-87. During this period a European Liaison Unit was set up in the Economic Development Unit to advise departments on how to take advantage of EC funding sources and inform them of important policy developments.

The Birmingham IDO was a major step forward, especially as the submission had been made later than in other parts of the UK. The ERDF element of the IDO programme was designated by Government as a National Programme of Community Interest (Commission of the European Communities 1987). The IDO reinforced governmental and city council priorities and drew other important public and quasi-public organisations into the process such as the Severn Trent Water Authority, West Midlands Passenger Transport Executive, the Midlands Electricity Board, British Rail and the British Waterways Board. The EC approved £203m of aid for the IDO for 1987–91. £128 m came from ERDF, £31 m from ESF and the remaining £44 m in loans from the European Investment Bank and the European Coal and Steel Community. The submission promoted three principal growth sectors: tourism, high technology and small businesses; and contained six action programmes relating to economic development, communications, business development, environment, tourism and manpower. The IDO is four times larger than other EC programmes in Birmingham.

Individual companies, especially in engineering and crafts, have been helped through European grants. Most research and development programmes have been channelled into the city's academic institutions. The University of Birmingham has had large research contracts with programmes such as BRITE (Industrial Technologies), CEAM (Concerted European Action on Magnets), and ESPRIT (Information Technologies). The university and the polytechnic collaborated with other academic institutions and a number of firms in the region in the COMETT programme which encourages the transfer of high technology training. The institutions supported the ERASMUS programme encouraging student mobility throughout the Community. Aston Science Park and Birmingham University's Research Institute received ERDF funding towards the cost of site infrastructure and unit construction. The city has benefited considerably from the EC. Resource allocations compare favourably with national and regional standards and fully reflect the severity of the city's social and economic problems.

The city's European strategy

Birmingham aims to become a successful European city. A city strategy report, 'Into the 90s', identified three ways in which Birmingham should enhance its international role and its status as the UK's leading regional city (Birmigham City Council 1990). First, it attempted to anticipate the effects of the Single European Market and help local firms to exploit the associated business opportunities. Second, the city indicated its determination to build upon Birmingham's growing reputation as a cultural centre. Finally, the city committed itself to working with key local agencies to promote a favourable external image and ensure that city interests are adequately represented on important issues such as the Channel Tunnel and airports policy.

Many of these objectives remain broad aspirations, but some of the mechanisms which will achieve them are in place. The European Liaison Unit plays a key role, ensuring maximum use of EC resources, informing departments of key EC policy developments and lobbying the EC through its own Brussels-based organisation. In the last decade the city council has increasingly been involved in European networks. Traditional twinning arrangements have been supplemented by a variety of economic linkages and membership of supranational networks. The council sees the 'Eurocities' initiative as the best vehicle for lobbying the EC, exchanging best policy practice and providing an umbrella for more specialised networks. Birmingham is an important player in the Motor Industries Local Authority Network (MILAN) which promotes awareness of the workings of the motor industry in different regions. The powerful local Chamber of Commerce played a key role by opening a European Business Centre and offering export services.

What future for Birmingham?

Birmingham has a number of advantages which enhance its prospects for the 1990s. It is centrally located within the UK and is at the hub of the UK motorway system which has extensive links with the prosperous south-east. The city is increasingly accessible from abroad. The Euro-hub terminal at the airport offers flights to major European business centres – Milan, Frankfurt, Paris, Geneva – as well as to destinations in the United States and Canada. Birmingham has Britain's fastest-growing regional airport with passenger numbers expected to increase from three and a half million in 1989 to ten million by the year 2000.

The concentration of manufacturing activity in the region and the associated pool of skilled labour has proved attractive to inward investors from Japan and Germany. The close understanding between the public and private sectors has spawned a number of ambitious joint initiatives such as Heartlands and given the city a reputation for being entrepreneurial and forward looking. Many of the city region's leading manufacturers are enjoying additional injections of capital and growing profitability. The city's further and higher education institutions, with local industrial interests, have encouraged technology transfer and a growing presence of small high-tech companies. The ICC and the expanding NEC will continue to raise the city's international profile. The city will continue to be Britain's most important provincial commercial centre, especially given sizeable recent additions to the office stock. The growing range of arts and tourist attractions and events plus quality hotel accommodation will consolidate business-related tourism, increase the mini-break trade and enhance the city's role as a base from which to explore the surrounding region.

Birmingham nevertheless faces a number of problems which could retard its development in the next decade. Despite improved economic performance and the renewed prosperity of larger firms, the city's economy as a whole is characterised by under-investment in research and development, high technology and training. The shortage of industrial land within the city could encourage the trend for new economic activity to locate on greenfield sites in the southern parts of the West Midlands region (Davies 1989). Out-of-town office parks are also growing and will compete with city centre locations. Birmingham still has difficulty in shrugging off its reputation as an unattractive city, dominated by bland 1960s architecture and designed for cars rather than pedestrians. Traffic congestion, particularly along arterial routes into the city-centre, will increase with the traditional over-reliance on road rather than rail transport within the region and the concentration of new development near the city centre.

The rapidly growing numbers of members of the ethnic minorities experience discrimination in housing and job markets. Ensuring that economic development benefits these groups and integrating all elements of the population into every aspect of civic life are growing concerns. There may be insufficient resources to counter increasing levels of poverty. There is not enough public and private investment to deal with a growing backlog of repairs to the city's substantial stock of pre-1919 housing and the design faults found in later public housing schemes. As a result, many residents are experiencing deteriorating living conditions.

Wider developments during the 1990s may also threaten the city. There are worries that the Channel Tunnel will benefit importers more than exporters because of the more extensive sidings, depots and collection points on the continent. Despite the airport's impressive growth, its expansion is currently being checked by the high ticket prices to continental destinations caused by Birmingham's relatively high landing charges.

Manufacturing industry faces a severe test in the 1990s. Despite the efforts of local agencies, many local firms seem unprepared for the Single Market. The shortcomings in national transportation policy and the impact of the Channel Tunnel may well favour continental competitors. Knock-on effects will be experienced in the service sector which is also less internationally orientated. Nevertheless, the completion of a series of infrastructural projects will enhance local facilities, improve the city's links with Europe and encourage local firms to be more outward looking. The city is efficient in hosting international business visitors and the surrounding region can attract mobile manufacturing plant given its skilled labour and range of quality housing.

In national terms, Birmingham should maintain its current position as Britain's primary provincial city. Internationally, the situation is more complex. In the short term, improved links seem likely to benefit foreign manufacturers more than local ones, given superior transport infrastructure and levels of investment in training and high technology. In the service sector, Birmingham is likely to capture more business-related travel and tourism. However, its financial sector will face stiff competition from other regional centres such as Manchester, whose corporate sector is perceived to be more internationally orientated. In the longer term, however, the city's centrality within the UK coupled with planned infrastructural improvements may give it the competitive edge it needs to protect its national and enhance its international status.

The final critical question is where will new economic growth take place within the region and who will be the beneficiaries? Here local factors could exert a critical influence. Unless problems of congestion, an unattractive environment and land shortages within Birmingham are tackled quickly, most development may take place on easy to develop, less congested greenfield sites near to the airport, Birmingham International Station, the NEC and the recently extended motorway network. In policy terms, Birmingham has never been viewed in its regional context and this will undoubtedly penalise the city and other parts of the conurbation. Enhanced economic status will, as is so often the case, be accompanied by uneven distribution of benefits in spatial, economic and social terms.

References

Birmingham City Council (1989a), Birmingham Economic Strategy, Economic Development Unit, Development Department.

Birmingham City Council (1989b), Poverty in Birmingham: A Profile.

Birmingham City Council (1990), Into the 1990s. The City Strategy Report.

Commission of the Bishop's Council of the Diocese of Birmingham (1988), Faith in the City of Birmingham: An Examination of Problems and Opportunities Facing a City, Exeter, Paternoster Press.

Commission of the European Communities (1987), Decision on grant of a contribution from the European Regional Development Fund towards a National Programme of Community Interest in the UK: Birmingham Integrated Development Operation, Brussels.

Davies, H.W.E. (1989), 'Birmingham' in Klaasen, L.H., Van Den Berg, L. and Van Der Meer, J. (eds.), The City: Engine Behind Economic Recovery, Aldershot, Avebury Gower.

DEGW Partnership (1988, 1989), 'The Highbury Initiative'. Proceedings of the Birmingham City Centre Challenge Symposia, March 1988 and September 1989. With Birmingham City Action Team and Birmingham City Council.

Peat Marwick & McLintock (1989), The Economic Impact of the National Exhibition Centre on the Birmingham Region and the UK Economy. Report prepared for the National Exhibition Centre.

Roger Tym & Partners (1988), Birmingham Heartlands: Development Strategy for East Birmingham.

Spencer, K., Taylor, A., Smith, B., Mawson, J., Flynn, N. & Batley, R. (1986), Crisis in the Industrial Heartland: A Study of the West Midlands, Oxford: Clarendon Press.

West Midlands Enterprise Board (1990), West Midlands Economic Review. Prospects for the Region's Economy.

Part II New core cities

4

Frankfurt

Klaus R. Kunzmann & Markus Lang

Before the reunification of Germany, Frankfurt was regarded as the only serious German candidate to become a global city. Although the population in the city proper was only 633,000 in 1990, its economic rank as a financial centre of global importance, its international fairs and its huge international airport made the city one of the leading European centres of communication and information exchange. The international image of Frankfurt is closely linked to the power of the German currency controlled from the Frankfurt headquarters of the German Bundesbank. It is primarily this institution which has contributed to the global rise of Frankfurt which was the seat of the first all-German parliament in 1848 and the birthplace of Goethe and the once influential Frankfurt school of sociology.

Frankfurt's current economic potential is rooted in history. It has always been a flourishing merchant city at the crossroads of European trade routes, with an influential Jewish community. In addition it benefited from post-war decisions such as the siting of the American military headquarters in Germany and the establishment of the 'Bank Deutscher Länder', the later 'Deutsche Bundesbank'.

Today the city of Frankfurt is the centre of the much larger Rhine–Main region which has a population of more than 3.4 million. In its densely populated, polycentric hinterland there are a number of medium-sized cities which perform special functions as industrial centres (Offenbach and Hanau), as research and development technopoles (Darmstadt and Heidelberg) or as administration and political seats of Länder governments (Mainz and Wiesbaden). Urban functions in the city region are divided among neighbouring cities and the various sub-regions.

However, like other urban areas in this book, Frankfurt is characterised by significant contrasts. It has one of the highest GDPs per capita in Germany but also the highest level of per capita debt. Unlike some parts of the wider city region which are rich suburban communities such as Kronberg and Bad Homburg, parts of its far outer fringe are assisted areas and receive financial support from federal regional policy programmes. It has the highest rate of foreign citizens (22.7 per cent) and one of the highest rates of drug-related crime. But it also has the highest rate of per capita expenditure for cultural activities. Although Frankfurt is a centre of bourgeois elites, it has a strong liberal, not conservative, tradition. It has always been a focal point of critical student protest in Germany and is today one of the pivotal political headquarters of the Green Party. Although Frankfurt is sometimes considered a financial centre only, the city region is an important industrial centre. Car production (General Motors/Opel) as well as chemical and pharmaceutical research and production (Hoechst, Degussa, Lurgi, Merck) are key employers in the regional labour market through their forward and backward regional linkages.

These contrasts make Frankfurt and its wider urban hinterland a dual city region, where urban and regional development has to be managed under rather difficult decision-making conditions. The city is bound into the complex mechanisms of the federal system as a whole, with its underlying principle of subsidiarity, and into highly sophisticated processes of decision-making amongst the various tiers of government. Benefiting from the traditional power of local government and driven by the economic power and influence of its key actors, Frankfurt is swiftly modernising its physical structure to maintain its international profile and become the international flagship and show-piece of the Rhine–Main city region.

Frankfurt's geographical context

The city of Frankfurt is the core of the Rhine–Main conurbation. The densely populated urban region covers territories belonging to four federal states. The city of Frankfurt, three other cities and ten counties have their regional administrative tier at the seat of the Regierungs-bezirk Darmstadt. Essential political, economic and infrastructural decisions, however, are made in the state ministries of Hesse in Wiesbaden, in Munich for Bavaria, Stuttgart for Baden-Württemberg and Mainz for Rhineland–Palatinate. Hence they carefully monitor the development dynamics of the Frankfurt and Rhine–Main city region, which have considerable impacts on regional and urban change in its neighbouring regions.

Because of its excellent geographical location, Frankfurt can easily be reached from other parts of Germany and Europe. Rail journeys to Stuttgart and Bonn take less than two hours, to Munich and Hamburg only three hours. The future TGV link will mean that Brussels can be reached within two and a half hours. Through its inter-city terminal at the airport, Frankfurt has, so far, the only international airport in Germany directly served by the national railway system. A dense network of six-lane motorways linking the city, the regional hinterland and the Rhine–Main city region to other large conurbations in Germany, means that the Frankfurt region is highly accessible by car. However, traffic congestion at peak hours is increasingly impeding the free flow of intra-regional traffic. As a result, travelling time is growing almost daily.

With its thirty million passengers in 1991, the international airport is Europe's second largest, after London. Ninety airlines link 216 destinations all over the world with Frankfurt. It is a traditional junction for passengers from the near and the far East travelling to North and South American destinations and vice versa. All major European cities have regular daily connections. As a freight terminal, the airport ranks as the first in Europe, handling over one million tons of cargo annually. Frankfurt is also well linked to the European waterway system through its inland waterway port. The city is connected to Rotterdam and Basle by the Rhine, and by the Main and newly built Rhine–Maine–Danube canal to Nuremberg, Regensburg, Linz, Vienna, Budapest, Belgrade and the Black Sea. As elsewhere in Europe, however, the relative importance of the port for the regional economy is declining, though it still handles over five million tons of cargo.

Few other city regions in Europe have such a favourable location and efficient multi-mode services to all parts of the continent. This is the result of heavy public investment throughout the century, achieved by the city's far-sighted policy makers. They have ensured that the city was amongst the first to profit from modern, forward-looking transport technologies, guaranteeing it an important position at the hub of the European transport network. Its only disadvantage is that political delays at the federal level mean that Frankfurt is not yet linked to the European high-speed rail network.

Historical development

Frankfurt's economic future is deeply rooted in its history. In 1240 the citizens of the then 'freie Reichstadt' Frankfurt organised their first fair, which became an important city asset and eventually developed into a centre of European-wide trade and financial activities. In addition, Frankfurt has always played an important role as a political centre. German emperors were crowned there between 1562 and 1792. With the (re-)invention in the sixteenth century of the block-printing system by Gutenberg in nearby Mainz, Frankfurt also became the German centre of printing and the book trade, a role it still retains. The financial strength of the city is very much linked to the successful banking activities of the Rothschild family.

Between 1817 and 1890 the population of Frankfurt grew from 41,000 to 180,000. From 1880 onwards, like other German cities, Frankfurt started to absorb neighbouring communities to enlarge its territory, facilitating further population and industrial growth. In the late 1920s the city became famous for its advanced architecture and city planning. The First World War did not really touch the city and Frankfurt's economy boomed in the post-war period. As a result the city's population grew from 467,520 in 1925 to 553,646 in 1939. However, the Second World War affected Frankfurt enormously. Its considerable Jewish community was deported and killed in the holocaust. Almost half of the existing housing stock was destroyed by allied bombing, leaving just 93,000 apartments for a considerably reduced population. After the war Frankfurt benefited from a number of external decisions, such as those to locate the headquarters of the American forces and the Bank Deutscher Länder (later renamed the Deutsche Bundesbank) in the city. The division of Germany brought new activities to Frankfurt, such as the annual international book fair and the car industry, with considerable spin-off effects for the local and regional economy. Although the city lost the competition with Bonn to become the country's political capital, it became the economic capital of West Germany.

During the 1950s Frankfurt absorbed considerable numbers of German refugees and expellees from Eastern Europe. In the 1960s it also attracted foreign guest-workers from Italy, Greece and Yugoslavia. Because of this, but also because of its considerable economic growth, the population of the city grew rapidly in the post-war period. In 1952 it reached its pre-war figure and growth continued up to 1970. From the end of the war until 1977, the city was governed by Social Democrats. The Christian Democrats held a majority for the next twelve years and in 1989 Frankfurt became the first major West German city with a 'red and green' coalition. However, up to the mid-1970s, the image of Frankfurt was that of a capitalist city – 'The most American city', 'The Chicago of Germany' – with a high crime rate (which was not true) and an anonymous unattractive inner city. But this has changed in recent years.

Frankfurt in the 1990s

Today Frankfurt is a boom town, economically and culturally successful with great ambitions to become a global city. The number of major development projects grows almost monthly. Such projects are used to attract further interest, projects and investments to the city. Most of the projects aim to create an easily accessible post-modern, inner urban stage for the performances of the resident and visiting international society. They aim to make Frankfurt a mecca of architects and urban designers.

Despite this, like many other cities in Europe, Frankfurt has been experiencing continuous suburbanisation during the last three decades which reduced the city's population from 669,000 in 1970 to 633,000 in 1990. During the same period the suburban communities in the regional hinterland grew considerably. However, since 1985 the city has been regaining some of the population it lost to the suburbs. This is partly due to reurbanisation caused by changing lifestyles and attitudes of the younger urban households. But reurbanisation is mainly a consequence of foreign immigration into Frankfurt. Between 1979 and 1989 the number of resident foreigners grew from 125,085 to 137,922. Like other large urban centres in Germany, Frankfurt is a favourite target for German refugees from Eastern Europe and the former East Germany.

The city of Frankfurt has to pay over six per cent of its budget on social support for deprived citizens since, in German law, the costs for supporting Germans and foreigners living below the poverty line and refugees waiting for political asylum have almost exclusively to be borne by the cities. This has created increasing sociopolitical tensions amongst the indigenous population, whilst ethnic minorities and low-income groups are concentrated in the less attractive parts of the metropolitan area.

Because of its economic growth, land values and real-estate prices have risen more than in most other German conurbations, except Berlin, and in recent years the shortage of affordable housing has become a crucial political and social problem. Rents have risen considerably and households often have to pay up to half of their income on housing, especially if they wish to live in the traditional residential neighbourhoods of the city. The waiting list for low-income, social housing is long. In 1990 there were 16,000 households registered for such housing. Rising rents and the growing number of households who cannot afford to rent apartments on the open housing market forced the city to pay up to 200 DM of housing allowance to each socially disadvantaged household.

To find affordable housing, families with children are constantly being driven out of the city to the distant semi-urban communities on the fringe of the Rhine–Main city region. They have to endure long daily commuting distances and limited access to public facilities. In these suburban communities choice of educational and cultural institutions is limited, while at the same time primary and secondary schools in the inner city have to be closed because of falling demand. The construction of affordable housing by private investors and housing associations or co-operatives in Frankfurt stagnated throughout the 1980s. In 1989 only 427 units were constructed, mainly because of the lack of land but also because the likely profits in this segment of the housing market are negligible. The number of homeless in Frankfurt rose in the early 1980s. In 1990 there were more than 3,200 registered homeless in the city living in hostels and low-grade hotels. Under public pressure the city has recently started negotiations with neighbouring communities to acquire land for subsidised housing. The red–green coalition agreed to focus on housing and to support new affordable housing projects on inner-city land.

In comparison with many other cities and regions in Germany, unemployment in Frankfurt is low. Favourable economic conditions in the country during the 1980s meant that unemployment declined continuously from the mid-1980s. The rate of 4.8 per cent in 1990 was far below the state average in Hesse or that of neighbouring industrial cities and the national level. Frankfurt's economy is dominated by the service sector. In the early 1990s seventy per cent of all jobs in the city were in non-industrial sectors, a figure which had grown from sixty five per cent in 1980. The region as a whole had a smaller industrial decline; in 1988 40.3 per cent of the regional labour force worked in the industrial sector.

Today there are three outstanding economic sectors in the city: banking, the airport and international fair activities. Over four hundred banks are represented in Frankfurt, including sixty-nine from Asia, forty-two from North America and twenty from Japan. Apart from the largest German business bank, the powerful Deutsche Bank, the headquarters of the Dresdener Bank, the union-owned Bank für Gemeinwirtschaft and the Deutsche Bundesbank are also located in Frankfurt. Their skyscrapers dominate the skyline of the city. One hundred and thirty national and international insurance companies are also represented in Frankfurt.

In the early 1990s almost 60,000 people worked in the city's banking and insurance industries. This in turn creates a substantial market for other services in consultancy, legal services, public relations and the design business. The presence of the Bank for Reconstruction and Development, which finances Third World development projects, and the federal government agency responsible for technical co-operation with Third World countries, has caused many consultancy firms to locate in the region. In addition, the Frankfurt Stock Exchange is the most important in Germany, handling two-thirds of the turnover of the eight German stock exchanges. The land and property market in the city is dominated by growing demand from the banking and insurance sector and related services. This is mainly responsible for Frankfurt's having the highest land values of any city in Germany and has an important impact upon urban and social development.

Driven by its own success and by international competition from London, Amsterdam and Paris, Frankfurt airport is continuously improving and expanding its wide range of facilities. In coming years new developments in the precinct of the international terminal will offer luxury shops, office, hotel and convention facilities, storage and parking and every other facility needed to keep a multi-purpose urban mega-machine at the airport physically and economically alive. Employment directly related to the airport passed 50,000 in 1990. After banking, the airport is the second largest sector of employment in the Rhine–Main region. However, this concentration of physical investment attracts considerable road traffic despite the excellent connections with regional and national rail networks, and is creating growing environmental problems.

The third feature of Frankfurt's economy is its international fairs. More than twenty international business and industrial fairs are organised annually by the powerful local 'Messegesellschaft'. A steadily growing number of exhibiting firms (32,145 in 1988, half from abroad) attract more and more potential visitors from all over the world; 1.38 million in 1988. The managers of the Frankfurt Fair exhibition have great architectural ambitions. When modernising the fair complex they commissioned leading international architects to provide comprehensive architectural improvements like the new entrance hall, the tallest skyscraper in Europe. Other important sectors of the Frankfurt economy are its media and publishing activities, its role as a world fur centre with more than 10,000 employees in 280 firms; its public relations industry, with more than 200 firms and 10,000 jobs and its considerable hotel and restaurant services related to its international activities.

Cultural policies

At an early stage, Frankfurt recognised and exploited the economic potential of cultural industries. The number of cultural facilities in the Rhine–Main conurbation is impressive. There are public opera houses and theatres with resident companies and orchestras and regular evening performances in Frankfurt, Wiesbaden, Mainz, Darmstadt, Heidelberg and Mannheim. Brilliantly promoted by its prominent former chief cultural officer, Hilmar Hoffmann, the city of Frankfurt is the only large city in the country which spends more than ten per cent of its budget on cultural facilities and activities. The city has numerous attractive art and historical museums. One hundred and sixty galleries are located in the city, offering a wide variety of arts to an affluent local clientele, for whom investment in modern art has become fashionable. The headquarters of the Deutsche Bank in Frankfurt itself includes a famous museum of modern German painting. Frankfurt has always targeted many of its cultural facilities and programmes towards younger citizens. The city is also known for its jazz-related activities and its annual guitar festival. It hosts the most important European music fair and its music-related education and training institutions are internationally recognised.

The most visible result of the impressive cultural policy of the city in the past is a range of new museums along the river Main, 'Museumsufer', designed by the most prominent international architects. In less than a decade, thirteen new museums have been built and others modernised, to attract middle-class residents as well as international visitors. The priorities in local cultural development perfectly reflect the requirements of the modern city and its affluent establishment. Culture is considered to be a means of improving the international corporate identity of the city and attracting tourists from abroad.

Key players in urban policy

The network of major players in Frankfurt reflects the region's economy. The fair and airport managers are particularly influential. Together with the Chief executive officers of the banking sector they set the international *Leitbilder* for the city, thus influencing local political priorities. These priorities, in turn, are heavily supported by those local vested interests who profit from the city's new investment activities, such as international and local developers, the larger construction companies, the media and public relations firms, the hotel business and the financial consultancy sector. By preparing and servicing land for new office developments in the inner city, the city government plays a key role. But the Federal German Railways too, one of the biggest landowners in the inner city has considerable importance for the future economic development of the city.

Monitored by the local media and the vigilant local Green Party, social issues and the protection of the environment have become important themes in the city. Occasionally the unions – the metalworkers' union (IG Metall) has its headquarters in Frankfurt – join the chorus of those warning the city leaders not to ignore the negative consequences of the booming city economy. But this provides them with a dilemma. City government is well aware that it is not the high property costs which are crucial for foreign investors, but the speed of decision-making and planning procedures and all the other contextual prerequisites for profitable investment. Hence it is a difficult task for Frankfurt's leaders to balance economic and social development in the booming city. Obviously it is a particular problem for red–green city government.

Economic development strategies

The explicit aim of the Frankfurt elites is to ensure the city's ongoing economic success and tailor all activities towards that goal. In their view the economic development of the city depends upon strengthening and expanding its role as a global centre of banking, finance and international information and communication. All their activities are concentrated on such international roles and aspirations. The city's physical, cultural, social and environmental development strategies which play a key supporting role in achieving these economic objectives are designed to improve the quality of life in Frankfurt and make it one of the pleasantest cities in the world to live in.

During the last decade a series of major urban development projects have been commissioned, designed and discussed. The most controversial included:

'Westend zwei', an ambitious idea to reconvert the one million square metre area of the inner-city railway goods terminal into a mixed inner-city office and high-income residential quarter;

'City West', an island in the archipelago city aimed at providing 'clean' office space for 20,000 jobs and improving the image of the run-down inner-city district 'Bockenheim';

'Hanauer Landstrasse', designed as an overspill office area for the overcrowded city centre; and

'Frankfurt Airport Centre', a project to add further offices, space for hotels (2,000 beds) and commercial activities and 11,000 parking lots to the existing multifunctional airport complex.

All these projects require immense public co-ordination because of the complex decisions necessary before existing users can be moved, before new railways, and extremely costly public pre-investment can be made. Only after this 'pump-priming' will private investors – increasingly foreign investors and developers from Sweden, Great Britain and Japan – be willing to build offices and commercial centres on such sites.

Social dilemmas

Although there have been discussions of the social, environmental and traffic-related impacts of major development projects, they are usually pushed into the background of local politics so as not to discourage potential investors. Outside the central city the main concern is to cope with the impact of the city of Frankfurt's international policy, to provide land and infrastructure for all those who have been driven out of the inner city, to avoid urban sprawl, to conserve the remaining islands of untouched 'nature' and to offer accessible recreation facilities for less affluent people.

Frankfurt's current social development strategies have two purposes. First, they aim to reduce the social problems of disadvantaged and ethnic minority groups. Second, they are designed to maintain local social peace by reducing social tensions among the local population. Such tensions, caused by immigration to the city region, remain a serious threat to the brilliant economic image of Frankfurt. As a result policies and projects are initiated and designed for the inner-city area to retain affordable housing and to construct new stock at an increasing rate. The policy requires extensive public intervention in inner-city land and property markets and costly investment in redevelopment sites, such as railway land or other inner-city land reserves. A variety of social policies are designed to improve basic and further education for immigrants, provide cultural facilities for ethnic minority groups and reduce drug trafficking and abuse, which are problems for the city's image.

Noise reduction policies in the city region have been less successful. Although noise-retention walls have been built along carefully maintained urban and intra-regional motorways and traffic calming policies enforced in a growing number of middle- and high-income residential neighbourhoods, noise is still a problem in the city region. Apart from the airport which is a steady source of environmental pollution, increasing traffic volumes pose continuing problems for the city's environmental planners and managers. Monitoring is carried out, but it cannot reduce the growing daily nuisance.

Intra-regional co-operation

Intra-regional co-operation in a dynamic, densely-populated area with numerous local governments in four different federal states is a difficult task. There are continual conflicts between the interests of Frankfurt in the dominant core, and those of the surrounding smaller and larger cities and communities, typically centring around land use, infrastructure and environmental issues. The city's constant efforts to become a greater Frankfurt are met with suspicion amongst the other communities of the region. They recognise that a division of labour in the region is necessary, but only if the assignment and distribution of tasks and functions is balanced and fair.

For the central region of the Rhine–Main conurbation, the Umlandverband Frankfurt, an intercommunal association of forty-three communities in two towns and six counties, has the difficult task of seeking a politically acceptable balance between economically justified land consumption and ecologically indispensable protection of open land in the region. The development pressure in the region is enormous and the system of local taxes and vested interests evokes considerable intra-regional competition. This makes land use planning in the region a constant process of bargaining and negotiating between the communities on the one side and the public and the private sectors on the other.

In 1987, after four years of negotiations and bargaining, the assembly of the Umlandverband finally approved the land use plan for the urban region. Although critics complain about the compromises which have been made during this process, the fact that the plan has finally got the approval of the forty-three communities is a remarkable success. An earlier effort of the agency, to develop a number of new towns for the expected overspill population at the fringe of the urban area, was less successful. The concept was abandoned in the early 1970s because population growth in the region stagnated, following the national trend, and the housing needs of the urban population changed. It may well be revived during the next decade.

Frankfurt in Europe

As a global centre of information and communication Frankfurt hopes to benefit from the expected economic benefits of the Single European Market. The city prepares for its international functions to meet the challenge of European competition. Its economic policy aims to retain the city's key financial functions in Europe by attracting the future headquarters of the Central European Bank to the city. Land has already been assigned and reserved for the project. The city's transport policy aims to keep its hub function in the European air, retail and road transport networks. Frankfurt's cultural policy aims to provide more cultural facilities and offer high-quality activities and events of international importance and interest. Its social policy is to retain its international credibility as a safe and profitable location for long-term capital investment and to avoid local social tensions and conflicts which may be harmful for its international image. Its urban design policy promotes the international skyline of its high-rise office blocks as an unchangeable image factor for the city. Finally, its environmental policy aims to conserve the urban and regional environmental quality of life, despite all the pressure coming from the further internationalisation of the city.

There are a number of European-related issues which particularly worry elites in the region. There is a fear that the concentration of political and administrative power in Brussels will work against Frankfurt's interests and that an additional upper tier of government adds further strain to the already time-consuming and costly bargaining procedures at regional and national level. A particular fear is that the state government of Hesse will take authority from the city to compensate for functions it is about to lose to the federal or European governments.

A further concern is linked to the impacts of the reform of agricultural policy in the Community. The expected reduction of subsidies to agriculture and the redefinition of assisted areas in Germany will also hit the rural parts of the wider city region. Agricultural land which is taken out of productive use will come under new development pressure in order to meet the increasing demand for land in the city region. It will accelerate rural gentrification and make it more difficult to resist vested interests in the land market. Their demands to assign more greenfield sites for overspill housing and for those industries which have been driven out to the urban fringe by the cost of land, will find decreasing opposition from local governments. Another concern is the scattered system of eight stock exchanges in Germany, which make it difficult for Frankfurt to compete with the other leading European stock exchanges in Paris and London. Leaders fear that the city may lose its European competitiveness unless German resources are pooled.

Future scenarios

There are six major problem areas or potential conflicts which will face the city managers of Frankfurt and their opposite numbers in the Rhine–Main city region during the 1990s.

The Central European Bank

For many years the city fathers of Frankfurt have been feverishly lobbying to attract the headquarters of the future Central European Bank to Frankfurt. Because of the heavy concentration of bank headquarters in the city and the strong German currency, they have good arguments. But there are other contenders and in recent years all urban development efforts in the city have been orientated towards this goal. The uncertainty about whether Frankfurt will win the race for this key institution is preventing local planners and politicians from proceeding with some of the other still controversial mega-projects. There is some evidence that the reunification and the resurgence of Greater Berlin has weakened Germany's and Frankfurt's chances in this race. This is a new challenge for Frankfurt and even more so for the local elites. How many of those activities which Frankfurt gained after the war due to the division of Germany are endangered? Which functions will have to be returned to Berlin and Leipzig for political reasons? The city managers are lobbying strongly to keep their city high on the international agenda, but in the end they will be forced to share these functions.

Social polarisation and segregation

The more successful the city region is in becoming a global city, the more it will experience the social impacts of the division of labour. This requires an army of semi-skilled and unskilled cheap and flexible workers to keep the financial steamship with all its services and entertainment requirements running. The quest for such cheap, flexible and non-unionised labour, the difficulty of finding such labour among the regional ethnic German population and increasing foreign immigration are clearly matched, and the spatial consequences of this are obvious. Migrants will be temporarily concentrated in scattered urban pockets in inner-city locations which are not yet under redevelopment pressure for offices and luxury housing. The lack of social facilities (schools, kindergardens) will further lessen the chances of ethnic minority groups escaping from the vicious circle of underclass conditions. Problems such as drug trafficking and crime already fuel the tensions between the foreign and the indigenous population, despite all efforts of the red–green coalition to promote the city as a liberal centre of the multi-cultural society.

Traffic collapse?

Growing use of the car and an increasing dispersion of city activities has put the road network in the Frankfurt city region under considerable stress. Congestion is a daily problem and travel times increase constantly. New industrial production processes such as 'just-in-time' procedures have added further congestion to the regional road system and theoretical and actual travel times increasingly diverge. Efforts to enlarge the capacity of the road network are limited, mainly because of environmental reasons and protracted participatory decision-making procedures. Because of relatively low housing densities in the city region, public transport cannot offer, at least not at a reasonable price, a real alternative to the private car. And so, gridlock at peak times, or under bad weather conditions, threatens to become a constant feature of Frankfurt. Technical solutions to the problem – more and wider roads, bridges – will not solve the problem, but other more radical solutions are more difficult to achieve politically.

Intra-regional conflicts

Growing development pressure and the scarcity of developed or developable land will inevitably increase regional conflicts. Given the present system of local taxes and local government sovereignty, the conflicts will make any well-balanced and fair intra-regional division of labour increasingly difficult. Issues such as waste disposal, airport extension, or new motorway construction projects already overburden the established local democratic system. Hence administrative and political actors at state level may increasingly be forced to intervene, a move which will create new tensions between the two tiers of government, with mutual blocking of decision-making procedures. There are no easy solutions to this structural problem. Greater co-operation amongst local governments is not easy to achieve and it requires qualified staff for the constant negotiation and bargaining processes amongst the many actors in the region.

Environmental degradation?

Frankfurt will be increasingly affected by the negative environmental impacts of accelerated economic growth and short-term profit orientated private investment. The public sector in the Rhine–Main city region will have to cope with the further environmental burdening of its scarce groundwater resources. Frankfurt will experience increasing traffic-generated air and noise pollution and the public sector will have to bear the costs of decontaminating soils at the many sites of the city region where earlier users – chemical industries, railways, army and so on – showed a lack of responsibility for the environment. Despite the recycling efforts of private households and industries, waste volumes in the region are growing and will continue to burden the environment. Given the prospects of a financially less powerful public sector and a dual private sector, the capacity to achieve sustainable development in Frankfurt may not be found in the long run.

Fiscal crisis?

There is some evidence that the favourable economic conditions under which the city of Frankfurt prospered in the 1980s may not continue. The impact of global economic recession will change the city. The costs of German reunification and pressures to contribute to the development of Eastern European communities will further burden national, regional and local budgets in Germany. This will have an impact on future urban development in the region. Public money for investment in transport facilities, in public utilities and social facilities, as well as for land clearance for new urban development will be less available from local and state budgets. Even finance for existing high-quality maintenance may not be available. Finally, subsidies and seed money for innovative technical, economic and social projects, to support structural transformation and to cushion the social and environmental impacts of private profit-orientated investments will also decline. So only a few of the urban dreams of the city of Frankfurt may come true. With the ending of the boom period which encouraged and enabled the public sector to initiate large projects in the inner city, a period of forced austerity can be expected. This, however, may also reduce the overall social consensus from which the innovative private actors in the region benefited so much during the 1980s.

Clearly, there will be changing coalitions in these and other areas. As long as intra-regional conflicts are repressed, the region will join forces against outside competitors. But all the social, environmental and economic impacts of the international race, from which the city cannot abstain, will further burden the already complicated system of intra-regional co-operation. The capacity of local and regional policy makers to negotiate and balance conflicting interests, and their skills in conveying their decisions to an increasing number of diverging urban interest groups, will determine whether social polarisation can be avoided and social peace be guaranteed, whether the quality of life can be maintained and whether Frankfurt remains an attractive location for international investors and can retain an innovative and highly-qualified labour force. The 1990s will bring the city many challenges.

Those challenges will be aggravated by ones which have emerged more recently; the current economic recession, the reunification of Germany and the opening of Eastern Europe to Germany which could all have major, negative implications for Frankfurt. For example, Berlin is now obviously a prime target of real-estate investment in Germany. But so too is Leipzig, the city in the former East Germany from which Frankfurt took over many functions after World War II. Frankfurt now has to share with those cities and in particular has lost some of its international attractiveness to the new (old) capital city.

Equally importantly, the costs of reunification were underestimated. State and local governments in West Germany are forced and squeezed by the federal government to demonstrate solidarity with cities and regions in East Germany. As a result, Frankfurt has been forced to reduce its sumptuous cultural budget, of which it had been so proud during the last decade. These cuts will have a negative impact on both the cultural life in the city and the building-up of Frankfurt's image as an international city.

For strategic and ethical reasons the intended changes to the German asylum laws are still uncertain. For a city like Frankfurt, a prime target and a traditional gateway for global asylum seekers, this uncertainty places a further burden on its social budget. In addition, Frankfurt was always regarded as a prime winner from the Single European Market. With the weakening of the European dream after

Maastricht, such expectations have to be slimmed down. As the decision for the location of the proposed headquarters of the Federal European Bank has not yet been taken, Frankfurt is still left in uncertainty.

All these developments will constrain the city's scope for innovative action, for improving its material and social infrastructure. The next decade may be one of modesty and muddling through for Frankfurt. The city's exemplary efforts to combine economic wealth with social freedom and responsibility for the urban environment will be seriously tested during the years to come.

5

Lyon

Patrick Le Galès

Lyon is a city of paradoxes. France's second city and the capital of the powerful Rhônes–Alpes region, it is an affluent place, located within one of the most scenic environments in Europe. But it suffers from several dilemmas. Lyon was once France's main city and a major European centre, but its influence declined with the rise of Paris. The city retains a complex about Paris and has an uneasy relationship with it. This emerges very clearly in its political affairs where Lyon often contradicts national political trends. Lyon also suffers from a lack of recognition from the wider region it is supposed to dominate. Rhônes–Alpes, a region created by the state in the 1960s, lacks historical legitimacy. The sub-regions around Saint-Etienne and Grenoble have retained their economic independence, supported by the French state, and have never accepted Lyon as their regional capital. As a result, the city occupies a difficult administrative position. Suzerain without vassals, it is an administrative capital with public services dependent upon Paris.

Lyon is located in a magnificent natural site, at the confluence of two rivers, the Rhône and the Saône, and surrounded by hills. It occupies a strategic position between northern and southern Europe on the Rhône corridor. However, it is mainly known for its huge traffic jams. The road system, developed in the 1960s, and the controversial planning of the city have given the city an ambiguous image.

Lyon is essentially a city for business, where its very powerful bourgeoisie has traditionally accumulated enormous wealth through trade. But whilst it is a rich city, it has some of the worst urban problems in France. Lyon's eastern working-class suburbs have become the symbol of the urban crisis in France in the 1990s, comparable not with the English inner cities, but with the peripheral estates in Glasgow. Lyon is divided amongst a rich city centre dominated by the traditional and powerful business bourgeoisie, the politically conservative western suburbs which are the residential bases for the middle classes, and the left-leaning eastern suburbs, where workers, employees and immigrants live amidst derelict buildings, tower blocks and bars built in the 1960s. The contrast between these areas is enormous – and they do not mix easily.

Finally, Lyon was an important centre for international trade during the sixteenth century, with links to Germany and Alsace in the north, the Mediterranean world to the south and traditional trading relations with Turin and Geneva. However, despite its history and locational strengths, Lyon is not an open city, but a complacent city closed in on itself. As a result of these features, historians regard Lyon as a mysterious and intricate city to analyse. But in recent years a major debate has been conducted across the urban area in an attempt to prepare a new strategy for the future of Lyon. An unusually wide process of mobilisation and thinking has led to a document, 'Lyon 2010', which sets goals for the city for the next twenty years. This chapter focuses on three main topics; Lyon's history and its political and administrative role, its diverse economic base and the absence, until recently, of a clear economic strategy. It ends with an assessment of the 'Lyon 2010' strategy whose purpose is to make Lyon a European city.

Powerful economy; weak politics

Lyon was once the leading French city. The historian Fernand Braudel has written at length about the competition with Paris which prevented Lyon from becoming the capital of France. If France had kept the Alpine territory it once occupied, for example in the Turin region, Lyon might have become the French capital instead of Paris. An exceptional natural location and a prestigious history are the two dominant characteristics of Lyon. Located on the Rhône corridor between the mountains of the Massif Central and the Alps, the city forms a natural link between the north and south of Europe. During the Roman era it was the key location in what was then La Gaule. Once part of the German empire, Lyon became part of the French kingdom in 1312. It was a relatively free city which became a major European centre for finance and trade, in competition with Geneva.

The sixteenth century, when the French kings tried to control Italy, was Lyon's golden age. For a short time, Lyon was the main economic centre of Europe, with a strong influx of Italian bankers. At this point Lyon was at the heart of the Renaissance and a centre for the silk industry.

Subsequently, Lyon's political and intellectual influence declined because of the rise of Paris, but its economic base remained a major asset. During the seventeenth and eighteenth centuries, Lyon made silk and traded it all over Europe. During the nineteenth century, three industries made Lyon's fortune; textiles, metallurgy and chemistry. The city was at the heart of the regional economy as it invested its capital in growing regional industries. This period also saw fortunes made by Lyon's 'grandes familles' and proved the beginning of some major Lyon industrial companies (Berliet, Rhône-Poulenc, Péchiney, Gillet) and banks (Crédit Lyonnais).

During the twentieth century Lyon built a diversified and powerful industry on these firm foundations. The city's economic dynamism is explained by the interaction of three factors; dynamic relations between the main industries and a variety of small firms, capital accumulation and the influx of a qualified work-force from the centre of France and the Alps. Chemistry, electrical engineering and mechanics became the three main economic sectors in Lyon during the 1960s. At this time, a mixture of the headquarters of international companies, branch plants and a range of dynamic middle-size industrial firms was the key to Lyon's economic development.

By contrast, Lyon's political and administrative weight has been reduced to that of a regional capital. National political structures have had a negative impact upon Lyon. In the past, its political influence derived from its ability to connect and influence cities in northern and southern Europe, from Strasbourg to Turin. The rise of the French state constrained the development of these connections. By contrast, Paris has imposed its own network on the nation. The Paris–south-east diagonal uses Lyon but does not respect the Rhine–Rhône corridor and therefore reduces Lyon's influence. Traditional rivalries between Grenoble, Saint Etienne and Lyon have also prevented the last from being a real regional leader. Despite its assets, Lyon has not managed to assert its political, cultural and intellectual influence regionally or nationally. However, the unification of Europe provides Lyon with a unique opportunity to revive its glorious past. The European dimension has become a powerful symbol behind a strategy which is seen as the only way to escape from the domination of Paris and from its own uneasy relationships with other regional cities.

Politics in Lyon invariably stand out from national trends. 'Apoliticism', or extreme moderation, have been the watchwords of Lyon politics throughout the twentieth century as a small number of notables dominated the city. This reflects the political dominance of Lyon's traditional bourgeoisie – industrialists, traders and bankers – and their desire to stay away from national political debate and the conflicting but continuing influence of the Catholic Church. In reaction to its dependence upon Paris, Lyon's politics has remained a private local matter, despite the size of the city. Just two mayors ran the city for most of the century. Edouard Herriot, mayor from 1905 to 1957, was from the centre–left party of the *laïc petit bourgeoisie*, slightly progressive and a national political figure in his party between the wars. Louis Pradel's reign, from 1957 to 1976, represented the triumph of 'apoliticism', the gentle but autocratic domination by Lyon's notables, built on close relations amongst local councillors, business interests and influential families. After 1977, Lyon's centre and 'non-political' parties moved decisively to the right, partly due to the rise of the left in the working-class suburbs. However, Francisque Collomb, the mayor from 1976 to 1989, and his successor, Michel Noir, both retained their independence from national political parties. Stability is, therefore, a distinctive feature of Lyon's political life.

As with every French city, it is important to consider the growth of the urban area beyond the central city. In keeping with national trends, Lyon's first period of urban growth occurred at the end of the nineteenth century, when the population grew from 130,000 inhabitants in 1875 to 318,000 in 1914. From this period on, especially after 1945, growth in the urban area took place on the east of the city, where factories and industries were located. During this time, major estates were built in les Rilleux, les Minguettes, Vaulx en Velin, Villeurbanne – places which were intended to be the symbol of urban modernity but have instead been characterised by urban crisis and riots. By contrast, high-quality private housing was built on the west of the city, accompanied by tertiary sector activities but no heavy industry.

In the 1960s, the national government decided to organise the expansion of the urban area. It imposed la Communauté Urbaine de Lyon (Courly), a compulsory intercommunal body bringing together fifty-five communes comprising 1.1 million inhabitants, which has since been run by the mayor of Lyon. In this growth period, it also created a new town, L'Isle D'Abeau. To establish Lyon as a major international city, an ambitious urban plan was formulated. The Government encouraged national and international bodies to set up their headquarters in Lyon. It supported a major urban programme, which included the business district of La Part Dieu, for public services, deconcentrated from Paris; offices, a library, an auditorium, banks and shopping centres. The renovation of the historic centre – St Jean, St Paul – was undertaken by the local authorities and supported by the Government. A metro was opened in 1978. So, from the late 1960s onward, the national government supported the renovation and redevelopment of Lyon as one of the 'métropoles d'équilibres' designated at that time. Lyon steadily lost population during the 1970s, with a decline from 500,000 to 414,000 in 1982. This figure has since remained stable and Lyon now constitutes forty per cent of the urban area. As in other cities, offices built in the centre and urban renovation projects have led to the departure of young and working-class people, leaving behind an ageing population. From the 1970s most of the growth took place in a ring outside the city centre as the overall population of the urban area remained over 1.1 million.

Economic development in Lyon

The French national economic crisis after the mid-1970s did not provoke the collapse of Lyon's economy. The strength and diversity of its economy prevented it experiencing major problems. Rates of unemployment remained consistently below the national average. However, the restructuring of the national economy reinforced the integration of Lyon's firms within international companies. Increasingly, company headquarters and command functions are leaving Lyon. An important feature of this process was the progressive reduction of Lyon's financial power. Even before the economic crisis, the financial market of Lyon had been reduced to regional status. Several companies that began in the Lyon region moved their headquarters to Paris – Péchiney, Rhône–Poulenc, Berliet. The growth of the universities, hospitals, banks and public services in the

1960s had reinforced Lyon as a tertiary sector city. But often these activities were dependent on Paris, which reinforced the administrative subjugation of Lyon to the capital.

A second trend was reinforced by the crisis – the relocation of firms away from the city centre to suburban or rural sites within the metropolitan area. Lyon and Villeurbane, the other major commune in the centre of the metropolitan area, lost 40,000 jobs in the 1970s. By contrast, the number of jobs increased noticeably in the east and south-east of the city. Between 1976 and 1981, the urban area lost almost fifteen per cent of industrial jobs. The restructuring process led to job losses mainly in the big companies in the traditional sectors – chemistry, mechanics and textiles. This decline reflected the fact that major companies in Lyon had either been bought by multinational companies or their headquarters had left Lyon. Many middle-size firms were also taken over by national or international firms during the period. The regional dimension of Lyon's economy disappeared, as firms became integrated into international corporations. But the change was difficult as international integration meant a loss of local control. The slow but steady rise of the service sector strengthened the importance of jobs in this sector of Lyon's economy. By 1981, service jobs accounted for fifty-six per cent of total employment (145,000), as jobs in manufacturing declined to twenty-six per cent (67,000). Although the city lacks jobs and firms at the upper end of the service sector (finance, international lawyers) Lyon has nevertheless has increased its role and weight.

In comparison with other cities where industry represented a more important part of their economic bases, Lyon did quite well despite the crisis. Of course, jobs were lost and firms closed in traditional sectors such as the building trade and textiles. But overall, the main industrial firms heavily involved in the Lyon area – Péchiney, Berliet, Rhône-Poulenc, Thomson, CGE–Alsthom, BSN and Elf–Aquitaine – restructured successfully and became successful French companies in the 1980s. Some middle-size firms went bankrupt and some were taken over, but the economic structure of Lyon reveals that this range of firms remains extremely competitive in the region and is a dynamic asset for the future. Lyon's economy remained solid, diversified and dynamic and went through the crisis without major damage. Outside Paris, the economic strength of Lyon and its region is unrivalled in France. These trends continued during the 1980s. The urban region represented 3.2 per cent of the French population but had 4.2 per cent of jobs in the manufacturing sector.

Within the Lyon urban region, more than 100 firms with a work-force over fifty belong to foreign companies, mainly from the United States, Great Britain, Germany and the Netherlands. These companies employ over 65,000 people. The number of urban–regional jobs in manufacturing declined through the 1980s. In the service sector, all main sectors experienced growth during the decade. Currently there are 108,000 jobs in the tertiary sector in the city of Lyon, and 203,000 in the wider metropolitan area. In the trade sector more than 10,000 jobs were created during the 1980s. In the private health sector 13,500 people work in the city of Lyon alone, with 22,000 in the metropolitan area. In the insurance–banking sector, 12,000 work in Lyon, 16,000 in the wider area. In the public sector, the hospitals employ 20,000 in the wider metro-politan area. It is clear that the economic base of Lyon remains dynamic and well-balanced amongst different sectors, public and private employment and large and medium-size firms. Positive indicators in the housing and office markets underline the dynamism of the Lyon area. Indeed the absence of major economic problems helps to explain the absence of an explicit economic development strategy in the area until the end of the 1980s.

This absence of an explicit economic development strategy can be explained by several factors: in addition to the lack of major economic problems in the region, mentioned above, there are the tradition of political pragmatism without coherent policies, the liberal-dominated politics which militated against economic inter-vention and the close relationship between political elites and business elites which left the Chamber of Commerce and Industry to its own devices in this sector. During the 1970s, as in other French cities, the priority of Lyon City Council (LCC) and the Courly was to build major infrastructure. As we have already seen, the national government also supported major urban redevelopment projects during this period. In contrast with other cities, however, infra-structural development remained the key priority of the council throughout the 1980s. Challenged by a young, ambitious Gaullist leader, Michel Noir, who later became mayor (in 1989), the then mayor announced in 1983 that Lyon had to transform itself into an international city. Since the national government's regional policy at that time was to develop the leading cities and new technologies, the city also decided to exploit new technologies to promote itself as an

international city. This emerged as a coherent integrated strategy as it
did at the same time in Rennes, Montpellier, Toulouse and even Lille.

The priority given to the international status of Lyon was in fact a
renewal of the priorities set by the national government in the
1960s. A series of major infrastructures were built in the 1980s to
give Lyon the major facilities which characterise an international city.
These included the development of the metro system, the renovation
of the Halles Tony Garnier, a new exhibition centre, a new station
for the TGV, which connects Lyon to Paris in two hours, and
prestigious schemes designed to strengthen Lyon's image. Lyon also
strengthened its transport network with the attraction of the TGV and
the development of its airport Lyon–Satolas.

At the same time, the city tried to develop its promotional
capacity and attract new firms and services to Lyon. The arrival of the
TGV and the end of *agrément*, which had restricted office building in
the Paris region, in 1985, constituted a double threat. The capital
was now only two hours away and one could expect decentralisation
to Lyon, but also a loss of services to Paris from Lyon. The city had
to respond to this threat and it maintained the role of the Association
pour le Développement de la Région Lyonnaise (Aderly). The
association had been created in 1974 to attract firms to the area. It
brought together representatives from the business sector, local
authorities, private and public bodies. Following the national trend
(though rather later than in other French cities) a science park policy
was also developed. Lyon planned to have three science parks, to
encourage firm creation and to build workshops for small firms
together with centres of research and the universities. However, the
main priority of the Aderly was to promote the urban region and
attract firms. Despite the creation of a weak committee for economic
affairs in the city council in 1983 – quite late in comparison with
more dynamic French cities – there was a consensus between
business organisations and the local authority to leave the economic
policy to the Aderly. In co-operation with this body, the city council
concentrated on urban planning, the development of housing
around the science park, and the renewal of La Part Dieu, offices
around the TGV station and Achille–Lignon Quay in the city centre.

Lyon, like Bordeaux, was one of the few major cities which was
not taken over by the left in 1977. And the city was still managed in
a traditional way in the early 1980s. Lyon was characterised by the
dominance of a well-established bourgeoisie which controlled the

Chamber of Commerce and Industry and, to some extent, the local council. As a result, local economic intervention was not pursued, in contrast to cities won by the left, where the middle-classes working in the public sector, particularly the universities, attempted to develop economic strategies incorporating a variety of local policies. In Lyon, economic policy was delegated to the Aderly and the CCI. It would sell the urban area and encourage prestigious urban pro- grammes. In this respect the science park policy did raise questions. It was argued that it was not really a policy to develop Lyon's innovative capacity, but more a public relations exercise to publicise Lyon's new technology base. In a number of fields, chemistry and pharmaceuticals, for example, Lyon's firms are world leaders and research is the key to their development. The chairman of the Mérieux company, the world leader in its field, is also a major political figure in the city and a dominant force in the business world. Again in contrast with other regional capitals, the universities and trade unions have always been political outsiders in Lyon. Lyon is known as a secretive, bourgeois city where outsiders are not easily integrated. The fact that the city has not had an economic policy until recently has not prevented its economic development. However, new questions have recently been raised as the city tries to define how it should achieve international status. It has tried to identify major trends and policy areas for the future and respond strategically to them to secure European status for itself.

Future challenges; which urban area, which international strategy?

Although it is only one of the priorities of the new plan for Lyon, the economic and social integration of the whole urban area (Courly) is the major challenge facing Lyon in the 1990s. The urban area must be desegregated. In the summer of 1981 major riots took place in Les Minguettes, a large estate east of Lyon. These riots changed national government thinking and led to the declaration of a national urban policy, Politique de Développement Social des Quartiers, for the coun- try's most troubled neighbourhoods. The policy was strengthened in 1988 with the creation of the Delégation Ministérielle à la Ville to co-ordinate government policies and concentrate major projects in 400 problem estates. Lyon's suburbs were one of the key priorities.

But in the autumn of 1990, in Vaulx en Velin, in the eastern suburb of Lyon, three days of riots again took place between young people and the police. Vaulx en Velin was supposed to be a model of urban renovation – at least of physical renovation. The death of a young handicapped immigrant following suspicious police action ruined years of efforts. Once again, Lyon's suburbs demonstrated the growing crisis in French cities. The Government reacted promptly, since the Socialist Government could not escape blame for the deterioration in urban economic affairs, and social conditions worsened during the 1980s. A Ministry for Cities was created and legislation passed to oblige rich local authorities, with environmentally-conscious firms, high proportions of the middle class and low taxes to support the communes with the worst estates such as Les Minguettes and Vaulx-en-Velin, and other large estates such as Duchére, Mermoz, Etats-Unis and entire neighbourhoods in Bron, Rilleux, Villeurbanne, Saint-Priest and Meyzieux.

Lyon's problems remained pressing. In the urban area, foreign immigrants constitute twelve per cent of the population. About half of these are from north Africa, especially Algeria. But these figures do not include second and third generations, born in France; les beurs. Immigrants and their families are heavily concentrated in the eastern part of the city, particularly in the big estates, distant from the city centre and isolated from public transport and most facilities. The riots underlined the point that physical renovation may be valuable, but an urban policy must involve education, jobs and a whole range of co-ordinated policies.

Lyon is characterised by social and spatial segregation which in the past has not been taken seriously enough. The metro is an obvious example. It provides good links to the the centre of Lyon but the periphery is largely neglected. The inadequate economic policy is a further example. Since most of the attention and resources of economic policy have focused upon attracting firms and prestigious urban programmes, it is hardly surprising that there has been little mobilisation of local agencies to achieve the economic integration of the problem estates. In fact, as a city closed in on itself, Lyon has never cared much for its suburbs. Most urban policies have been carried out either by the national government or by local communes on the left who do not have the financial resources of Lyon itself.

Despite the existence of the Courly, no integrated policy has been developed for the whole metropolitan area. The Courly has negotiated with individual communes over projects, and it has also allowed some financial redistribution amongst communes. To some extent, social amenities were provided in the east because of this redistribution. The urban planning agency associated with the Courly did intervene after 1982, for instance in Vénissieux, but not on a very large scale. For years, the city of Lyon and even the Courly did little for the estates and the communes facing the worst crises. These problems were left to national government intervention, especially in the 1980s. These communes were politically on the left and preferred direct negotiation with the national government to avoid becoming politically dependent upon Lyon.

Despite government urban programmes – which with only 300 million francs for the whole national programme are not substantial in any case – and support for social housing renovation, Lyon's problems are worsening. The social and economic integration of the urban area must be the first priority. If nothing is done and the state and local agencies do not prevent the worsening of the urban crisis, social tensions will lead to further disorder, the image of Lyon will suffer and its strategic European ambitions will be threatened. This has been recognised by the mayor, Michel Noir, who has made the social and economic integration of the wider urban area one of his priorities. He appears ready to undertake a real metropolitan-wide policy, starting with the transport system. However, he is also more concerned by the future of the lower middle classes that he wants to keep in Lyon than by the future of the local estates. The future of the strategy remains uncertain.

'Lyon 2010'; reclaiming European status?

The question of Lyon's traditional role as an international city emerged vigorously in the debate about the city's strategic plan. The definition of a European strategy to make it a 'Eurocity' like Frankfurt, Stuttgart, Munich, Turin, Milan and Zurich, lies at the heart of all the strategic thinking in Lyon of the late 1980s and early 1990s. By playing the European card, Lyon hopes to escape domination by Paris and its uneasy relationship with its regional competitors. The quest for European status is a motivating factor in Lyon's search through its past for the keys to its future. If it can reassert its role in the Rhine–Rhône corridor and develop relations with Italy,

Lyon may rediscover the strategic importance it once had.

The first part of the strategy was to identify the international performance of Lyon and to compare it with other European cities. A number of key points emerged. Lyon's foreign population, apart from immigrant workers, is smaller than that of any other major European city. There are significant numbers of official diplomats. Two international organisations have their headquarters in Lyon, Interpol and the International Centre for Research against Cancer. But in the economic field, Lyon suffers from the absence of headquarters of large industrial or financial firms like Mercedes–Benz, Porsche and Bosch in Stuttgart, Fiat and Olivetti in Turin and Migros, Altusuisse, Jacobs Suchard in Zurich. Paris has attracted the bulk of economic command and control functions. Some studies show Lyon lagging far behind Geneva, Zurich and Barcelona. According to these kinds of criteria, Lyon is comparable with Turin, Düsseldorf, Manchester and Stuttgart. It does not have an important role as a centre for congresses and business meetings.

In terms of transport, Lyon is uniquely placed at the heart of the motorway and rail system. But its airport, with 3.8 million passengers in 1989, suffers from competition with Geneva. In the cultural field, Lyon attracts a significant number of foreigners and its main assets, the orchestra, the theatre and the ballet make regular appearances outside France. But in the intellectual field, despite its 75,000 students and important cultural infrastructures, Lyon has a low national profile, partly explained by the fact that the university has never been regarded as part of the city or integrated in local networks.

From this list of strengths and weaknesses Lyon's urban elites concluded that Lyon was the only French city apart from Paris which could be one of the great European cities, because of its size, economic strength and diplomatic and cultural amenities. However, Lyon also had weaknesses to overcome. The strategic plan 'Lyon 2010', completed before 1989 and the election of Michel Noir as mayor, represented an opportunity to mobilise local actors around key goals. Most attention was devoted to attracting exhibitions, 'metropolitan functions', a new opera house, a business district with all the signs of 'modernism', telecommunications, cable, and the headquarters of multinational firms and international organisations. The plan's first priority is economic development, to make Lyon more competitive in the European market-place. Prestigious urban programmes and attracting firms and organisations were predictable

priorities. The main new element is the recognition of the importance of universities and research for the 'Eurocity'. Their development and integration within the urban area is the second priority of
the strategic plan. Lyon was already one of the major university cities
in France; the idea is, therefore, to raise its international status.
Universities and centres of research were dispersed across the wider
urban area. After the election in 1989, the new mayor proposed a
number of urban projects to bring as many faculties as possible back
to the centre of Lyon and to raise the profile of the universities.

Under this scenario, Lyon would become a truly international
European city. The major weaknesses would be overcome. The new
transport and road system would remove all the current problems.
Universities and centres of research would become integrated in to
the city and would acquire international fame. The airport Lyon
Satolas would be connected to the city and would ensure regional
leadership by catching up with Geneva airport. Some multinational
firms and international organisations would relocate to Lyon. Economic prosperity, new housing schemes and the new transport
system would ensure the social balance of the urban area, aided by
state urban programmes. The new opera house and the new museum
would give Lyon an international cultural profile. It would attract
firms and residents from all over Europe and the United States; it
would be an international city. The significance of the strategic plan
has to be underlined, since it is the first time that such an exercise
has occurred in Lyon, demonstrating the mobilisation of local actors
around the issue. However, the plan reflects the interests of Lyon
business and the middle classes – including sections of the lower
middle class – at the expense of the eastern suburbs.

Lyon played the card of competition amongst European cities
rather late, in comparison with other French cities. The defeat of the
incumbent mayor in 1989 and the election of the dynamic Michel
Noir confirmed that the previous leader had not taken into account
European competition amongst cities and the complex strategy of
economic development. He had been overcome by the scale of
economic problems and his lack of leadership and projects for Lyon
had upset local urban elites who were increasingly concerned by
European competition. In contrast Noir concentrated upon enhancing Lyon's international status. Business interests in Lyon, whilst not
facing a major crisis, realised they had to open up the city and that
this was a unique opportunity.

A clear reservation about the plan is that although they want to escape domination by Paris, the urban elites of Lyon are adopting Parisian strategies, such as the business centre or the construction of a new opera house and *grands travaux* to enhance the prestige of the city. The Lyon strategic plan may be too close to national techno-cratic ways of thinking. Certainly the European strategy which has been adopted has not yet assimilated ways of thinking or planning seen in other European cities. In terms of the future, it is also revealing that although Lyon wants to be the corridor between northern and southern Europe, it mainly sees itself as the point where northern Europe enters the south. Since it is on the Rhône corridor, in the light of the economic crisis in Marseille, Lyon would become a prime location for Mediterranean immigrant workers in the future. This trend has not been taken into account. Finally, the preparation of 'Lyon 2010' led many local actors to suggest that Lyon should assert its regional leadership, a major asset in achieving European status. This policy has had some effect, as Saint-Etienne has signed an agreement with Lyon. But there is little sign that Grenoble, with its famous university and successful science park, would accept the regional leadership of Lyon. That challenge remains.

Along with the strategic plan 'Lyon 2010', the election of the new mayor, Michel Noir, represented a major breakthrough for Lyon. For the first time, the city elected a national political figure, with international ambitions for the city and presidential ambitions for himself. But the future is not yet clear. On the one hand, Noir was supported by local interests anxious to develop Lyon's international ambitions. In this respect, he accelerated existing programmes such as the renovation of the opera house, the creation of an international business centre in collaboration with the private developer SARI, the new automatic metro, at a cost of 350 million francs, and a new private road tunnel. Changes also occurred in the marketing efforts of Lyon City Council. The promotional budget was increased from twenty-nine to forty-nine million francs in the year after the municipal election. Since the mayor is a national figure, Lyon has become an important political centre in France for the first time, illustrating the new kind of grand notable playing the European and regional card.

At the same time, the mayor has not overemphasised the great projects for economic development at the expense of social housing or investment in schools and education. In this sense, his relationship with local business is more ambiguous than was originally thought. He behaves like a real leader of a whole city, a new experience for Lyon, and local business interests may be challenged by his lack of dependence upon them. Significantly, Noir is not one of the local bourgeoisie but comes from 'la Croix Rousse', a former working-class area.

Some uncertainties remain about Noir's future role. His position in Lyon's politics became complicated by internal party divisions within the RPR which has led to a split in the support for the mayor. A number of right-wing local business interests have mobilised in opposition against him, and this has partially destabilised the public–private consensus in the city. This has slowed down Noir's capacity to deliver the flagship projects at the pace originally intended, leaving question marks about their long-term future.

A series of questions remain concerning Lyon's European future. Private developers in Europe are currently wondering whether Lyon will really pursue its ambitious strategy or not; a doubt shared by politicians, journalists and rival French cities. The question is still posed whether Michel Noir will manage to change Lyon's traditions, to open the city to international influences? In terms of image, economic promotion and the organisation of international events, Lyon has an aggressive strategy and change is on the way. However, it is not clear that Lyon's local actors all share the enthusiasm for their mayor. Lyon will probably attract the necessary major infra-structures. It is a rich region and its economy remains dynamic. But to transform Lyon into an attractive, interesting city is another story, and it is difficult to see how the social traditions of the city and the domination of old families in the business world will be challenged.

A second question concerns the future of Paris. The decentralisa-tion reforms of the 1980s gave Lyon and its region unprecedented room for political manoeuvre. But the recent growth of the Paris region (especially if the new strategy for the Ile de France concen-trates on competition with London, New York and Tokyo) would be a threat to the region. If economic and political decentralisation were undertaken, Lyon would be able to exploit that trend. But during the past five years administrative decentralisation in France has gone hand in hand with economic reconcentration.

The third question concerns the future of Lyon's immigrant population and the widening gap between eastern suburbs and the city centre. Lyon relies heavily upon national urban programmes and the communes to deal with this issue. Intercommunal co-operation is limited on other issues and the strategic plan has few positive proposals. But Lyon is already the centre for urban riots in France and they could occur in the city centre in the future. This is a crucial outstanding challenge.

The fourth issue concerns co-operation in the government of the metropolitan area. The relationship between Government field services, the City of Lyon, the Courly, the Département and the increasingly influential region is not stable. The mayor modified the structure of the local authority, the Courly and a number of semi-public agencies, and is now clearly in charge in this area exercising direct control over most institutions. But uncertainties remain. It is not clear that Lyon will develop a policy for the whole urban area, including an economic policy. Urban elites in Lyon are still tempted to let the national government look after the eastern suburbs. A mayor who wants to raise his city's international status may also be tempted to concentrate on the city centre. Also, the regional council and its dynamic chairman are playing an increasing role in regional economic policy and relations between Lyon and the region remain tense.

Lyon has benefited from the introduction in 1989 of the *contrat d'agglomération* initiative which provides national government funds to support strategic policies aimed at reducing social and economic exclusion at a metropolitan-wide level. This has led to increased collaboration between the communes and a growing concern with the whole urban area of Lyon. Nevertheless, it is still too soon to assess the impact which the scheme will have upon the depressed neighbourhoods of Lyon. Uneven development within the metropolitan area remains a pressing dilemma.

A final question concerns the likely success of Lyon's international strategy and new infrastructure. The future of the airport, on the east of the city, probably illustrates most clearly what is at stake. The plan is that it would become the region's only real international airport and enhance Lyon's regional role. There are plans to connect the TGV and the port and divert air traffic away from Paris, and possibly Geneva. Further plans aim to create a public transport line from the airport to the city centre. The success of this project would put Lyon firmly in the forefront of the European transport network, especially if further TGV lines to the south are built.

Lyon is at a crossroads. European integration and a new generation of urban elites with a new mayor and new chairmen of the CCI, the Département and the region make it an important period for Lyon. It will be able to raise its profile and to strengthen its role and influence. But it is by no means certain that it will become one of the main European cities and deal with the most serious urban crisis in France.

6

Milan

Franco Bianchini

Milan is the capital of the Lombardy Region, which extends from the Po Valley to the Alps. Bounded to the north by Switzerland, to the west by Piedmont, to the south by Emilia–Romagna, and by Veneto and Trentino to the east, the region covers 23,800 square kilometres, and comprises landscapes of remarkable diversity, from the mountains of the north to the fertile plain of the Po River in the south. The picturesque lakes, Garda, Como and Iseo act as a magnet for tourists while the southern part of Lombardy is either industrialised or given over to intensive agriculture.

The region comprises nine provinces; Bergamo, Brescia, Como, Cremona, Mantua, Milan, Pavia, Sondrio and Varese. It is Italy's most densely populated region with a total population of almost nine million. Population density varies markedly from the mountainous Sondrio to the highly industrialised provinces of Milan and Brescia. The area between Milan, Como and Varese is now completely built-up and the Milanese urban sprawl engulfs nearby towns such as Vimercate, whose economy is dominated by IBM, Cinisello Balsamo (Toshiba), Legnago (Montedison), Arese (Alfa Romeo) and Monza (Singer, Candy).

Lombardy is well linked to the rest of Europe and the south of Italy by road, rail and air. It is connected by rail and road to Switzerland and France by the Simplon Pass, and to Switzerland and Germany by the Gotthard Pass. More than a third of Italy's international traffic goes through the border railway stations of Domodossola, Luino and Chiasso, all of which are well connected with Milan.

Milan has two international airports, Linate and Malpensa, the second and third largest in Italy, after Rome, for numbers of passengers and goods. However, Milan is still relatively small as an airport city compared with some of its European counterparts. In 1987 the average number of weekly direct international flights from Milan was slightly less than Rome and considerably less than London, Paris, Frankfurt, Amsterdam, Copenhagen and Brussels.

Economic development

Milan is the centre of a complex urban region extending across the central section of western Lombardy – a huge conurbation with a high degree of integration between the regional capital and a dense network of urban centres in which six out of ten Lombards live. The Milan Metropolitan Area (MMA) is a complex of 106 municipalities (comuni) which are closely integrated with the Milan urban core in economic, cultural and spatial terms. In 1986, the population of the urban core was 1,495,260 and that of the MMA 3,221,325.

The metropolitan area has been transformed since the end of the Second World War. (Beltrame *et al.* 1988) During the phase of rapid development between the end of the war and the beginning of the 1960s, the process of industrialisation in the MMA accelerated considerably. Industrial expansion, coupled with demographic growth, fuelled by immigration from the south of Italy, were not confined to the capital but began to encroach on the municipalities on the MMA borders, especially to the north. Large-scale industry led the growth process by exploiting the existing urban network and a well-established public transport system. While industry occupied a ring which followed the railway network, residential expansion took in new areas beyond this ring, shaping the demographic expansion of the comuni of the northern fringe of Milan. At this stage, the process of suburbanisation was determined by demand for housing, which was met by private speculative building, often of an extremely low quality. This phase of development soon resulted in a growing strain on the transport network as the working population found themselves increasingly pushed to the periphery. Milan's solution was to prioritise private transport, by massive investment in roads and motorways. Public transport policy also favoured buses over trains. These choices were partly influenced by the growth of the Italian car industry, which needed to expand its domestic market.

The second phase, from the early 1960s to the early 1970s, was characterised by urban congestion, resulting largely from the strategic choices made during the previous fifteen years. For housing and industry, location in the capital was no longer convenient because of increasing congestion and the high cost of sites, and industry began a massive process of decentralisation. In its place, service activities and expensive housing flourished at the centre of the metropolitan area. Urbanisation and industrialisation spilled over into previously agricultural areas, especially to the south and the north-east of Milan.

The explosion of private car ownership went hand in hand with the intensive development of local roads. Between 1963 and 1972, the road network in the province of Milan increased from 3,264 km to 4,048 km, with a rise in the number of vehicles from 494,000 to 1,204,000. By the end of this phase of intense development the MMA had basically assumed its present shape. These processes resulted in a shift in importance away from the capital and towards the whole of the metropolitan area. New suburban centres attracted some of the services and functions that were previously the mo-nopoly of the capital. There were many new public housing initiatives in peripheral areas, resulting in the gradual creation of self-sufficient neighbourhoods.

The third phase of Milan's development, beginning in the mid-1970s, saw an end to expansion and the start of a process of greater integration and homogenisation of the MMA. The growth of the comuni which had expanded during the previous two decades slowed down, in some cases to the point of losing population, while the southern area of the MMA attracted further development. The crisis of large-scale industry involved on the one hand deindustrialisation characterised by the restructuring and reorganisation of plants and, on the other, deurbanisation. Population decline in the urban core was accompanied by a fall in industrial employment of 104,000 between 1971 and 1981. In the rest of the metropolitan area the trend was in the opposite direction (Gario 1989).

Urban morphology

Milan evolved in distinct concentric circles which radiate from its historic core. The innermost circle (cerchia dei Navigli) follows the original medieval walls. It contains banking and business districts, the shopping areas, the main tourist attractions and the most exclusive residential districts, like Via Montenapoleone. The area is not thoroughly gentrified and it is possible to find pockets of cheaper housing and more 'downmarket' shops. A second circle, the viali or bastioni, encloses other fashionable residential and business districts. The areas between the viali and the city's ring road are becoming increasingly popular as residential districts. Beyond the ring road are the working-class suburbs, the factories and modern office and residential complexes such as Milanofiori to the south-west and Segrate, Milano San Felice and Milano 2 to the east, near Linate airport. Further out, between the northern boundaries of the Milan municipality and Lake Como, the historic town of Monza and parts of the hilly countryside of Brianza have virtually become suburbs of the city.

The strong upward demographic trend which characterised post-war Milan and its hinterland was interrupted in the 1970s when the birth-rate began to fall. The drastic decline in immigration into the area, due mainly to industrial restructuring and the tertiarisation of the economy, contributed to this trend. Milan, like many other European cities, went through a process of suburbanisation and deurbanisation. Population decline in the city of Milan has been constant since 1971. Between 1971 and 1986 the Milan municipality lost 238,000 inhabitants − 13.7 per cent of its 1971 total. The population of the MMA, on the other hand, grew by about two per cent between 1971 and 1981 but declined by an average of about 1,000 per year in the first half of the 1980s.

The pattern of population movement is one of suburbanisation at the urban level but concentration at the regional level. People have followed the movement of industry, leaving the centre after the decline of traditional heavy industry and moving to the periphery. Milan and its conurbation are increasingly linked with the Turin–Ivrea conurbation in Piedmont, forming a bipolar nexus specialising in high-tech industry (Turin) and financial and commercial services (Milan). The growth of outlying parts of the MMA does not compensate for the outward flow of population from the centre − the Milan conurbation is gradually deurbanising. The falling fertility rate, which is at the core of this phenomenon, has many socio-economic implications. On the one hand, it causes a fall in demand for goods and services normally provided by the female component of the employed work-force while, on the other, it is the reason for the increase in the number of women, especially married women, seeking work. The school system is also affected. From 1986 to

1991, the age cohort within compulsory education decreased by around thirty per cent in Milan and twenty per cent in the province. The growth of the elderly population – a relatively new phenomenon – will bring about increased demand for new services for this age-group.

Key problems

Traffic congestion is a serious environmental problem in the MMA, with important implications for the area's long-term economic performance. At the beginning of the 1980s there were 410 vehicles per kilometre of road in the MMA compared with 135 in Lombardy and 71 in Italy as a whole. This problem reflects the high concentration of production and service activities in the central part of the metropolitan area and the radial structure of the public transport network, which lacks adequate horizontal links. This means that some peripheral areas are handicapped by poor accessibility. Similarly, decentralisation of productive activities is in many cases hampered by inadequate transport links with the periphery.

Congestion imposes considerable economic costs on people living in the MMA and has a negative impact on their quality of life, encouraging deurbanisation. Commuting also draws income away from the metropolitan area, where it is earned, to outlying residential areas, where it is spent. Traffic exhausts combine with fumes emitted by industrial plants to produce serious atmospheric pollution. The concentration of sulphur dioxide in the air is amongst the highest in Italy, especially in winter when it reaches peaks ten times higher than the national average. One desperate measure adopted in 1991 was the banning of cars on a rota basis determined by their number plates.

Milan lacks land for neighbourhood services and other public amenities. Land for residential use is also scarce, despite decentralisation and the city's demographic decline. Over forty per cent of families experience difficulties in finding suitable accommodation. In the 1980s, fifty-five per cent of residents in the outer ring lived in overcrowded accommodation. Twelve per cent lived in conditions of overcrowding described as 'critical'. There has been very little new public or private investment in housing in the urban core, and the gap between housing cost and its affordability for first-time buyers is

growing. Particularly in the centre, the lack of affordable accommodation is exacerbated by the increase in the number of single-
member households and by the tendency to convert residential units
into offices and shops. About 130,000 dwellings which in 1971 had
been used for rented accommodation were owner-occupied or used
for different purposes in 1991 (D'Agostini 1988).

High accommodation costs pose serious difficulties for low-
income families. Poor housing quality, however, still affects a
considerable minority of the population and neither the market nor
public provision has been able to address the problem effectively.
The difference in housing prices between the central and the outer
areas of the MMA is increasing. However, prices in those areas
immediately beyond the central core and in outlying *comuni* are
becoming more homogeneous. There were 37,140 housing evictions between 1983 and 1986, the highest rise in Lombardy. In one
year alone, evictions in the city of Milan rose by 19,000. Finding
adequate accommodation, rather than regular employment, is the
single greatest problem for the growing number of immigrant
workers from the Maghreb and Senegal. In some districts, local
residents have protested against the municipal provision of temporary accommodation for immigrants. Immigration, from North
Africa as well as the former Yugoslavia and other central and east
European countries is likely to become an increasingly important
issue in the urban policy debate in Milan. The city council has none
the less been able to respond to growing immigration pressures
more effectively than its counterparts in Rome and Florence.

The local economy: structure and international position

Large-scale mass production dominated the industrial development
of Italy between 1945 and the beginning of the 1970s. Large
industrial plants were concentrated in the Milan–Turin–Genoa trian-
gle, which acted as a magnet for immigration from the south of the
country. The MMA developed in three phases. Between 1945 and
1963, rapid industrial growth saw manufacturing employment rise
from 458,000 in 1951 to 640,000 in 1961, mostly in sectors such as
engineering (from 180,0000 to 263,000), chemicals (49,000 to
80,000), metallurgy (27,000 to 34,000) and shoemaking (6,000 to

13,000). Some sectors remained static or declined gradually – for example, textiles, from 49,000 to 45,000 (Pisani 1989). The most significant increases in employment resulted from the development of light industry, particularly in the plastics sector, which did not require large investment or complex technology. This spread throughout many comuni of the metropolitan area, without a specific geographical concentration. The localisation of light industry, more generally, resembled a leopard-skin pattern, where large concentrations in Milan and Sesto San Giovanni evolved adjacent to agricultural areas.

During the second phase, from 1963 to 1972, manufacturing employment rose from 640,000 to 681,000. Engineering played a vital role in this growth, particularly the production of consumer durables and vehicles. In all other sectors there was either marginal-growth (chemicals, rubber), or decline. The MMA became a site of massive investment in methane pipeline networks, motorways and roads. For the first time the municipality of Milan lost its attractiveness for industrial plants. Between 1961 and 1971, manufacturing employment in Milan fell from 427,000 to 353,000.

The 1970s were years of crisis and restructuring for manufacturing industry in Lombardy. Total industrial employment in the MMA declined for the first time, from 681,000 in 1971 to 596,000 a decade later. Declining demand in the national market and increased competition from abroad induced firms to compete more and more on a global scale. Under such unfavourable market conditions the large corporations concentrated on the maximisation of existing assets and a radical reorganisation of logistics and relationships with suppliers and sub-contractors. The state-controlled corporations in particular faced heavy pressure because they lacked self-financing capacity and were making large losses. They were forced to invest in new technology, which contributed to reducing their work-forces.

One part of large-scale industry adopted typical strategies of crisis restructuring, characterised by the concentration of functions within the enterprise, limited investment in rationalisation and limited increases in turnover. Another responded to the crisis through more sophisticated types of investment, the widening of the production mix, increased product differentiation, expansion of services, diversification of end markets and decentralisation of operational responsibilities. The structural economic changes of the 1970s also affected inter-firm relationships. The clear distinction between large-scale enterprises and medium or small ones gave way to greater integration, interdependence and complementarity between firms. The dynamics of innovation and development in small and medium-sized enterprises (SMEs) were no longer subordinated to and imitative of large firms. Instead, SMEs emerged as important actors in the industrial system of the MMA.

The main manufacturing sectors in Lombardy today are machine tools, car components, leather goods and furniture, paper, jewellery, textiles and garments. Among the older, more traditional industries with large work-forces, those still of major importance include rubber (Pirelli), chemicals (Montedison), bioengineering and textiles (SNIA), electro-engineering (Magneti Marelli at Sesto San Giovanni), steel (Falck), agro-industrial products (Ferruzzi), pharmaceuticals (Carlo Erba, Enichem, Formenti and Glaxo). IBM is also a large local employer.

In 1981 there were 1,699,700 people employed in the province of Milan – ten per cent of Italy's work-force. The service sector had overtaken manufacturing industry in terms of employment – 56.1 per cent services, 42.9 per cent industry and 1 per cent agriculture. Compared to the rest of Italy, Milan has a greater than average percentage employed in the chemical industry, engineering, electro-mechanics and electronics, and in the financial and business services sectors. It has a smaller than national average employed in agriculture, construction and public administration. Comparisons between Milan and Lombardy show that the city increasingly specialises in the provision of services for enterprises at both local and national level. The relationship between Milan and its region is different from that between Italy's other regional capitals and their hinterland. For example, Turin in Piedmont, the other major industrial centre in northern Italy, has an occupational profile which is more similar to that of the region as a whole. Of those employed in Milanese industry 61 per cent work in firms with fewer than 1000 employees, 29.3 per cent in medium-sized firms (100 to 1,000 employees) and only 9.7 per cent work in firms with over 1,000 employees – in line with the national average. Turin presents a different picture, with 22.9 per cent employed in large firms, and 77.1 per cent in SMEs – 28.1 per cent in medium-sized firms, and 49 per cent in small ones. Turin is dominated by two major industrial groups, Fiat and Olivetti, which act as poles of attraction for the whole region, while Milan has a more diversified economic base centred on SMEs and endowed with greater flexibility and a significant presence in all vital sectors of the national economy.

SMEs grew considerably during the phase of restructuring of large-scale industry in the Milanese hinterland in the late 1970s. Today they face increasing competition from large-scale industry, especially in sectors characterised by high capitalisation and advanced technology. Since the mid-1980s in particular, SMEs have struggled to hold on to their position. Their competitive performance depends on their capacity to introduce new technology faster and more efficiently than large-scale industry, and to market high-quality specialised products instead of mass-produced standard ones. Innovations requiring large injections of capital and, therefore, extensive borrowing are largely beyond SMEs.

The province of Milan also has a significant number of artisan firms. They increased from 29,400 in 1957 to 97,700 in 1983 and eighty-five per cent are considered as an integral part of the industrial system (artigianato di produzione). The highest rates of growth in artisan firms has occurred outside the MMA. In 1957 for every two artisan firms in Milan there were three in the province, but by 1983 the proportion was two to six. Thirteen per cent of artisans in the province work in engineering, ten per cent in plant installation, nine per cent in construction, eight per cent in woodworking and six per cent in clothing. The geographical position of Lombardy in Europe both stimulates and favours the ability of artisans to innovate and exchange information so that they are not marginal workers but rather at the centre of the production system.

The MMA is relatively specialised in certain industrial sectors, for example, in engineering, precision mechanics, electronics, chemicals, computers and printing. These sectors do not, however, provide the basis for an expansion in employment because of the highly productive, new-tech and qualified nature of the work-force. In the service sector, the MMA is highly specialised in financial auxiliary services, research and development, oil and gas piping, office equipment hire including computers, public relations and advertising. Expansion in the MMA has been particularly strong in already highly specialised activities, such as services to enterprises and insurance. The primacy of Milan in innovative and advanced economic activities guarantees that the MMA will remain the economic and financial capital of Italy, and an important European centre. Milan is a well-established pole of tertiary activities, particularly for those services linking the local and national economies with European and international markets. For example, the import/export service sector is especially developed because of high volumes of international activity by local, regional and national firms throughout the 1980s. The potential of the service sector, however, has not been fully realised. For instance, the degree of internationalisation of banks and trading companies is still fairly low.

A high-tech future?

High-tech industry is the newest and most advanced sector of the Milanese economy. Over the last two decades it has become concentrated in a large area to the north-east of the city, including part of the Milan municipality. Its development was favoured by the existence of a good road network, efficient public transport services, including the underground, and the presence of research institutions such as the Departments of Informatics at the State University and at the Polytechnic. Almost half of the high-tech firms located in this area are controlled by foreign capital. To sustain processes of rapid innovation, these firms often adopt systems of flexible automation, easily convertible in response to changes in production. The main sectors utilising high-tech production are pharmaceuticals, advanced precision instruments, telecommunications and electronics for medical use.

The first project for an Italian science park originated in the MMA twenty years ago, with proposals made by the municipality of Milan for the creation of a high-technology complex near the town of Gorgonzola, twenty kilometres from the city. This project, although never implemented, led to the concentration of small, private high-tech companies in the area, and to the establishment of branches of the National Research Council and the Polytechnic of Milan. In the 1980s, as a consequence of the failure of the public sector to implement the scheme, it was taken over by Pirelli, Italy's major tyre and rubber goods producer. The initiative was relocated to the 740,000 square metre Bicocca area of Milan where Pirelli have a presence dating back to the First World War. The scheme, renamed Project Bicocca, involved the dismantling of a huge redundant industrial complex in collaboration with Milan City Council and the Lombardy Region, for the creation of a new technological pole. Initially, the transfer of the Department of Electronics of the Polytechnic to Bicocca was seen as an 'incubator' for new firms, to which commercial offices, technology transfer agencies, venture capital enterprises and research laboratories would be added. Although not all of this happened, the objective of creating a multifunctional and technologically integrated science park, capable of providing jobs in research and development for about 5,000 people, still remains. Employers in Bicocca include informatics and bioengineering firms and a teleport owned by Reuters. The eventual investment is expected to be over 1,000 billion Lire. This project, once implemented, should lead the way for new initiatives and serve as an example for other regions in Italy. Planning permission for the first phase of the project, which includes a residential scheme and the construction of premises for academic research institutions, was given by Milan City Council in 1992. Progress in the implementation of the project is currently blocked by the political crisis in the city administration, which will not be resolved at the earliest until after the municipal elections to be held in June 1993.

Labour market and employment

Between 1971 and 1981, manufacturing employment in the province of Milan fell by eight per cent and this trend continued into the 1980s. When the total number of employees is broken down into categories of employment, a more complex picture emerges. Between 1981 and 1986, there was a fall of only 7.5 per cent in the number of white-collar workers, while the number of skilled and unskilled manual workers fell by 27.5 per cent and 23.2 per cent respectively. In the same period the number of middle managers grew both in relative and absolute terms. In 1982, 56 per cent of employees in industry were described as manual workers, decreasing to 51 per cent by 1986. This fall was counterbalanced by rising numbers of clerical, white-collar and management staff. In 1982 these comprised 41 per cent of the industrial work-force and in 1986 46 per cent. In sectoral terms, the most marked decline affected metalworking (32.4 per cent), followed by textiles (18.7 per cent) and engineering (16.8 per cent) (Luciforo, 1989).

In general, manual employment has declined whilst white-collar employment has grown. The employment structure of the Milan area is characterised by high numbers of managers and middle managers.

In all sectors, the proportion of managers in the MMA is higher than in Lombardy as a whole. The proportion of technicians, administrators and professionals like accountants and business consultants in the MMA is also higher than the regional average. Milan has fifty-seven employees for every 1,000 residents in the health and education sectors, as against forty-one in the rest of Lombardy, reflecting the centralisation of administration in these fields.

The rate of unemployment for the Milan municipality in 1990 was 5.5 per cent (Montanelli & Cervi 1990). It had been 8.5 per cent in 1981 and 8.3 per cent in 1986. The figure for the MMA in 1981 was 5.7 per cent, an increase of over 4 per cent since 1971. Estimates suggest a fall in employment for the first five years of the 1990s of between 115,000 and 120,000. Increased unemployment will especially affect the peripheral areas of the MMA, partly because of the specialised nature of the new jobs expected to be created there. The attractiveness of the city centre to employers is expected to remain strong, chiefly because of the availability of infrastructures, amenities and cultural facilities. The service sector is expected to consolidate its dominance of the local economy. Forecasts suggest it will grow by ten per cent, from about forty-eight per cent to fifty-eight per cent of all jobs.

Milan's national and European contexts

The primacy of Milan within the Italian economy, particularly in governing Italy's relationships with European and world markets, is evident in a number of sectors. In the financial sector the share of international transactions conducted by banks with headquaters in Milan, as a percentage of those conducted by banks with headquarters in Italy, grew from thirty-seven per cent in 1978 to 57.6 per cent in 1984. Moreover, as many as thirty-two of the thirty-four branches of non-Italian banks in Italy in 1985 were based in Milan (Camagni 1988). Research expenditure by local firms is far higher than in any other Italian city. In the advanced services sector in 1985 36.9 per cent, 26.5 per cent and 19.7 per cent of all Italian marketing consultancies, business management consultancies and advertising companies respectively were based in Milan. The position of Milan in 'cultural industries' sectors such as publishing, fashion and design is similarly dominant (Camagni & Pio 1988).

Recent research confirms that Italy's international economic functions are increasingly centralised in Milan, particularly in the fields of technological innovation and telecommunications. Camagni and Pio estimate that Milan is the most important of twenty-five cities located within the area of influence, but excluding Rome. More particularly, they argue that Milan, followed by Zurich, Frankfurt and Munich, is the top city for strategic functions measured through indicators including the volume of airport passenger traffic and the number of headquarters of major industrial companies. Milan also comes first in commercial functions – indicators include number and turnover of trading companies and of visitors to trade fairs – and technological and industrial functions. In financial functions, Milan ranks third, after Munich and Zurich but, somewhat surprisingly, before Frankfurt. The city also has the best composite ranking, followed by Frankfurt, Munich, Zurich and Turin.

Further research by the Agnelli Foundation into the position of forty-eight cities in the urban hierarchy of the European Community suggests that Milan is a 'command city' of European importance. Along with Frankfurt it is endowed with innovative potential and industrial structures of a superior level and occupies a position in the urban hierarchy which is inferior only to London and Paris. The same research, however, also highlights some important weaknesses of Milan compared with Frankfurt and even with lower-tier cities such as Turin and Stuttgart. For example, the percentage of the industrial work-force in Milan employed in the most innovative sectors is 33.3 per cent, considerably less than in Frankfurt (39.3 per cent), Turin (41.5 per cent) and especially Stuttgart (57.2 per cent).

Key actors, projects and strategies. The 1990–95 programme of Milan City Council

Between the end of the Second World War and 1991, all Mayors of Milan belonged either to the Socialist Party (PSI) or to the Social Democratic Party (PSDI). In November 1991 the municipal administration led since December 1986 by a Socialist politician, Paolo Pillitteri, a relative and close associate of PSI leader Bettino Craxi, was swept away by a tide of corruption scandals. Local magistrates brought charges including payment and receiving bribes (tangenti) related to public procurement contracts against Pillitteri and a number of other local politicians. The most prominent of these politicians was another Socialist, Carlo Tognoli, Pillitteri's predecessor as Mayor and former Minister for the Problems of Urban Areas. The scale of the corruption revealed by the magistrates' investigations was so huge that Milan was soon nicknamed by the press *Tangentopoli* ('Bribesville'). Investigations into kickbacks paid to politicians on public sector contracts rapidly extended from Milan to other cities. Charges were brought against a number of national political figures, including PSI leaders such as Craxi himself, former Foreign Secretary Gianni De Michelis and former Justice Minister Claudio Martelli.

Between the June 1990 local elections and November 1991 the municipal administration led by Pillitteri had been supported by the Socialists, the PDS (Democratic Party of the Left, known until early 1991 as the Italian Community Party), the Greens, and the Pensioners' Party. The priorities of the new administration, dubbed the *rossoverdegrigia* ('red, green and grey') were spelt out in a programmatic document for the 1990–95 period. The document put social policy and quality of life issues at the forefront of the city's agenda and paid less attention to economic development and the city's future international role. Such emphasis was in keeping with the tradition of PSI-led municipal policy-making in Milan. The most interesting policy innovations introduced by the local authority in Milan over the last two decades are to be found mostly in the social policy area. One example was the introduction in the late 1970s of an experimental system of Area Social Accounting (*Bilancio Sociale di Area*, or BSA), designed to plan the delivery of municipal social services so as to reduce inequalities between different areas within the city (Martinotti 1989).

The 1990–95 municipal programme emphasised imaginative proposals to convene a city-wide forum to redefine the opening hours of shops, places of work, municipal services and public transport facilities, to meet the needs of working women in particular. Other proposals included the establishment of a municipal agency to help women wishing to enter or re-enter the labour market; a multifunctional centre for young people, with cultural facilities, counselling services, meeting spaces and a database on the condition of youth in the city; a 'social project' targeted at immigrants from outside the EC, including the provision of temporary accommodation and assistance in finding regular employment; and the provision of 10,000 new homes, to be created through a programme of new building and reuse of existing buildings.

There was also a well-developed cultural policy, including proposals to found a new museum of contemporary art and a detailed plan to enhance the city's environmental sustainability. The 'green strategy' of the municipality included several important commitments. The first concerned a plan to revitalise redundant or underused areas, most of which had traditionally been used by industry. With the decentralisation of manufacturing plants, about three million square metres of land (twenty per cent of all industrial space in the Milan municipality) were available for redevelopment. The *Comune* undertook to devote half of the revitalised areas to collective uses, with green spaces taking the lion's share (Vicari & Molotch 1990).

The City Council's policy on traffic and public transport completed its green strategy. It was proposed to extend the city's pedestrian zones and its network of cycle lanes and to widen the areas where car access was restricted. There were plans to strengthen public transport infrastructures with major projects including the completion of a third underground line, the creation of radial LRT systems and, perhaps most importantly, an underground high-speed railway 'through line' to link three existing rail stations, through an eighteen kilometre route from the north-western to the south-western periphery of the city.

This polycentric vision of the city's future informed aspects of the municipal programme concerned with land use planning and the delivery of local authority services. Under the Tognoli mayorship in 1984, the City Council had prepared a plan (a *Documento Direttore*), which considered the implications of the creation of the *passante* for urban settlements. In particular, the *Documento Direttore* promoted the formulation of four specific 'area projects' with a strategic relevance for the future of the MMA. The four projects are being implemented by the Pillitteri administration through the 1990–95 municipal programme.

The first area project, Portello–Fiera, involves the expansion of Milan's international trade fair. Milan is one of the most important European cities for trade exhibitions, with the second highest annual number of exhibitors, after Paris (Secchi & Alessandrini 1990). However, the fair's competitive position is undermined by inadequate accommodation in an area close to the city centre, difficult access for cars and lorries because of heavy traffic and insufficient outdoor exhibition space. Under this *progetto*, the Fiera is expanding into the adjacent, ex-industrial area of Portello, previously occupied by Alfa Romeo. A project for the decentralisation of some of the Fiera's structures to outer areas is subject to competing proposals from Milan's three major developers, Giuseppe Cabassi, Salvatore Ligresti and Silvio Berlusconi. Conflicts between local interests have meant that no decision has been reached on a new location for the Fiera.

The second area project, the Bovisa–Farini–Repubblica, aims at integrating the emerging Garibaldi–Repubblica business district into a new green-space system. It comprises new premises for the Lombardy Regional Council, the stock exchange and various financial companies. The new business district will include a wide range of public amenities. The *Documento Direttore* specifies that forty per cent of land and cubic volumes should be allocated to finance, credit and public administration, with the remaining six.y per cent divided between hotels and business services (thirty per cent), culture, leisure and information services (twenty per cent), and retailing (ten per cent).

The third and fourth projects (Sud Est and Nord Ovest) are wide frameworks for the regeneration of peripheral areas, in which the existence of large redundant industrial zones provides opportunities for environmental improvements and the development of advanced services and high-tech industrial activities. The Sud Est project includes Montecity, a pole for service activities created by Montedison on its land near Linate airport. It will be expanded to comprise new parks and new premises for the Policlinico Hospital and the State University of Milan. The Nord Ovest project will contain new premises for the Polytechnic of Milan. The implementation of both projects has been blocked by the City Council's political crisis.

In January 1992 Piero Borghini, a former Communist politician who had recently left the PDS to create an independent centre-left grouping within the council, formed a new administration (Borghini I) involving the PSI, the PSDI, the Christian Democrats, the Liberals, the Pensioners and one defector from the Northern League, an anti-corruption, anti-Rome, anti-South and anti-immigrant protest party whose influence on Milanese, Lombard and northern Italian politics was rapidly growing. The Borghini administration relied on a wafer-thin majority and collapsed because of disagreements within the coalition in June 1992. In July 1992 Borghini succeeded in forming a new administration (Borghini II), which was supported by the same political parties which had backed Borghini I and involved some non-party political experts (*tecnici*). Once again, the coalition was too weak and divided to last and in March 1993 the Mayor was forced to dissolve the city council in order to overcome the political impasse. Milan is currently administered by a Commissar appointed by the Prefect. A new city council will not be created until after the local elections to be held in June 1993. The *tangentopoli* scandals have seriously undermined the credibility of mainstream parties such as the PSI and the Christian Democrats and the Northern League are widely expected to achieve an electoral triumph, as they already have in local elections recently held in other Lombard towns like Monza, Varese and Mantua. The 1990–95 municipal programme, prepared by a coalition which has now virtually no chance of gaining power, is therefore now a largely meaningless document. A wide range of voluntary associations, business groups, public–private partnerships, pressure groups and consortia is vigorously promoting urban development projects in contemporary Milan. Paolo Fareri (1990) suggests that a variety of factors explains this remarkable activism. First, the 1980s saw a growing awareness of the importance of the quality of urban life among opinion makers and the public. This was reflected in flourishing neighbourhood associations which campaigned on local environmental issues and against the penetration of the Mafia and other forms of organised crime, as well as in the growing influence of such publications as Il *moderno* and *Societé civile*, which devoted much space to debate about the future of the city.

Second, construction companies and other public and private enterprises were keen to obtain contracts for major development projects financed by the public sector before the creation of the Single European Market in 1992. Italian entrepreneurs feared that, after that date, the pressure of competition from their more efficient European counterparts would increase considerably. The establishment of building consortia like Milano Sviluppo and Costruire Milano can partly be explained in this context. Another example is the leading role of the Italian telephone company, Sip, in launching and financing the *Lombardia cablata* project, for the establishment of an optical fibre telecommunications network primarily aimed at businesses throughout Lombardy.

The third important reason is the growing inability of the

municipality to formulate strategies to address the increasingly complex problems of the city's development. This derives from a combination of political instability, the constant need for municipal politicians to concentrate their energies upon time-consuming mediations between different interests and the inadequate number of specialist policy-makers within the local authority. Moreover, the traditionally narrow concern of municipal town planners with land use regulation and the built form is increasingly inadequate for the purposes of integrating different sectoral policies and interventions into a coherent urban strategy.

Finally, the construction industry is no longer the central actor in the urban development process, as it was, in alliance with political parties and factions, until the late 1970s. Particularly for major projects, an increasingly important role is being played by large public, quasi-public or private corporations, such as Sip (*Lombardia cablata*), Pirelli (Bicocca Technology Park), Montedison (Montecity), Fiat (indirectly involved in the Consorzio Palasport) and the IRI group.

Issues for future urban policy and strategy development

It is difficult to predict if, when and in what form the urban development projects planned by the city will be implemented. Delays and uncertainties affecting implementation are partly the product of the peculiar nature of the Italian political system. As Vicari and Molotch explain, 'in the Italian situation, things happen because the political and bureaucratic mix is right, and nothing happens if they are not' (1990, p. 617).

There are, however, more specific problems related to the capacity of municipal technical bureaucracies to implement policies, which the city council would need to address through internal reforms. More general problems, related to the inefficiency of state bureaucracies, are being addressed by the *Consiglio metropolitano*, a pioneering experiment launched by the city's Prefect. Second, co-operation between Milan and the municipalities of its hinterland is not always easy to achieve (Dente 1989). However, Law No. 142 of June 1990, which among other major reforms of the structure of Italian local government institutes a strategic authority for the MMA, may help to solve this problem. However, an agreement between relevant municipalities, provinces and the regions on the boundaries of the strategic authority still has to be reached. The provisions of the law related to the new metropolitan authority, in short, are still very far from the implementation stage. Third, central government has traditionally shown little sensitivity to the problems of Milan. It has equally little understanding of the need to sustain and develop the city's functions as an engine for stimulating innovation throughout the national economy and as a gateway between Italy and international markets. There are various examples of central government's reluctance to finance urban development projects in Milan, even when they could arguably have enhanced the competitiveness of the national economy. Finally, scarce financial resources significantly constrain implementation, especially for projects led by the city council. The 1990 reform of local government may provide some help, by widening the revenue-raising options of the comuni and encouraging them to form more solid partnerships with the private sector and different tiers of government.

Foreign policy issues

Ironically Milan, despite its well-established function as a link between Italy and the world economy, lacks a strategy aimed at refocusing and further developing its international role. There is no coherent effort co-ordinated between local public and private sector agencies to promote the city abroad and no systematic monitoring of perceptions of the city by outsiders. The city's image, formerly associated with style, good design, fashion, opera, efficiency and hard work, has been badly damaged, internationally, by the corruption scandals. Until the institution in 1990 of PROMOS by the Chamber of Commerce and the Association of Industrialists for Lombardy, there was not even a one-stop agency co-ordinating Milan's approach to attracting inward investment.

Conclusions

A diverse economic base, a lively civil society, a commitment to the locality by innovative companies such as Pirelli, the presence of a strong system of universities and research centres, and a clear national hegemony in most advanced services and many high-tech sectors are obvious signs of the considerable future economic potential of Milan. Without denying the numerous problems described earlier, Milan City Council, with its emphasis on social policy and quality of life issues, has succeeded in reducing the impact of social inequalities and deprivation. The Comune, however, has perhaps paid too little attention to the vital need of developing the city's international role and has not been able to integrate its 'area projects' into a vision of the city which is more than the sum of its parts. Moreover, the technical shortcomings of the council's policy-making structures have contributed to delaying the implementation of urgent projects like the expansion and decentralisation of the Fiera.

Policy-makers in Milan have also largely been unable to capitalise on the potential synergies between the city and its regional hinterland. Necessary projects like Lombardia cablata and new high-speed rail links along the Turin–Milan–Venice line, for example, are still a long way from being implemented. It seems likely, however, that a thorough debate about the potential role of Milan in its region will not take place for some years, until the controversial questions of the boundaries of the new MMA authority created by the June 1990 reform of local government is settled. The council should also play a greater role in encouraging the city's universities to co-operate and in dealing with the shortage of graduates in technical and scientific subjects that Milan suffers from. In short, a range of problems principally related to the weakness of the municipal decision-making process and of the Comune's capacity to implement projects suggest that Milan is at a relative disadvantage in the very intense competition between European sub-continental regional capitals. At the same time, the centrality of Milan in the Italian urban system and in its relationships with Europe and the world have been further strengthened.

Shifting the focus from national and international competition to issues of internal functioning and sustainability, it is possible to argue that Milan is in a good position to meet the challenges of responding to growing presssures from immigration, reducing traffic congestion and generally improving its environmental quality. In this sense, demographic decline, the deurbanisation process and the availability of large redundant areas for use as green spaces and other public amenities, provide a mix of opportunities too good to be missed. Uncertainty, however, dominates any current discussion about the future development of urban policy in Milan. It is, impossible, at this stage, to predict the political priorities of the municipal administration which will emerge from the local elections in June 1993. *Tangentopoli* has discredited and removed from public life an entire political and economic establishment. It remains to be seen whether Milan has sufficient resources to overcome the current crisis and democratically regenerate its political and economic life.

References

Beltrame, Gianni et al. (eds) (1988), Trasformazioni territoriali e organizzazione urbana, IReR-Progetto Milano, 9, Milan, Angeli.

Camagni, Roberto (1988), 'La capacità di risposta dinamica della area metroplitana milanese', in Predetti, Adalberto and Camagni, Roberto (eds), La trasformazione economica della città, IReR-Progetto Milano, 8, Milan, Angeli.

Camagni, Roberto & Pio, Allesandro (1988), 'Funzioni urbane e gerarchia metropolitana europea: la posizione di Milano nel sistema dell' Europa centro-meridionale', in Predetti, Adalberto & Camagni, Roberto (eds).

D'Agostini, Sergio (1988), 'Edilizia residenziale', in Beltrame, Gianni et al. (eds) (1988).

Dente, Bruno (1989), 'I processi di governo nella metropoli', in Pastori, Giorgio, Balboni, Enzo & Dente, Bruno (eds), Istuzioni e nuovi modelli di governo urbano, IReR-Progetto Milano, 10, Milan, Angeli.

Fareri, Paolo (1990), 'La progrettazione del governo a Milano: nuovi attori per la metropoli matura', in Dente, Bobbio, Fareri & Morisi.

Gario, Giuseppe (1989), L'Area metropolitana milanese, Milan, CNR.

Luciforo, Claudio (1989), 'Struttura e dinamica occupazionale nell'industria milanese', in Dell'Aringa, Carlo (ed.), Lavoro e nuove professioni nella città che cambia, IReR-Progetto Milano, 11, Milan, Angeli.

Martinotti, Guido (1989), 'Urban change, urban services and the quality of life' in Eurocities Conference, 21st and 22nd April 1989, Barcelona, Eurocities.

Montanelli, Indro & Cervi, Mario (1990), Milano ventesimo secolo, Milan, Rizzoli.

Pisani, Ignazio (1989), 'Il terziario: le trasformazioni storiche 1840-1970', in Beltrame, Giannini et al. (eds) (1988).

Secchi, Carlo & Alessandrini, Sergio (eds) (1990), L'impatto dell'europa 1993 sulle attività terziarie delle grandi aree urbane, Milan, Associazione Degli Interessi Metropolitani.

Vicari, Serena & Molotch, Harvey (1990), 'Building Milan: Alternative machines of growth', International Journal of Urban and Regional Research, 14, 4, December.

7

Montpellier

André Donzel

'A city of private incomes amidst a sea of vines'. These were the terms in which Montpellier was described at the beginning of the 1960s. Three decades later, this sleepy provincial city is more like a beacon for the new European sunbelt which some commentators have recently perceived rising up all along the French Mediterranean coastline, stretching as far as Catalonia and northern Italy (Brunet et al 1988). For the last few years, the city has been breaking all records. Benefiting from sustained population growth dating back to the last war, Montpellier has risen from the twenty-second largest town in France in 1962 to be the eighth largest. The growth in the level of employment within its sphere of economic influence also indicates a level of economic activity well in excess of either the regional or the national average. With the completion of its ambitious architectural projects together with the staging of major sporting and cultural events, the city has become an important centre of urban activity whose reputation extends far beyond the immediate region. These changes are all the more remarkable in that, even in the mid-1960s, they appeared extremely unlikely.

The viticultural tradition

Viticulture was undeniably the most important factor in the regional growth of Languedoc–Roussillon during the pre-industrial period. The region is still the major centre of wine-production in the world. The wealth of its architectural heritage, in both the countryside and the town, bears eloquent testimony to this fact. At the dawn of the twentieth century, however, the first signs that the market for viticultural products had reached saturation point could be detected as wealth and economic power were drawn irresistibly towards the concentrated urban and industrial zones of northern Europe. At this point the south of France went into its long period of economic stagnation.

For want of an alternative, viticulture continued to occupy a significant proportion of the region's resources until quite recently. In 1962, a record year for wine production in the region, Languedoc–Roussillon accounted for almost half of the total French output. Employing 160,000 people, viticulture provided employment for nearly thirty per cent of the region's active work-force. But this persisted only at the price of a continuing decline in the income of the rural worker, a trend which makes Languedoc–Roussillon one of the poorest regions in France. This phenomenon has been reinforced by the fact that meridional viticulture was only belatedly the object of efforts to regulate the wine market. It was only with the entry of viticulture into the Common Agricultural Policy at the beginning of the 1970s that an organisation was created to achieve this policy.

As a result, at the beginning of the 1960s, industrialisation and urbanisation were at an embryonic stage in the region. Vestiges of industry could be found only at a few isolated poles in the hinterland, particularly on the edge of the Cevennes Mountains, based on the traditions of mining (Alés, La Grand Combe) and textiles (Ganges, Le Vigan). On the coastline Sète, the principal port for the Languedoc economy, was of only modest importance in comparison with other French ports.

The regional urban fabric, whilst extremely dense because of a Languedoc tradition of grouping settlements together, remained highly dependent on the rural environment. As a result there was no real urban hierarchy. Although a few towns stand out from the rest – Nîmes, Montpellier, Perpignan, Carcassone – it was because of their administrative functions at the departmental level, not because they could assert an undisputed right to leadership. Montpellier was unique in that it possessed a long-established and well-known university, but its demographic and economic significance did not provide it with claims to leadership either. Even including the fourteen surrounding communes, which form the District of Montpellier, in 1962 the town had a population of only 136,000 inhabitants – less than nine per cent of the population of the region. This proportion remains very low in comparison with other French regional capitals. This also explains why Montpellier, although the designated regional capital in the recent administrative decentralisation of French local government, failed to benefit during the years from 1960–1970 from the application of the 'métropoles d'équilibre' policy, designed to create competition between the larger French towns within a European context. If we take all these various handicaps into account, the reversal of the downward trend in the region's economic potential which occurred in the 1960s appears all the more remarkable.

The birth of a new pioneer frontier

In recent years, a number of crucial events – the repatriation of French citizens from North Africa, the development of the Languedoc coastline for tourism, the establishment of IBM at Montpellier – marked a turning point in the social and economic fate of Languedoc–Roussillon. These changes can be seen first in demographic terms. The region, which was for so long a land of emigrants as the exodus of the rural population fed the more industrialised regions of France and its colonies overseas, became increasingly a land of immigrants. Starting with the return of the 'pieds noirs' to the French mainland following the independence of Algeria in 1962, this phenomenon has continued to gain strength. Between 1965 and 1990, the number of inhabitants of Languedoc-Roussillon increased by 500,000 because of immigration. The most urbanised regions of the wealthier parts of France increasingly provide the greatest proportion of the region's immigrants. Between 1975 and 1982, of a total of 133,000 immigrants from different regions of France, nearly a third originated from Paris and nearly a quarter from the two great south-eastern regions – Rhônes–Alpes and Provence–Côtes d'Azur.

An important factor in this process of migration has undoubtedly been the area's attractive climate and privileged lifestyle. This is especially the case since the government opened up the Languedoc coastline for tourism, a policy dating from the mid-1950s. This has markedly improved the viability of the region and its 180 kilometres of beaches which are almost unspoilt, except perhaps for the mosquitoes. Implemented by the offices of the 'Compagnie Nationale de Bas Rhône–Languedoc', followed by the 'Mission d'Aménagement du littoral Languedoc–Roussillon', these policies were intended to improve the general amenities of the region, especially its water supply, and promote the Languedoc coastline through the setting up of six tourist areas capable of accommodating one and a half million visitors. The economic repercussions of the new 'French Florida' have none-the-less failed to live up to early expectations. Although Languedoc–Roussillon, with more than three million visitors, was the second most popular tourist destination in the summer of 1981, the number of tourists has not exceeded this figure since 1983. In addition, because of its seasonal nature, the income generated by tourism has never contributed more than modestly to the wealth of the region; the sums involved are less than those contributed by agriculture.

Given the weight of the agricultural heritage and the long-term decision of the public authorities to intervene directly in order to encourage tourism, the principal factor in the economic revival of Montpellier and its region came from a relatively unexpected quarter: industry. The initial impulse was provided in 1965 by IBM who opened a new factory employing some 2,800 people on the outskirts of Montpellier. Originally intended to manufacture mainframe computers, today it forms one of the four industrial units of the company in France. IBM has also been directly responsible for the creation of a further 1,500 jobs in the region through its dealings with sub-contractors. This trend has been consolidated by the establishment of a multitude of small and medium-sized companies, often as a result of local initiative, in those sectors involving a large technological component such as robotics (ABX), electronics and telecommunications (ASM, Cégelec, Eurofarad, Transpost), pharmaceuticals (Laboratoires Chauvin, SANOFI, Hygiéne Diffusion) and agronomy (Richter, Phytodif). Closely linked to university research work, these constituted the beginnings of one of the principal centres of 'high tech' in the south of France.

Since then, there has been a clear shift in the course of the development of the regional economy. The gross domestic output of Languedoc has had the highest annual growth rate of any French region. The added value of industry is rising just as fast. The region has also created the highest number of new jobs in relative terms, particularly in the industrial sector. Between 1976 and 1981, the level of industrial employment declined in every region of France with the exception of Brittany (+ 2.4 per cent) and Languedoc–Roussillon (+ 3.6 per cent) (Duche & Savey 1987). More recent figures confirm these trends. The increase in gross domestic product for the region remains higher than the national average. The contribution of Languedoc-Roussillon to the gross domestic product, which was at 2.4 per cent in 1978, increased to 2.6 per cent in 1981 and reached 3 per cent in 1988. The growth in the rate of employment remains above the national average even though there is a tendency for the region's energies to become concentrated around the reservoir of employment formed by Montpellier. The city benefited from nearly sixty per cent of the 33,000 jobs created in the region between 1981 and 1988.

A similar tendency exists in the number of new companies created. Languedoc–Roussillon is second only to the Ile de France in this respect. If the number of new companies created is combined with the number of companies which are still in existence after four years, the region has the highest level of vitality of any region in France (INSEE, November 1990). Thus, Languedoc–Roussillon nowadays appears to be a new pioneer frontier of economic development. Although at the beginning of the 1960s, this phenomenon was given a massive boost by external investment, its enduring quality in the 1980s owes much to the ability of its local actors to promote a more endogenous model of regional development. In the past two decades there has been a dramatic shift in the local political culture.

The revival of local political elites

From the inter-war years to the 1970s, the political debate in Languedoc–Roussillon centred on the alternative claims of the tradition of viticulture and modern tourism. The former was largely supported by left-wing parties whose traditional support lay in the powerful viticultural corporatism. The latter was largely the prerogative of right-wing parties whose support was drawn from the shopkeepers of the towns and villages. Throughout the 1960s the growing crisis in the wine industry, together with disillusionment created by the implementation of the policy of stimulating tourism, did much to contribute to decline in the powers of the traditional parties to mobilise public support. The emergence, at the end of the 1960s, of an *occitaniste* movement, and the inroads made by regionalism in the political debate in Languedoc was one manifestation of this phenomenon.

The changes which have occurred in the economic apparatus and fabric of regional urbanisation have, however, given them a new *raison d'être*. The rise of new social classes linked to economic change – managers, university lecturers, research workers, technicians – demanded political spokespersons prepared to introduce the new legislation required by these transformations. Montpellier, the main theatre of this new regional economic energy, was at the heart of this revival. This has been symbolised since 1977 by a political personality who has become a central figure in the political landscape of Languedoc, Georges Frêche, Mayor of Montpellier, Deputy for Hérault and, more recently, Secretary of the Departmental Federation of the Socialist Party.

A clear product of his educational background – he attended one of the most prestigious Parisian business schools – he typified the rejection of the natural right of the nobility ('légitimité notabiliaire') to play a decisive role in local affairs in France in favour of the natural right of the working and middle classes ('légitimité managériale') (Grémion & Muller 1990). Frêche none the less has firm roots in the 'deep South', with a regionalist rhetoric always likely to attract that part of public opinion willing to challenge the legitimacy of Parisian central government. A lecturer by profession and still an active member of the Faculty of Law and Economic Science at Montpellier, he appeals to the needs of the local elites, themselves in the main university-educated, as a way of differentiating themselves. An assiduous reader of Plato, Aristotle and even Hippodamus of Miletus, his political model is that of the Florence of the Quattrocento, a dream he would like to recreate for Montpellier. Under Fréche, Montpellier has pursued a new political direction. Following Grenoble in the 1970s, Montpellier became, in the course of the 1980s, one of the centres for the implementation of what has been termed 'the urban face of socialism', the new culture of left-wing local elites in France. This attempts to combine high-quality urban development, economic success and a highly developed sense of social communication (Garnier & Goldschmidt 1978).

Urban renewal

Montpellier's urban transformation is most obvious in terms of public amenities and services. In the mid-1970s, Montpellier had all the dysfunctional characteristics of a city which had grown too large, too late. The steps undertaken by the municipal council between 1959 and 1977 to cope with the doubling of the population were too limited to achieve a coherent urban framework. The town was described in these terms at the time:

The proliferation of public housing programmes only accentuates the fundamental lack of balance between a centre which is too small and congested and ever increasing suburbs. This disequilibrium is manifest on several levels and is the result of the selective appropriation of space: to the South, secondary employment and shopping centres, low-cost housing either in the form of housing schemes or individual dwellings; to the North, the university and hospital complexes and exclusive residential dwellings. To the West, some 6 kilometres from the centre, La Paillade, with its 4,000 HLM (low-cost public sector housing) constitutes an ill-equipped and isolated city of its own.

(Cholvy 1989)

The election of a new municipal government in 1977 can be seen as the result of a desire to address these functional and social imbalances. To break down the partitioning of the urban landscape, measures were taken both to improve access to the town centre and to distribute urban amenities around the outskirts. Montpellier now boasts the largest pedestrian precinct in Europe around its restored historic centre and the Place de la Comédie has been freed of traffic by an underpass. Access to the town by public transport has been remarkably improved. In the ten years between 1979 and 1989, the public transport company more than doubled its number of routes and passengers. At the same time, renovation schemes have affected most of the 11,000 homes which constitute the town's social housing programme. Public amenities in the form of the 'Maisons pour tous', multi-purpose buildings for social, sporting and cultural activities have multiplied in the different districts.

Municipal urban policy also encouraged large-scale development projects which have been a major factor in creating the avant-garde image which the city of Montpellier enjoys today. This is especially true of the 'Antigone' scheme, launched in 1977, in which a vast complex of dwellings, offices and open spaces, designed by the Catalonian architect Ricardo Bofill, sprang up to cover some twenty-five hectares of land on the edge of the town centre. Antigone was judged by the review Urbanisme one of the ten most important architectural projects in France during the 1980s. Another project deriving from 'Antigone' was that of 'Port Marianne', intended to link Montpellier with the sea, some ten kilometres away. On the banks of the Lez, a modest stream which had been enlarged so as to allow its navigation by pleasure boats, a whole new district was created. Consisting of some 4,000 dwellings and 150,000 square metres of office space, this is seen as a portent of the vital role of development that the town will represent during the twenty-first century. In the town centre, the opening of the 'Corum', a combined conference centre and opera-house capable of seating 2,000 and of a quality equivalent to that of the Bastille project in Paris, places Montpellier in the forefront of French towns in conferences and the promotion of culture.

Montpellier has made remarkable progress in the field of cultural policy. Through the use of festivals or more permanent theatrical productions, cinema performances, music and dance, the town will in future constitute a coherent cultural ensemble. A dozen festivals are held in the town throughout the year, though especially important are the Festival de Radio–France Montpellier and Montpellier–Danse (for music and dance), the Festival of Mediterranean Cinema, the festivals of Jewish and Chinese cinema, the JIPAMs for photography and video. The town is equally well-equipped in cultural amenities. Because of its two opera companies, the Comédie and the Berlioz, and its Philharmonic Orchestra, the town is in the first rank of provincial cities for musical performances. In addition, the town possesses two schools of national standing for theatre and dance, the Centre Dramatique National, directed by Jacques Nichet, and the Centre Choréographique National, directed by Dominique Bagouet. Contemporary and rock music are equally well represented by the 'Zénith' and the 'Espace Rock', both capable of accommodating the largest international concerts.

The technopole strategy

These developments obviously could not have taken place without a corresponding improvement in the town's economic performance. Of the twenty-two regional capitals of France, Montpellier experienced the highest increase in the rate of employment between 1975 and 1987; 23 per cent, ahead of Rennes (+ 19 per cent) and Toulouse (+ 17 per cent) (INSEE, March 1990). Montpellier, so long peripheral to the great axes of industrial development, is now in a more favourable position to take advantage of the new factors which affect the location of firms in a technological era. It has an attractive environment, high-level university research facilities, a network of small and medium-sized companies of a highly innovatory nature and the presence of an established multinational corporation capable of playing a leading role in the economic development of the region. Montpellier possessed all these potentials, but it was still necessary to bring them together and to harness them.

This was achieved by an association called 'Montpellier LR Technopole'. Developed in keeping with an organisational model to manage science parks, as in Sophia Antipolis near Nice, this association is one of the most successful partnerships between the private and public sectors at the local level in France. Initially no more than a municipal office responsible for the management of the development zones created by the town, it has evolved since 1985 into its present hybrid form, bringing together local elected representatives and professionals entrepreneurs, researchers, university teachers. Montpellier LR Technopole plays an increasingly significant role in stimulating and promoting the local economy.

Governed by a steering committee representing the different partners of the association, the Technopole is structured along five principal poles which reflect the different specialist activities of the companies and research centres established in the town:

(a) the pole 'Euromédecine' combines operations concerned with health – pharmaceuticals, medical research;
(b) the computer pole combines computer technology, automation and artificial intelligence;
(c) the 'Agropolis' pole conducts agronomic research;
(d) the 'Antenna' pole specialises in the application of new methods of communication;
(e) the 'Héliopolis' pole promotes tourism and leisure industries.

LR Technopole is responsible for encouraging relations between industry and research at a local level and promoting local firms at the national and international level. It has offices in Paris and Brussels and is in contact with all the towns which are members of the international association of technopoles. Each centre is responsible for convening an annual international conference. The most important of these, Euromédecine, held each year in Montpellier, attracts nearly 20,000 doctors. In close contact with the seed-bed of firms which it has helped to created, Cap Alpha, it also plays a role in helping and advising companies who wish to set up or develop further in the region.

A 'tuned-in' town

Montpellier's successes are encouraged by a strategic policy of external and internal marketing. 'Every event which occurs in Montpellier has an inherent media-worthy dimension', Frêche has written. It stands out as a pioneer town in the field of urban marketing in France. As a result of its economic success, quality of life and cultural radiance, the town has acquired an image of excellence which has set the standard for the advertising campaigns in the national media – 'Over-Endowed Montpellier', 'Montpellier: Capital of the South', 'Montpellier Eurocity'. The town now enjoys such a reputation in France that, according to one survey, two-thirds of the French population would like to move there.

Besides campaigning in the national media, Montpellier has sponsored a number of projects to twin itself with towns abroad which also serve as a network to promote its image on the international stage. The most elaborate of these has joined the town with the German city of Heidelberg. Beginning with a twinning of the universities, it has gradually spread over the last twenty years to incorporate all aspects of the town until exchanges are almost everyday events. The Maison d'Heidelberg, in the centre of the old town, where exhibitions and meetings as well as German lessons are held, has a counterpart in Heidelberg, the 'Montpellier Haus'. At the beginning of the 1980s, Montpellier reactivated an agreement dating back to 1963 to twin itself with Barcelona, thus consolidating long-standing cultural and economic relations with the neighbouring capital of Catalonia. Besides these bilateral relations, Montpellier has also taken part, on both the national and international scale, in numerous cultural, economic or scientific associations. It is a member of the Eurocity network which unites over sixty EC towns and cities. It has formed a partnership with Barcelona and Toulouse. It is a major player in the International Association of Science Parks in which one of Montpellier's leading figures, Michael Lacave, played a crucial founding role.

If Montpellier pays a great deal of attention to external communication, it pays no less attention to internal communication. The reason for the success of its communication policy is that it has transformed the town's 210,000 citizens into 210,000 ambassadors for Montpellier, Frêche has argued. As a result of municipal publicity, the whole population sees itself as an elite sales force in the service of the city. Unlike many towns, the Municipality of Montpellier makes every effort to share information with its citizens. Montpellier was one of the first towns in France to be completely linked by cable. It abounds in different means of disseminating information. Hoardings all over the town advertise its virtues: 'People work better under a blue sky', 'In Montpellier, intelligence isn't only artificial', 'Over-endowed. Who, me?' Municipal information is further disseminated by four publications delivered free to every household. Two are of general interest; *Montpellier notre ville*, which proclaims itself to be as the town's official newspaper and describes in great detail every item of municipal business; *Montpellier-Hérault Synergie* offers, in the same spirit, information on the events in the district of Montpellier. Two other more specialised newspapers are intended for the young (*Mach 2*) and the elderly (*Age d'or*). These publications, in addition to conveying news, play a key role in the construction of a common identity. Everyone is made aware of the records broken by the town until the 'technopolitan' culture eventually impregnates all strata of the population. From the pensioner to the housewife to the university teacher, no one can avoid coming into contact with its jargon: 'synergy', 'cross-fertilisation', 'expansion', 'optimisation', 'percolation'.

The disconcerting ease with which the town and its surrounding area have exchanged the culture of the 'large glass of cheap red' for that of the 'Big blue' underlines the points in common with the old cultural traditions. Under the guise of modernism, the technopolitan culture, like everything else, depends on two deeply-rooted local characteristics. The first is the aptitude for local co-operation in a region of small local producers who had been the bastion of the co-operative movement in an agricultural context. The second is the particularly precocious commercial sense of a region which formerly had to export all its production.

The price of excellence

If the signs of Montpellier's success are clear, it does not mean there are no difficulties. The rapid development of the town masks the extremely volatile nature of its economy. The town may hold the French record for the establishment of firms, but their failure rate is also very high. The same contradiction can be seen with employment, which has risen consistently since 1974; but not only has Montpellier not managed to halt the rise in the rate of unemployment, this has consistently increased at a higher rate than the national average. The rate of unemployment in Montpellier increased from 2.2 per cent in 1962 to 13.9 per cent in 1982 whilst, at the same time, the working population increased by 62 per cent (OELR 1989). One result of the ability to attract a better and better qualified work-force, often from outside the town, is an increase in unemployment and precarious employment amongst less well-qualified workers.

This trend would certainly have been magnified if the sharp rise in the cost of living in the town had not been responsible for some decline in the rate of population growth since 1975. Montpellier has become one of the most expensive metropolitan areas in France. In 1977 its cost of living was amongst the cheapest of the larger towns; since 1985 it has become the third most expensive, surpassed only by Paris and Ajaccio. A more detailed breakdown of living expenses indicates that price rises have been particularly significant in basic necessities, especially rented accommodation, food and clothing, all of which tend to penalise lower-income households (INSEE, May 1990).

The result of these trends is that the profile of the town and the region have become increasingly divided at both a social and economic level. Whilst the labour market in Languedoc–Roussillon is marked by decline in its specialist sectors and their level of profitability – agriculture, construction, retail trade, administration – Montpellier continues to attract highly qualified people and high value-added products. This progressive divergence in the labour market at the regional level produces increasingly uneven distributions of household income. In 1985, the average household income varied on a scale of 1 to 3.7 between Montpellier, the richest commune, and Grand Combe, the poorest in the region. As a result, relations between Montpellier and departmental and regional institutions have become increasingly strained in recent years. Regional institutions have had to make collective decisions which are less advantageous to the regional capital. At the same time, they also have to consolidate their own still fragile economic foundations.

Although Montpellier has been in the lead in implementing a developmental strategy, this may now be under threat. The 'stratégie technopolitaine' which developed in Montpellier has found numerous converts in many other towns in the south of France, Aix-en-Provence, for example, or Avignon or Nîmes. All offer similar advantages. Moreover, several of France's larger cities, now confronted with the problems of economic restructuring, have recently woken up. There is a risk that future investment will tend to concentrate on areas with long-standing industrial roots. Montpellier may soon lose the advantage of its own innovations. This is one important reason why the town has sought so insistently to 'go European'. It is ironic that the capital of one of the regions of France which less than a decade ago was the most hostile to the European ideal is now an unequalled champion of the increased co-operation between towns across the EC.

Languedoc and Europe: from confrontation to co-operation

Dependent as it was on a single product, wine, the region was initially extremely suspicious of the prospect of a Single European Market. In 1970, even if it provided some hope of new guarantees with respect to the regulation of that market, the entry of viticulture into the Common Agricultural Policy left Languedoc having to compete with other extensive wine-growing areas in the EC. Competition from Italian wine was seen as especially serious. The prospect of Spanish and Portuguese entry also added to the general unease. The 1970s and early 1980s were thus marked by an increasing vociferousness amongst those engaged in the wine-growing industry against what was portrayed as the sacrifice of meridional viticulture on the altar of Europe. Committees for the protection of viticulture were set up throughout the region. Under their control, the protest of the viticulturists took on such a radical dimension that it sometimes appeared as if a 'wine war' was in progress. Spectacular and occasionally violent protests were organised throughout the region; 'ghost town' campaigns, the occupation of administrative buildings, the blocking of main roads against lorries transporting Italian wine, the emptying of vats belonging to wine-merchants suspected of illegally importing wine.

These events, though regrettable, helped to bring the attention of the public authorities to the predicament of wine production in Languedoc. In 1976 the French government began to study proposals for the creation of a body whose role would be to stabilise prices in the viticultural market. At the same time, a system of aid for wine producers was instituted at the European level under the auspices of FEOGA. Large bonuses were offered to wine growers who would uproot vines and so prevent the risk of over-production. Similarly, a scheme intended to improve the quality of wine was inaugurated. Viticulturists were encouraged to renew their vines and restructure their vineyards along less extensive lines. As a result, Languedoc is nowadays no longer a region which just produces cheap red wines; it also produces an increasing proportion of high-quality wines.

The establishment of the EC's Integrated Mediterranean Programmes in 1986 improved local perceptions of the benefits of European unity. For the first time, these programmes incorporated local and regional collectives directly and assisted the Mediterranean regions of France, Italy and Greece to adapt to the new conditions created by the entry of Spain and Portugal into the EC. These programmes had a major impact on economic investment, the development of infrastructures and the most effective use of human resources in these regions. Languedoc–Roussillon is the French region which has benefited most from the programme. During the first stage of PIM (1986–88), community subsidies to the region were 620 million francs, as opposed to 484 million francs for Provence–Alpes–Côte-d'Azur, 478 million francs for Aquitaine, 457 million francs for the Midi–Pyrénées, 374 million francs for Corsica, and 176 million francs for the departments of Drôme and Ardéche. Between 1965 and 1987, before the application of the PIMs, the region received 6.7 per cent of the financial aid given to France by the European Community under ERDF. The financial aid now received from Europe is the highest on a per capita basis of any region in France. As a consequence, regions in the south of France now show much stronger signs of attachment to the European ideal.

Montpellier – a Eurocity

The substantial financial aid received by the region is not the only reason for this change of attitude. The links between the region, and especially Montpellier, and European institutions now go far beyond a simple matter of assistance. Montpellier is one of the most active supporters of the construction of Europe and its enthusiasm cannot be explained merely in terms of economic opportunism. For Frêche, for example, the construction of Europe and the growth of its towns are indissolubly linked.

It is the cities which will be its driving force. Large enough to act on a European scale, yet posing little threat to the State. A Europe of cities is a matter of political wisdom, because they alone will allow Europe to develop without calling into question the necessary political pre-eminence of the various States.

(Frêche 1990)

The university and commercial traditions of the cities also encourage the sense of openness which exists towards the outside world. Against the tide of regional opinion which for a long time was hostile to the entry of the countries of the Iberian peninsula into the European Community, the city of Montpellier signed a charter to twin itself with Barcelona as early as 1963.

Montpellier can also claim to be the bedrock of the negotiations to set up the PIMs which were entered into from 1986 onwards between the region and Brussels. On this occasion more personal relations were established between the town and the European institutions, as a whole series of meetings between local officials and those from Brussels followed. One result of these discussions was a modification in the policy of the PIM to favour Montpellier; which obtained support for three large-scale projects regarded as essential for it to be considered an international technopolis; the enlargement of the airport, the construction of the conference centre and assistance for the LR Technopole in developing its scientific and technological poles.

In addition to these important projects, Montpellier conducted an extremely active campaign to attract Community programmes for research and development – SPRINT, ESPRIT, BRITE–EURAM, RACE, FLAIR, ERASMUS, COMETT. It established a service to provide support for firms, universities and research centres to help them make maximum use of these programmes. A monthly newsletter

informs potential users of the current programmes. European officials are invited to Montpellier to present these programmes to local
decision makers. This policy has proved so financially viable that
over forty firms in the town have now established links with
Brussels. In this way Montpellier's search for excellence has been
realised on a European level. But at the same time, through a number
of innovatory projects requiring federal co-operation, European
influence has become increasingly important at regional level. When
Jacques Delors, President of the European Commission, visited
Montpellier in 1990, he declared 'In Montpellier, we can see Europe
has arrived'.

Conclusion

The experience of the PIMs has clearly indicated, at least in the case
of Montpellier, the need for an interface with the towns in the
implementation of regional community policy. By proposing
innovatory federal projects, Montpellier has contributed by showing
the constructive and respectable face of local political balance. None
the less, if this policy is to become more far-reaching, tensions could
appear between the collective objectives which will continue to tie
the hands of the regional and departmental institutions because of
their links with the rural community and the competitive goals of a
regional capital anxious to maintain its rank in that race towards
excellence in which every city has to take part in order to attract
investment.

It would seem, however, that a compromise might be possible
due to the co-operation which exists between towns at a regional
and inter-regional level. This provides a means by which they can
avoid wasteful competition. Montpellier, in reviving the tradition of
urban federalism particular to Languedoc, is conscious of the need to
spread growth across the other towns of the region. It has recently
provided an indication of progress in this direction by signing an
agreement of co-operation with its long-time rival and neighbour,
Nîmes. Under this agreement, each undertakes to harmonise their
cultural policies and to work together to improve the motorway links
between the two towns.

In the longer term such projects may well spread beyond the
regional framework. The whole of the French Mediterranean is

characterised by a very dense and extremely dynamic urban fabric. But there is every reason to think that the constellation of towns which extends from Montpellier to Toulon passing by Avignon, Aix and Marseilles will constitute one of the major poles of urban development in Europe in the twentieth century. There are a number of factors behind this; the existence of an attractive environment and climate, the presence of an important port (Marseille–Fos) and a diversity of tertiary and industrial activities, together with a constant increase in population due to migration from both the south and north of Europe. The prosperity of the north sea coastal towns was founded on their ability to co-operate. This is particularly true with respect to the Dutch 'Ransdtad' whose territorial configuration presents numerous analogies with that of the towns of the Rhone delta on the Mediterranean coast. The restoration of European equilibrium between north and south will depend no doubt on European opinion, but it will also depend in large measure on their own desires.

References

Brunet, R., Grasland, L., Garnier, J-P., Ferras, R. & Volle, J-P. (1988), *Montpellier Europole*, GIP RECLUS–Maison de la Géographie.

Cholvy, G. (1989), *Histoire de Montpellier*, Toulouse, Privat.

Duche, G. & Savey, S. (1987), 'Changement industriel et croissance des périphéries; le cas du Languedoc–Roussillon', *Revue de l'économie méridionale*, 138, Montpellier, CRPEE.

Frêche, G. (1990), *La France ligotée*, Paris, Belfond.

Garnier, J-P. & Goldschmidt, D. (1978), *Le socialisme à visage urbain: essai sur la local-déocratie*, Paris, Editions rupture.

Grémion, C. & Muller, P. (1990), 'De nouvelles élites locales?', in *La France politique*, Esprit 9.

INSEE (March 1990), 'Communes, Métropoles, Régions: l'espace français', *Economie et Statistique*, 230.

INSEE (May 1990), 'Les prix dans 23 agglomérations en 1989', INSEE Première 69.

INSEE (November 1990), 'Survivre: premier souci des jeunes enterprises', INSEE Première 110.

Observatoire Economique du Languedoc–Roussillon (1989), *Bilan 1988 de l'économie du Languedoc–Roussillon*, Montpellier, INSEE.

Part III Peripheral cities

8

Dublin

Jon Dawson

Peripheral cities face formidable challenges as economic competition between European cities increases. The economic performance of peripheral cities is comparatively weak and, very often, constrained by overdependence on technologically underdeveloped industries, relatively small local and regional markets and inadequate communication links to the European 'core' and other peripheral cities (Dawson 1992). This chapter and the next explore how Dublin and Seville are responding to the challenges of economic peripherality and assess their prospects for the future.

Dublin is one of the most peripheral cities in Europe. Its surface links are particularly disadvantageous; there are two seas between the city and the European mainland. As the capital city of the Republic of Ireland, Dublin is the centre of the social, economic, political and administrative life of the country and is the hub of Ireland's communication links to the rest of Europe. But the city faces many of the challenges characteristic of peripheral cities in developing regions. Although Dublin possesses a strong cultural and telecommunications infrastructure and reaps benefits from its capital city status, it has severe locational, transportation and inner-city problems. It also has an acute and deepening economic crisis. It has lost many industrial jobs whilst employment created in new industries and the expanding service sector in recent years only partially offsets these losses. The need to revitalise the local economy and to avoid widening polarisation between social groups and between different parts of the city underpins the complex web of challenges facing policy makers working in Dublin.

The centralised system of government in Ireland greatly influences the delivery of public policy to its capital. Local authorities, like Dublin Corporation, have more restricted fiscal autonomy and fewer powers than many other European cities. These financial and institutional constraints limit the capacity of local actors to regenerate the city. Moreover, national policy making and delivery is typically conducted on a sectoral rather than a spatial basis. As a result, multidisciplinary approaches to urban areas generally, and Dublin in particular, have been limited.

Even so, an array of important urban initiatives have been pursued in Dublin. The 1986 Urban Renewal Act and its tax incentive policies to stimulate property-led regeneration, the Custom House Docks and its International Financial Services Centre (IFSC) – Dublin's urban renewal flagship – and strategies to develop a cultural quarter in the heart of the city demonstrate a concerted urban focus. Revitalising the city centre, boosting its economic performance and improving the built environment are the cornerstones of local development policy. However, establishing effective links between new developments and disadvantaged inner-city communities remains an important challenge.

The chapter presents a picture of the key demographic, economic and social characteristics and trends in the city region. A knowledge of the processes and impact of urbanisation, suburbanisation, inner-city decay and renewal is critical to understanding contemporary Dublin, its urban problems and the responses made by policy makers. The chapter then sets out the institutional context in which development and change in the city takes place. The next section of the chapter examines the key urban development strategies and projects implemented in the city. It also discusses the crucial economic development role of the Industrial Development Authority, efforts to modernise the city's infrastructure and address its peripherality constraints and the important role which the EC plays in developing the city. Finally, the chapter identifies a series of issues and policy priorities which will shape Dublin's future and appraises its prospects as a city located on Europe's westernmost fringes.

Demographic trends and spatial patterns of urbanisation

As in other developing regions in Europe, rural–urban migration was a major dynamic of urbanisation throughout the 1960s and 1970s. Equally, emigration trends, particularly to Britain, have been significant and remain a highly sensitive political issue. However, with the faltering of the British economy and enhanced employment opportunities in urban areas at home, migration patterns have increasingly emphasised rural–urban shifts within the nation state. Moreover, Dublin is an attractive location for returning migrants, especially younger people in professional socio-economic categories.

In 1961, the city and its suburbs had a population of 665,000. By 1971, its population had reached 778,000, whilst the city region totalled 852,000. By 1979 the city region's population had risen to 983,000 and continued to grow, passing the one million mark in 1986 (NESC 1981). But the spatial distribution of growth was uneven. Whilst the wider metropolitan area grew, there was depopulation of the urban core. For instance, between 1966 and 1971, while the suburbs grew, many inner-city wards lost over ten per cent of their population. Infrastructural investment and a consistent policy emphasis favouring new development on greenfield sites encouraged the process of suburbanisation.

The organisational framework for the suburbanisation of Dublin derives broadly from the Wright Report on the Dublin Region in 1966 and the subsequent 1971 Dublin County Development Plan. These led to the designation of three 'new towns', Tallaght, Lucan/Clondalkin and Blanchardstown to the west of Dublin city, to accommodate the city's spiralling population. Each was intended to be a major urban centre of some 100,000 people with a full range of commercial, industrial and social facilities. All three grew rapidly. Tallaght, for instance, was transformed from a small settlement of 8,000 in 1971 to a major town of over 56,000 in 1981 and over 73,000 in 1986.

Future urbanisation trends are more difficult to predict. Nevertheless, the most likely scenario is a stabilising of population levels in the city region and a continuing depopulation of the urban core in the absence of comprehensive initiatives to check decline. Moreover, due to Dublin's youthful population profile – almost half of all Dubliners are under twenty-five – emigration trends seem set to continue as more young people enter an already overcrowded domestic labour market.

Economic trends

During the 1980s Dublin was one of the few cities in Europe to experience population growth and economic decline simultaneously.

Between 1981 and 1987, industrial employment fell by 25.5 per cent and unemployment doubled in both absolute and percentage terms. At the same time, service sector employment – almost 74 per cent of the work force in the Dublin region – remained relatively static in the 1980s, although it rose by 12 per cent in the rest of the Republic. The city's relatively high unemployment rate masks even worse concentrations of joblessness in particular areas. For instance, in the north inner city, unemployment rates were 28.7 per cent in 1986 while unemployment rates of over 50 per cent occur in Ballymun, a council estate housing 20,000 people, about four miles from the city centre, and in parts of Tallaght.

The labour market will continue to grow throughout the 1990s. However, even with high rates of emigration, anticipated net employment requirements contrast starkly with the city's economic performance. Between 1981 and 1987, the number of jobs in the city region's economy fell by an average 5,000 each year. Dublin's economy closely parallels the Irish economy as a whole and as a result the omens for the city are not encouraging. During the 1980s the performance of the Irish economy was particularly bad in comparison with other EC nation states. Indeed, Ireland's cumulative percentage growth in GDP/GNP from 1980 to 1987 was the lowest in the EC.

Although the performance of the economy as a whole has disappointed, some economic sectors are expanding and prospering. However, foreign-owned firms dominate these growth sectors. Indigenous industries are broadly locked into the less dynamic sectors of the economy. Indeed, evidence suggests that with endemic low levels of research and development, Irish companies will become further disadvantaged as the European and global economies become increasingly competitive (NESC 1989). There is, however, a disparity between levels of innovation and technology in the economy and Dublin's potential to exploit a highly skilled labour resource. Dublin has three universities and an Institute of Technology that together provide higher level education in the science and engineering disciplines to over 6,000 students. If Ireland and Dublin fail to harness this potential effectively, they will continue to lose one of their richest resources. The talents of an educated work-force will move instead to overseas firms that, although located in Ireland, repatriate their profits, or disappear altogether through economically induced emigration.

These economic trends, together with land use planning policies, have induced spatial shifts within the Dublin city region.
Residential suburbanisation has been paralleled by the suburbanisation of employment opportunities. Most of Dublin's industry and
new investment are now located on peripheral industrial estates.
Industry no longer concentrates in the inner city. During the late
1970s the Industrial Development Authority (IDA) estimated that
at least 2,000 jobs were lost annually from the inner city due to the
closure, shrinkage and relocation of businesses (MacLaren &
Beamish 1985). By contrast, in the inner city there has been
dramatic growth in office development and land use. Seventy-eight
per cent of new office space developed in Dublin between 1960
and 1985 was located in the inner city. But there are also spatial
imbalances within the inner city itself. Dublin's office development
has concentrated in the more prosperous parts of the south inner
city.

Housing issues

Unlike many European cities, the most extensive housing problems
in Dublin occur in the private sector stock, rented and owner-
occupied. Problems of dereliction and decay, especially in the inner
city, are mounting. However, much of the city's public housing is of
a high quality, including inner-city housing built since the 1970s
and residential development in the peripheral new towns. Even so,
some areas of the city suffer from poorer quality municipal housing
and overcrowding, for instance, the multi-storey blocks in Ballymun
and the highly degraded apartment complexes in the south inner
city.

Many residential areas are spatially segregated by social class. The
lack of a private housing market in the inner city has almost
exclusively confined new house building there to the public sector.
Moreover, public and private sector housing developments in suburban areas are well defined in a way that starkly segregates social
classes. Bannon (1988) stated that 'Dublin's housing is rigidly
segregated in a way which not only segregates social class, but loudly
proclaims that segregation to the disadvantage of the poor in our
society.'

Urban government

Urban change and development in Dublin takes place within the context of limited local government autonomy, few community powers or resources and an austere fiscal climate. The highly centralised system of government limits the contribution that local actors can make to Dublin's urban regeneration. Major policy decisions on, for example, economic development, environmental improvement and the promotion of tourism, which have a significant impact upon the city, are taken at national level on a sectoral basis. Economic development is primarily the responsibility of the IDA, with board members appointed by the Minister of Industry and Commerce. Tourism policy and initiatives are determined by Bord Failte Eireann (the Irish Tourist Board) whose chairman and board members are appointed by the Minister for Tourism. Transport and environmental policy and initiatives are predominantly the domain of the Department of the Environment. Moreover, the Department of Finance dictates the scale of sectoral policies, allocating resources to the various departments in the annual budgetary process. This sectoral approach to policy delivery prevents a coherent multi-disciplinary approach to urban policy in Ireland. Whilst there may be interdepartmental co-operation on particular schemes, there is a tendency for each department to plough its own furrow, relatively independent of the others.

Although local authorities prepare development plans which provide a land use development framework, their freedom of action is tightly constrained. Central government significantly reduced the autonomy of local authorities in 1977, when it abolished the local rating system for private housing and replaced it with central government grants. Local government, therefore, not only has limited powers but is also highly dependent on central government funding. Hence, local authorities in Dublin argue that significant initiatives can only take place with the support of national government (Drudy 1989).

Regeneration strategies

Central government is the major influence on urban change and development in Dublin but the local authority does play a part. This section examines the key sectoral strategies of strategic infrastructural development, economic development and housing which impact on the city, discusses the key area-based strategies developed in the city and highlights the EC's role in supporting strategic development goals.

Strategic infrastructural development policy

The IFSC is the showcase for the Irish government's concerted campaign to help redress some of the disadvantages of geographic peripherality by investing heavily in telecommunications infrastructure. From possessing one of the most primitive telecommunications systems in Western Europe at the end of the 1970s, an investment of 650 million IR£ in the early 1980s, with considerable assistance from the European Regional Development Fund (ERDF), provided Ireland with a sophisticated digital telecommunications system. Effectively, it transformed telecommunications in Ireland. From a reliance on the technology of the 1920s, Ireland and its capital now benefit from state-of-the-art systems.

The Irish Telecommunications Board (Telecom Eireann) offers a wide range of national and international business services which connect Dublin to Europe and the rest of the world. Its services include a mobile telephone service, computer-to-computer file transfer, networking, international video conferencing and fibre-optic lines to the UK and European mainland. The new telecommunications services are an integral part of the IFSC's viability and form a central plank of the project's marketing agenda. Whatever the success of the IFSC, there is no doubt that Ireland's advanced telecommunications system will be a vital resource to enable Dublin to compete in the European urban system.

In terms of international transport connections, Dublin's accessibility depends on the efficient functioning of its sea- and airports. The city's air links to Europe are reasonable. There are particularly frequent links to London, with twenty-five flights daily. The development of direct air links with other European cities, although still limited, has always been an important objective at central government level (Killen & Smyth 1989). The rapid growth of total passenger traffic through Dublin airport in recent years reflects the increasing importance of air links to the city. In 1988, the airport handled 4.4 million passengers compared with 2.6 million just three years earlier.

Dublin's port suffers from poor access within and through the city. The construction of the Channel Tunnel and the planned upgrading of the north Wales road network, provide an additional incentive to resolve this long-standing issue. A port access route was first suggested in the 1971 Dublin Transportation Study and remains one of the most important strategic transportation issues in the city. However, the city's 1987 draft development plan includes no such proposals. Proponents of an access route to the port argue that the environmental costs of the scheme could be minimised. Indeed, it could not only significantly improve Ireland's links with Europe but, at the same time, vastly enhance the environment of the inner city and the central business district by reducing heavy commercial traffic there.

Economic development policy

The Government's leading agency to promote and facilitate economic development in Ireland is the IDA. In terms of interventionist local economic policy and development, the IDA is the key actor in Dublin. It performs national and regional industrial planning and provides grants, other financial incentives and advice for new and existing manufacturing, internationally traded services, technical services and small industries. It develops and manages industrial estates and in partnership with the private sector constructs industrial premises and promotes joint ventures.

Until 1976, the IDA's policy and activities were biased against Dublin as it aimed to promote economically the more peripheral areas of Ireland. Dublin's economy was considered sufficiently strong to succeed without intervention. However, this judgement proved overly optimistic. The city lost many jobs with inner-city industries particularly badly affected. In 1976, therefore, the IDA radically reversed its policy. It began to promote the city as an industrial location, by acquiring land for industrial development and by providing factory space around the periphery and in the inner city. Approximately a third of the IDA's expenditure is upon projects and initiatives in the Dublin city region.

The economic development strategy of the IDA attempts to marry expected growth sectors and labour-intensive sectors with specific areas of the city region. Expected growth sectors, broadly, include the food industry, engineering, electronics, and services. Its spatial specialisation of economic activity envisages developing a range of labour-intensive industries in Tallaght and promoting the food sector in the Lucan/Clondalkin area. It has earmarked the peripheral town of Blanchardstown for initiatives focusing on electrical engineering, electronics, data inputting, pharmaceutical and software developments. Finally, the focus of development in the inner city is on developing small businesses and internationally traded services.

Housing policy

The contemporary inner-city housing policy of Dublin Corporation has had some success. It includes encouraging tenants to purchase their dwellings through a subsidised Tenant Purchase Scheme, building low-rise medium density housing in traditional styles and pursuing a programme of refurbishment and modernisation of pre-war blocks of flats. However, insufficient resource to tackle the often severe housing problems remains a major obstacle to more rapid progress. Slum clearance policies, quality new build housing at lower densities, together with the increased supply of purpose-built apartments in the suburbs and falling average family size, have significantly reduced overcrowding problems. However, there is a widespread consensus in the city that reversing the decline of the inner city must comprise a wider strategy than simply building local authority housing. Mixed tenure housing to promote social diversity is considered essential.

Current housing policies, however, restrict the refurbishment and improvement of the existing private housing stock and favour new build housing. For instance, the grant and mortgage subsidy systems have favoured new housing and encouraged development in peripheral areas on greenfield sites where costs are lowest (Drudy 1989). In recent years, however, incentives favouring new building have been reduced while inducements to invest in refurbishment have increased. But these are limited in scope and are unlikely to stem the tide of decay (Blackwell & Convery 1989). If appropriate policies and initiatives are not taken soon, Dublin will continue to lose some of its prime assets. The continuing deterioration of the city's

Georgian architectural heritage threatens the attractiveness of the city for tourism and inward investment. Its restoration would not only enhance the quality of life of inner-city residents but could also boost economic development prospects in the city.

Area-based strategies: the Custom House Docks Development Authority (CHDDA)

The first efforts to introduce an urban policy in Dublin came relatively late, in the mid-1980s. The 1986 Urban Renewal Act, introduced by central government, led to the establishment of the Custom House Docks Development Authority together with a complementary scheme of tax and rating incentives to encourage redevelopment. Under the Act, the Minister of the Environment designated further areas for urban renewal. These area-based initiatives mark the beginning of an explicit, if limited, urban policy for the city.

One of the most significant urban redevelopment initiatives in recent years took place in the CHDDA. The Custom House Docks became redundant as a port facility as port-related activity became physically separated from the rest of the city. The twenty-seven-acre site lies on the north bank of the River Liffey close to the city centre. Recognising its potential, the Government established the CHDDA to redevelop the area. The Authority is a comprehensive development authority with streamlined and flexible planning and financial powers. Its remit is to secure the redevelopment of the site and spearhead the regeneration of other decaying, derelict and obsolete quayside areas along the river. The site was earmarked for the development of the IFSC. Financial incentives there include capital allowances, rent allowances and rates relief together with a favourable rate of corporation tax for international financial services.

The IFSC is the centre-piece of the development. Other elements of the high-profile project include office, residential and retail accommodation, as well as a museum, hotel and conference centre and, following the extension of the CHDDA area in 1988, a National Sports Centre. The CHDDA is the first example in Dublin of a formal partnership between the public and private sectors. Public-sector incentives are being used as a catalyst to encourage private-sector involvement and to lever private-sector investment in urban renewal programmes and projects. The key actors in the funding, developing and marketing of the scheme include the developers – the Custom House Docks Development Company Limited – a consortium comprising three private-sector property developers and the CHDDA.

The IFSC has successfully attracted tenants. The Centre now has a work-force of over 1,300. Amongst these companies are some of the world's leading financial institutions, including three of the five leading Japanese banks. But the CHDDA has its critics. As with the Urban Development Corporation experience in Britain, its approach has raised important questions about its relationship with the local government and adjacent communities. And the difficulties for local people, who endure crippling rates of unemployment, in accessing quality jobs in the new service sectors has not been resolved.

The 1986 Urban Renewal Act also designated three inner-city areas with fiscal incentives – less generous but broadly similar to those available in the CHDDA area – to encourage urban development. To support this central government initiative, Dublin Corporation set up an Inner City Development Unit. The Unit promotes the incentives and encourages development and refurbishment in the designated areas. Its Development Advisory Team gives planning and architectural advice to those wishing to develop there. It also prepares feasibility studies for sites owned by the Corporation prior to marketing them. A Corporation marketing campaign seeks to stimulate residential development in the inner city and there is an information service for investors in residential property and for potential home buyers.

At designation, the areas were characterised by under-used and derelict land and deteriorating buildings with little prospect of immediate private development in the absence of incentives. Indeed, in the decade prior to designation, there was not a single planning application for the quays alongside the river Liffey; a surprising fact given the area's development potential. Few European cities possess such an expanse of developable waterfront property adjacent to its urban core. Following designation, however, developer interest soon emerged. The Liffey Quay area attracted most attention whereas investment was more difficult to generate in the north inner city.

Encouraged by these partial achievements, the Government substantially extended its urban renewal scheme to several new areas in the inner city. However, developments in the original areas, though encouraging, are limited. The widespread extension of incentives to new areas on this scale may, therefore, prove precipitate. The relative lack of developer interest in the north inner city supports this view. It also suggests that the mere existence of tax incentives in depressed urban areas may not be an adequate inducement for their regeneration through profit-led development. Tax breaks specifically targeted on residential development have also influenced developments in Dublin. Available on a nation-wide basis, Section 27 of the 1988 Finance Act allows investors in residential property to write off the development costs of new or refurbished units against rental income for tax purposes. The financial incentives offered by Designated Area status have had some success in attracting office development. However, there are concerns that much of the built office space remains vacant. In 1992, thirty per cent of the newly built office floorspace in the Designated Areas − outside the Custom House Docks − was unoccupied. On the housing front, the incentives have, in part, been a successful catalyst for development of private-sector housing, a sign that a housing market is re-emerging in the inner city.

Temple Bar cultural quarter

In 1991, The Temple Bar area of inner-city Dublin became the latest area to acquire designated status. To exploit its tourist potential for the benefit of Dublin and the nation, the development of a 'cultural quarter' at Temple Bar is under way. It is a central plank of strategies to boost tourism, improve the quality of life in the city and promote economic activity there in the arts and associated services. In 1990 Dublin Corporation adopted an Action Plan for the area, which subsequently became one of the EC's pilot projects, under the auspices of the Directorate General for Regional Policy. The 9.4 million ECU project provides for pedestrian links between two parts of the Temple Bar area, new public squares, lighting and street furniture, the Irish Film Centre and research and marketing. The EC meets fifty per cent of the costs. Central and local government and the private sector pay the balance.

The 1991 Finance Act and the Temple Bar Area Renewal and Development Act extended the area and made available an array of financial incentives to stimulate a cultural quarter. The legislation established two companies, Temple Bar Renewal Limited and Temple Bar Properties Limited. The former is the policy-making body which oversees development and administers the financial incentives. The latter is the executive company responsible for physically developing the project. The project is a partnership between the public and private sectors, the EC and the local community, the last having representation on the board of Temple Bar Renewal Limited. The completion of developments there is anticipated to take five years.

The nature of the Temple Bar scheme makes gentrification likely. Without safeguards in the overall framework, particularly for affordable housing provision, the local community could be disadvantaged by the scheme. Policies to promote links with surrounding areas in terms of physical and cultural access and employment should be a priority. The development should be inclusive and not exclusive if it is to benefit local communities as well as those visiting from outside or those moving to live and work in the Temple Bar area.

Dublin in Europe

The geographical peripherality of Dublin, in the European context, is of particular interest to the EC. The Commission has a strong commitment to strengthening its social and economic cohesion by tackling problems of regional disadvantage. The EC's involvement in Dublin through its structural funds is an important dimension of this objective. The EC classifies the whole of the Republic of Ireland as an Objective 1 region for structural fund purposes. In other words, the country is categorised as one of the less developed regions in the Community.

Two crucial factors influence the impact of the EC on Dublin and bear upon any evaluation of the effect of EC funds in the city. First, the negotiating and allocation of funds is highly centralised. National government negotiates with the EC and national government disburses expenditure. The city authorities have little involvement in obtaining or allocating EC resources. Second, the Government administers the allocation of EC funds on a sectoral rather than a spatial basis. EC funds, therefore, are allotted to industry, tourism, infrastructural development on a national basis and administered through the relevant government department. It is, therefore, extremely difficult to obtain accurate figures about, let alone evaluate the impact of the use of EC resources in the city region.

Nevertheless, EC funding has been an important element in public expenditure in Ireland, and therefore in Dublin. On a national basis, up to 1988 Ireland had received 2.4 billion IR£ from EC structural funds since joining the Community in 1973. Between 1975 and 1988, Ireland was allocated some 884.7 million IR£ in grant payments for infrastructure and industrial development from the European Regional Development Fund (ERDF).

The Community Support Framework for Ireland (1989–93) also allocated resources on a sectoral rather than a spatial basis. The total cost of the priorities adopted by the Community and the Irish Government is 8.4 billion ECU, with budgetary assistance from the Community comprising 3.67 billion ECU. Again, however, because of the sectoral nature of the agreed Community Support Framework, it is not possible to separate accurately the EC resources to be devoted to the Dublin city region. Nevertheless, on the reasonable assumption that around a third of available funds will be channelled to Dublin, the city region stands to gain significant additional resources.

Broadly, the key areas and priority action agreed in the Community Support Framework which relate to Dublin are tourist development; support for industry and services, particularly for traded goods and services subject to international competition; measures to offset the effects of peripherality, including improvements to physical and telecommunication infrastructure; and training and employment measures targeted at developing skills in economic growth sectors.

Future scenarios: problems, opportunities and prospects

Whether the cities of Europe will succeed or fail in the 1990s will depend largely on their ability to secure functional economic roles in the new European system. Whilst local politicians, representatives and the private sector are broadly optimistic about the future of the city of Dublin, its position in the European urban system is not assured. According to the report by Cheshire et al (1987), Dublin ranks 101st in a comparative assessment of urban problems, out of 117 functional urban regions. Moreover, the city was one of only 14 areas identified as having seriously deteriorated since 1974. At the same time, the city continued to grow, exacerbating social and economic problems. There are some signs that the city's fortunes are beginning to improve. However, its ability to compete in the Europe of tomorrow is essentially uncertain.

The logic of the Single European Market provides some clues as to how Dublin will engage in an increasingly competitive economic climate. The economic sectors which are likely to form the vanguard of Dublin's future economic role are those which have long-term growth prospects and an availability of complementary skills and resources. However, there is a shortage of a dynamic indigenous industry with enterprises in the expanding sectors of the economy. The IDA's strategy to link these growth sectors to specific areas of the city is an innovative attempt to counter this imbalance and to forge an economic development policy which goes with the grain of emerging market trends. Even so, poor intra-urban transport infrastructures restrict the efficient functioning of the city. In particular, the inadequate internal links to Dublin's port threaten the city's transportation movements to its external markets.

The expanding economic importance of the service sector is a trend that is likely to continue throughout Europe in the foreseeable future. There is a clear intention from national government, with support from local actors and the private sector, to promote Dublin's competitiveness in this field. There is an expanding range of commercial, financial and industrial services. The city's telecommunications facilities, for which the IFSC is its shop-window, are a strong asset in this context.

Increasing leisure time throughout the Community is likely to facilitate a continuing expansion in the tourist market. Dublin has much potential in expanding its share of this market, especially as urban tourism becomes more popular. The Temple Bar project is a cornerstone of its tourist policy. It should be a major magnet for tourists and help to mitigate the disincentive to visitors of the decaying urban environment right in the heart of the city. Environmentally, there are many attractive areas in the city region, including Phoenix Park, the largest enclosed urban park in the EC. Moreover, air quality will improve following the recent introduction of clean air legislation to ban the burning of coal in the city. Dublin also has a high cultural reputation with its wealth of historic buildings and literary associations.

Whatever the effect of the forces which will shape the new European economy and its spatial outcome, Dublin faces a number of deep-seated urban problems and policy issues. Unemployment will remain a major issue in Dublin for many years. Dublin's less competitive industries are likely to suffer as European economic integration compounds unemployment problems. Moreover, the expected influx of large numbers of young people into the city region's labour market is unlikely to be fully assuaged by outward migration. Unemployment has already reached crisis proportions in some pockets of the city region and has been accompanied by poverty, drugs, crime and other welfare problems. The spatial concentration of multiple deprivation, for instance in the inner city, the new towns and Ballymun, calls for a multidisciplinary approach to regenerate such communities. A co-ordinated strategy bringing together social, economic, environmental, cultural and property development initiatives is vital.

However, a spatial approach to development raises the thorny issue of accountability and local autonomy. The centralised structure of the political system in Ireland does not readily lend itself to locally specific development strategies in Dublin. Such strategies, if they are to be responsive to local needs and fully exploit local capacity, require the involvement and empowerment of local actors from the public sector, the private sector and the local community. But this involves the centre relinquishing some of its control, which would require a major transformation in Government attitudes to local democracy. However, there are signs that the Government is beginning to recognise the need for change. Although it is in its very early days, a committee with links to central government, embracing local government officials and politicians and community representatives has been set up to promote an integrated approach to development in the Liberties quarter of the south inner city (Dawson 1993). The organisational structure for the Temple Bar development embraces a similar partnership. In view of the traditional form of policy delivery in Dublin this is a significant breakthrough. These initiatives will encourage participation and co-operation between the various actors involved in the area. But they are new initiatives and their impacts on the delivery of policy and their effectiveness in alleviating the problems and exploiting the opportunities in the area are uncertain.

Whatever the outcome of these initiatives, experience elsewhere suggests that even if the Government's inner-city development schemes are successful in their own terms, conflicts of interest are likely to arise between different interest groups. These conflicts will be greatest in the centre of the city. Local communities, the wider city and the nation state all have an interest there. Parts of the inner city are attractive to urban tourists and to people from other parts of the city and current developments there will enhance its pulling power. Equally, developments in the heart of the capital offer the potential to expand commercial economic activities. At the same time, there are closely knit communities which have severe social pressures and their own local needs and wishes. They will not always be compatible with the agenda of the wider city and the nation state. The challenge for policy makers in Dublin will be to recognise these competing demands and resolve them.

In summary, Dublin's capacity to benefit from the emergence of the Single European Market is restricted by its location in a developing and peripheral region. Moreover, the city faces a litany of urban problems. However, Dublin also possesses a number of strategic strengths which will enhance the city regions's competitive position in the changing European urban system. If Dublin is to fulfil its potential in the future European urban system it must address these problems and build on its strengths. Constructing working partnerships between central and local government, the private sector, local communities and, where appropriate, the EC would enhance its ability to succeed.

References

Bannon M. J. (1988), 'Modern Dublin' *The Resource Source: Exploring Dublin,* 16, Department of Environmental Studies, UCD.

Blackwell J. & Convery F. J. (eds) (1988), *Replace or Retain: Irish Policies for Buildings Analysed,* Resource and Environmental

Centre, UCD.

Cheshire, P., Hay, D., Carbonaro, G. & Bevan, N. (1987), *Urban Problems and Regional Policy in the European Community,* Commission of the European Communities.

Commission of the European Communities (1989), *Community Support Framework 1989–1993: Ireland,* CEC.

Dawson,J. (1992), 'Peripheral Cities in the European Community: Challenges, Strategies and Prospects', *Public Policy and Administration,* 7, 1, 9–20.

Dawson J. (1993), 'Dublin: South Inner City' in Dawson, J., Froessler,R., Jacquiers, C. & Perez, J. (eds) *Final Report of Quartiers en Crise 2nd Programme.*

Drudy, P. (1989), 'City Report: Dublin', in Klaasen, L., van den Berg, L. & van der Meer, (eds) *The City: Engine Behind Economic Recovery,* Avebury.

Killen, J. & Smyth, A. (1989), 'Transportation' in Carter, R.W.G. & Parker, A.J. (eds), *Ireland: A Contemporary Geographical Perspective,* Routledge.

MacLaren, A. & Beamish, C. (1985), 'Industrial Property Development in Dublin 1960-1982', Irish Geography, 18, 37–50.

National Economic and Social Council (1989),*Ireland in the European Community: Performance Prospects and Strategy,* NESC.

National Economic and Social Council (1981), *Urbanisation: Problems of Growth and Decay in Dublin,* NESC.

9

Seville

Jon Dawson

Seville is an example of a peripheral city which is striving to modernise itself and to overcome its economic and geographic disadvantages. This process was dramatically demonstrated by massive investment in the prestigious Universal Exposition held in Seville in 1992, and in its complementary infrastructure. Expo 92, to give the festival its popular title, has recently dominated urban policy and development activity in Seville. The city is the capital of the Autonomous Community of Andalusia and the seat of the regional and provincial governments. It is the fourth largest city in Spain and the principal industrial and tertiary centre in its region. Seville has undergone a rapid transformation as national and regional policies designed to prepare Spain (and Andalusia) for the challenges of the Single European Market have targeted resources at areas with the highest potential for economic growth.

The Expo was one of a trinity of major events that maintained a high European and world profile for Spain in 1992; Barcelona hosted the Olympic Games and Madrid celebrated its being named as European City of Culture. These three major events in three major cities heralded Spain's relatively recent emergence as a modern democratic state and its status as a full partner in the European Community. Expo 92 presented an outstanding opportunity to secure the long-term future of Seville in the European urban system. The intensive development of physical and telecommunications links coincided with important plans to transform the Expo site into a leading international location for research and development.

This chapter examines the impact of Expo 92 on Seville and its region, the effect of European Community investment on the city and the ability of the local economy to adapt to the demands of the

1990s. First, however, it sets out the social, economic and demographic trends which have shaped the city and which will continue to influence Seville's position in the European urban system.

The development of Seville

The rationale for the initial development of Seville was its location at the highest navigable point on the river Guadalquivir. Situated on the extensive plains of the Guadalquivir the city was, and still is, an important crossroads linking towns and villages to the west and east of the river. It is Spain's only river port and has historic links with the early sailings which led to the European discovery of America in the fifteenth century. Indeed, Seville's early wealth was built on trade with the New World.

Seville's first wave of urban development took place within its city walls. As well as being defensive fortifications, the walls acted as a vital flood barrier when the Guadalquivir burst its banks. The city grew significantly at the beginning of the twentieth century, but, despite the flat topography of the area, not in concentric fashion. To avoid newly developed areas becoming flooded, urban expansion primarily took place to the east of the river. Flood danger dictated, until very recently, that the Isla de la Cartuja (the site of the Expo) remained undeveloped, despite its prime location close to the historic core of the city. The construction of a canal, which removed the threat of flooding, made the site developable for the first time.

Expo 92 is not the first international trade fair to influence urban development in the city. In 1929 a major Ibero-American Exhibition was staged and, although it plunged Seville into a fiscal crisis, it bequeathed to the city many architectural treasures and effectively opened up the south of the city for development. In the post-war years, urban expansion occurred in industrial and residential zones along the main arterial routes of the city. Although city plans in 1946 and 1961 proposed the development of infrastructure to accompany the city's rapid expansion, it was only after the third city plan in 1987 that infrastructural requirements began to be met.

Demographic trends

In common with many cities in southern Europe, the population of Spanish cities rose sharply in the post-war years until the early 1980s. The twin processes of rural–urban migration and high rates of natural increase triggered strong urbanisation trends. Seville was no exception to this pattern. The population of the city increased dramatically from 374,000 in 1950 to 645,000 in 1981. In the same period, the population of the wider metropolitan area almost doubled from 498,000 to 915,000. Three-quarters of this population expansion was due to natural increase, with the balance primarily the result of continuing rural-urban migration.

However, birth-rates have fallen sharply in the last decade. The rate of natural increase in the middle of the 1980s was less than half that of the previous decade. This led to a significantly reduced rate of population growth throughout the metropolitan area. Nevertheless, Seville still has a youthful demographic profile, a consequence of high birth-rates in previous decades. Although the city and its metropolitan area grew rapidly from the 1950s until the 1970s, there were strong net out-migration trends in the wider Province of Seville. Between 1951 and 1975, approximately 200,000 people left the province for other areas of Spain and abroad. This same pattern was apparent at the regional level. The weakness of the Andalusian economy, unable to provide work for labour that had become superfluous to the modernised agricultural economy, together with high rates of natural increase, provoked a massive population exodus. Between 1955 and 1975 almost 1.5 million people left Andalusia. Migrants travelled primarily to Barcelona, which now has a large Andalusian population, and secondly to Madrid. Migration out of the country was also significant and Germany attracted many migrants from Seville (Román, 1987).

There have been marked intra-urban shifts of population within Seville (Cruz 1986). The most pronounced trend was an exodus from the historic core of Seville to the suburbs. By far the largest exodus from the inner city was from the densely packed, traditional working-class area of the city. The population also fell in the wealthier area of the urban core. However, the dynamics underpinning population decline in these two areas differ considerably. The loss of population from the wealthier districts was primarily a response to changing economic functions and land use in the area.

As commercial activity became more prevalent, so residential use diminished. Many residents moved out to new apartments in the emerging middle class neighbourhood of Los Remedios on the opposite bank of the river.

By contrast, the loss of 85,000 residents from the established working-class district reflected aspirations for better housing conditions away from the historic core. Typically, working-class housing in the core was very overcrowded and in a poor state of repair. In recent years, however, the population of the urban core stabilised and even began to rise. Urban growth on the periphery is due to three factors: rural–urban migration, depopulation of the historic centre and high rates of natural increase, the last amplified by the high proportion of young couples moving to peripheral housing areas.

Although demographic predictions may prove unreliable, a study by the Gabinete de Estudios Metropolitanos suggests that the population of Seville and its wider metropolitan area will continue to grow in the 1990s and beyond. But the rate of growth will probably be much slower than in the past. The city's population is expected to reach 740,000 by the beginning of the next century with the metropolitan area home to an estimated 1.1 million.

Economic trends

Seville's leading political, administrative and economic role in Andalusia requires economic trends to be seen in their regional context. Andalusia has a population of just over seven million, but its land area is comparable to that of Portugal and twice the size of Denmark or the Netherlands. The contemporary Andalusian economy displays all the hallmarks of underdevelopment. Productivity rates, levels of investment and income per capita are low, whilst rates of unemployment are high. The economy of Andalusia endured a particularly severe crisis in the first half of the 1980s. But in the latter years of the decade, economic recovery has been impressive. Until 1984 the Andalusian work-force was consistently shrinking, but in the following years employment steadily expanded. Nevertheless, because of an influx of young people into the labour market at this time, the high rates of unemployment did not begin to fall until 1988.

In the later 1980s the performance of the regional economy

turned around. Economic growth in Andalusia between 1987 and 1989 was double that of the EC average. Andalusia's contribution to Spain's expanding gross national income increased marginally from 13.6 per cent in 1986 to 14 per cent in 1989. External investment in Andalusia also rose dramatically. Between 1985 and 1989 there was a consistent increase in annual totals of inward investment. In 1989 foreign investment in the region was 150 per cent above the previous year's total. In 1990, 13 per cent of all inward investment in Spain was in Andalusia. But Andalusia still ranks a poor third in the league table of inward investment totals. Madrid and Cataluña are the dominant centres for foreign investment, together accounting for 65 per cent of inward investment in 1989.

Although rates of Andalusian economic growth were impressive in the later 1980s, claims of an economic renaissance should be treated with caution. Growth was from a relatively low level of activity. Moreover, much of Andalusia's economic growth and increased productivity reflects the heavy infrastructural construction programme supported by the public sector and improved efficiency in a previously highly inefficient agricultural sector. The use of new technologies, except by foreign-owned firms, is far from widespread. This weakness is widely recognised and policies to correct it form the basis of economic development strategies for the region.

Seville is the engine of the Andalusian economy. At the provincial level, Seville contributed a quarter of gross regional income in 1988 and its rate of economic growth has outstripped the Andalusian average in recent years (Lasarte 1989). The metropolitan area of Seville is the most dynamic economic area in the region. Despite its pre-eminence within the region, however, Seville did not avoid the economic crisis which afflicted the region from 1972 to the early 1980s. This era of severe economic crisis had a profound impact on the city's economy. The industrial and construction sectors were particularly hard hit, suffering massive job losses and business closures. Between 1981 and 1986, over fifteen per cent of the industrial and construction labour force was lost. By contrast, the service sector, despite general economic decline, expanded by 40,000 between 1970 and 1986.

There are now more than 320,000 jobs in the metropolitan area. Data compiled by the Gabinete de Estudios Metropolitanos (1989) shows that the tertiary sector accounts for 64 per cent of jobs, industry and construction employment for 31 per cent and agriculture for

5 per cent. The tertiary sector also generates 60 per cent of total gross added value. Seville has the highest proportion of tertiary activity in Spain's five largest metropolitan areas. It has the lowest incidence of industrial activity, although the construction sub-sector is proportionately more significant. Productivity in the industrial and construction sectors approximates to the national average but productivity in services is below average.

Public administration accounts for a significant component of the service sector. This is not surprising given the city's status as the regional administrative capital. Public sector employment also accounts for much of the growth in services in the 1980s. The secondary sector, including the construction industry, employs 90,000 workers. Seville is the most important industrial economy in Andalusia. It is also the most diversified. Even so, most activity is concentrated in a few sub-sectors. Approximately 20,000 work in industries related to metalworking, the aircraft industry, shipbuilding and car components manufacture. A further 14,000 are employed in the food, drink and tobacco industry, a vital exporting sub-sector with direct links to the regional primary sector and of strategic importance to the local economy. Finally, 7.5 per cent of employment is in construction and public works.

Despite expansion in the economically active population, the influx of large numbers of young people into an already crowded labour market has given Seville one of the highest unemployment rates in Europe. By 1986, unemployment in the metropolitan area had surpassed 100,000, a rate of 32 per cent. Youth unemployment was even more acute with a rate of more than 50 per cent. Unemployment rates in Seville fell as the economy expanded. Whilst evidence of local economic recovery is patchy, the loss of enterprises and jobs clearly halted in the later 1980s. There were indications of significant economic growth, due in part to a more favourable national and international economic climate and the economic impulse afforded by Seville's status as the regional capital and as the host city of the Expo.

Private-sector confidence in the Seville economy increased. Industrial investment in Andalusia in 1989 was 26.7 per cent higher than the previous year. More than half of this investment was in new industries. At the provincial scale, Seville was the most attractive area for private capital, with the province receiving over 27 per cent of total investment (OPE 1990).

In summary, the economic situation in Seville, as in Andalusia, improved in the late 1980s. Unemployment fell, there were high rates of economic growth and the city attracted significant inward investment. Nevertheless, severe structural constraints in the economy remained. Small and medium-sized enterprises remained technologically underdeveloped, the work-force typically lacked the skills necessary for firms to compete effectively in the Single European Market and there was a fragmented communications infrastructure. However, the Expo development and the associated infrastructural provision enhanced the city's economic attractiveness to both external and internal capital. The next section examines the Expo, its economic influence and the opportunities it offers Seville and Andalusia.

EXPO 92 – an internationalisation strategy

Expo 92, held in Seville between April and October 1992, was the first event of its kind to be staged in Europe since 1958, when Brussels was the host, and only the fourth world-wide in the last four decades. Ostensibly, the event marked the fifth centenary of the discovery of America, but the significance of Expo 92 is more than as a temporary, albeit high profile, event. Its impact extended far beyond the boundaries of the Expo site. The Expo acted as a catalyst for the comprehensive modernisation of Seville's physical and tele-communications infrastructure. The Expo site would continue to be used as a prestigious science and technology complex. This innova-tive and ambitious scheme aimed to capitalise on the international attention and kudos gained from hosting such a global event and to exploit fully the new developments, on and off-site, associated with it (Dawson 1992).

The Expo took place on the previously undeveloped Isla de la Cartuja which lies on the west bank of the original course of the Guadalquivir river, on the other side from the city centre. It was an appropriate venue. Columbus prepared for his first voyage to America from the monastery which stands on the site and was restored for the Expo. The Expo relied primarily on central govern-ment finance. A government-appointed Commissioner General was the Expo's senior executive. The 'Sociedad Estatal para la Exposición Universal Sevilla 92, Sociedad Anónima' (State Corporation for the

92 Seville Expo), operating under the Commissioner-General, prepared, organised and managed the Expo. The site underwent massive
development. Over a hundred pavilions were constructed by partici-
pating countries, international organisations, the seventeen Autonomous Communities of Spain and the organisers themselves. Some
remained as permanent features. The high architectural level attained
by many of the pavilions reflected the involvement of many of the
world's leading architects.

An extensive network of cultural, sporting and leisure facilities
was also developed. These included an open-air auditorium, a
'Palenque' (an innovative air-conditioned marquee), mini-theatres,
an open-air cinema, an 'Olympic' stadium and watersport facilities.
The arts and leisure facilities hosted a number of complementary
programmes of activities encompassing theatre, music, dance, film,
street performances and sporting events. The Expo's high-quality
entertainment schedule and its new infrastructure overflowed into
the city. The Expo bequeathed to Seville its first opera house and the
Lope de Vega theatre (a legacy of the 1929 Exhibition) and the
cathedral hosted important cultural events. Despite the massive
public investment on the site, the organisers hoped that an anticipated eighteen million visitors and thirty-six million visits would
ensure that the Expo broke even. In the event, there were forty
million visits and, whatever the final balance sheet reveals, the Expo
has enhanced the future development prospects of the Cartuja site
and its potential as an economic resource for Seville and Andalusia.

Infrastructure development

Expo 92 had an impact far beyond the boundaries of the Isla de la
Cartuja. It acted as a catalyst for a massive programme of infrastructure development. This long-awaited transformation of the physical
and telecommunications infrastructure in the city and its region
which elsewhere would occur only after decades of evolution was
completed in just a few years. As a result, a region whose infrastructure was typical of the least developed regions of the Community
now has an infrastructure more appropriate to develop a modern
economy. It has a much improved road, rail and air transport system
which, together with a state-of-the-art telecommunications infrastructure, enhances the accessibility of Andalusia, and especially

Seville, to the European economic core. In accordance with national and regional economic development policy these projects, at the least, ensure that the city and its region are not excluded from the benefits of European integration because of inadequate infra-structural capacity.

Although Seville lies at the centre of the developed infrastructural framework and is the focus for new resources, the infrastructural investments and the Proyecto Cartuja are linked to an economic development strategy for Andalusia as a whole. They are not intended to develop the regional core at the expense of the periphery. However, some commentators (e.g. Cruz *et al.*, 1985) question the strategy, fearing that it will accentuate existing divisions between the relatively prosperous western part of Andalusia, particularly Seville, and the economically disadvantaged and geographically remote eastern sector.

Paying for development

The hierarchy of government in Spain and the division of functions along horizontal rather than vertical lines of responsibility, means that development costs are shared according to the proportion of works deemed to be of local, regional or national significance. The breakdown of estimated costs in 1988 of road, rail, air and infra-structural expenditure between regional/national government and the Sevilla municipal authority was in the ratio of 5:1. European funding has also played a key role. Seville has benefited substantially from Spain's entry into the European Community. Andalusia is an Objective 1 region under the EC's structural funds. But it has exploited its status and has had considerable success in attracting more ERDF and ESF resources, in total, than any other of Spain's Autonomous Communities. Seville's role as the Andalusian capital and as the hub of the region's road, rail and telecommunications infrastructure biased resources in its favour.

EC structural fund support for Andalusia now forms part of the agreed Community Support Framework (CSF) for Objective 1 regions in Spain. The CSF is divided into a series of 'sub-frameworks'; one multi-regional framework and a framework for each of the Objective 1 regions, including Andalusia. The multi-regional framework totals 10.9 billion ECU with EC contributions of 5.7 billion

ECU. The agreed regional framework for Andalusia provides 2.1 billion ECU, of which EC contributions total over 1 billion ECU. Matching funding under this programme comes primarily from the regional government. The resources are set against a series of key development objectives. These include infrastructural developments to further improve the accessibility of remoter towns in Andalusia and links between the eastern and western sectors of the region. Support to industry and the artisan sector is also significant. The programme aims to address the traditional lack of productive dynamism in small and medium-sized enterprises and to tackle the spatial and sectoral concentration of activity.

Andalusia has also secured resources under the National Programme of Community Interest for Motorways (NPCIM) in Spain. The Programme, co-financed equally by national government and the EC to the tune of 135 billion pesetas, is divided between four major projects with the largest single expenditure (52 billion pesetas) directed at the motorway linking Seville and Madrid. The STAR programme, which assists the development of less-favoured regions by improving their access to advanced telecommunications systems, has also benefited Andalusia and Seville; 16 billion pesetas has been invested under the programme in Andalusia.

There are three key categories of infrastructure developments which have transformed Seville's accessibility; physical communication projects in Seville and its metropolitan area, similar projects in the wider region and telecommunication developments.

Physical communication projects in the Seville metropolitan area

Within Seville, a new road network links up with the city's existing radial system, developed after lying dormant (as plans) for many years. The network also includes the ambitious construction of seven new bridges over the Guadalquivir river and its new canal. There was a tripartite agreement between MOPU (the central government's Ministry of Public Works), the Andalusian Regional Government and the Municipality of Seville for the construction of the outer ring road. Because of their distinctly local function, the inner ring roads are the direct responsibility of the Municipality. All these road projects accord with proposals in the General Urban Development Plan for Seville.

A four-way public-sector partnership underpins developments which have remodelled the city's existing rail network. The three tiers of government together with RENFE (the National Railway Company) co-operated to provide the city with a modern and efficient rail system. The project capitalises on the strengths of the existing facilities whilst eliminating their obsolete features. Developments incorporate an inner city line for the exclusive use of passengers and centralises all rail services at a new central station, the Santa Justa Railway Station. The new station replaced pre-existing rail terminals at Plaza de Armas and San Bernardo. It provides a new focus of activity in a previously neglected part of the city.

Many of the millions of visitors to the Expo arrived by air. Increasing the capacity of Seville's airport was, therefore, a priority. Under the auspices of the Ministry of Transport, Tourism and Communications (MTTC) the airport was expanded and reorganised, with a new terminal building and a cargo terminal to handle goods traffic generated by the Expo. Other important developments have also taken place in the city. The Expo induced some of the projects whilst others were accelerated in the rush to have the city in pristine condition by 1992. These included private-sector developments to provide new accommodation for participants and visitors to the Expo, the rehabilitation of parts of the historic city centre and a major renovation programme to restore the city's architectural legacy. The Consejeria de Cultura of the Junta de Andalucía largely co-ordinated and financed the last programme.

Physical communication projects in the region

Major strategic infrastructural links, which focus on Seville, have emerged rapidly throughout Andalusia. Creating a comprehensive regional road network permits faster intra-regional and inter-regional journey times. The new arterial road network provides more effective connections between Seville and the other major urban centres in Andalusia and provides better access for Seville and Andalusia to other major road networks in Spain and beyond. Significantly, the overwhelming majority of ERDF resources have been targeted at the modernisation and improvement of the regional road infrastructure. The motorway project linking Seville, Granada and Baza received the largest ERDF support in Andalusia, 4 billion pesetas. Moreover, the NPCIM-sponsored project will complete a strategic road axis connecting Seville to Madrid and Barcelona and link them through France to the European core.

The development of the new high-speed rail link between Seville and Madrid has the highest international profile. By reducing travel times between Madrid and Seville to three hours it gives Seville close surface travel links to the national capital for the first time. The Seville–Malaga line has also undergone improvements to cut travel times between the two cities to two hours. These improved road and rail communications enhanced the accessibility of Expo 92 to visitors, but they also provide Seville with an important economic resource for the 1990s and into the next century.

Telecommunications

Expo 92 acted as a catalyst for major public investment which transformed Seville's telecommunications infrastructure. The telecommunications projects are impressive and ambitious and are intended to make Seville an important international communication node. The city now possesses a digital network and complementary fibre-optic cable routes, which link the major urban centres throughout Andalusia to each other and to international telecommunications systems. An International Communications Centre (ICC) for voice, data and video transmissions is a key component of the new infra-structure. The ICC incorporates an automatic international exchange, with digital technology, linked to an Integrated Services Digital Network to handle continental and global traffic, a teleport and a satellite communications complex (Sociedad Estatal Expo 92 and IFA 1989).

The speed of the transformation of Seville's infrastructure is exceptional. However, the future economic benefits that may accrue to the city from heavy investment programmes are not the only potential legacy of Expo 92. Innovative plans for the post-Expo use of the Isla de la Cartuja will also exert a considerable economic and social influence. Fully to exploit the Expo event and the infrastructural transformation accompanying it for the economic benefit of Seville and Andalusia, the site is being partially reused as an internationally significant science and technology complex. Designated as 'Proyecto Cartuja 93', the scheme is the single most important economic development initiative in Seville.

Proyecto Cartuja 93

Expo 92 bequeathed a high-quality urban environment complete with parklands, sporting facilities and prestigious buildings providing a unique economic resource. The site lies at the heart of an advanced system of transport and telecommunications. These valuable resources will be exploited more fully by the Proyecto Cartuja 93. This joint venture, a central plank of economic development strategies for Seville and Andalusia, brings together the Instituto de Fomento de Andalucia, the state agency in charge of the Expo, Seville local authorities and expert advisers from Spain and abroad. A strategic priority of the proposals is to bridge the technological and skills gap in the Andalusian economy. Despite capacity shortages which frustrate its ability consistently to generate products with high added value, Andalusia has comparative advantages in several economic sectors. Cartuja 93 plays a key part in incorporating technological advances in key sectors of the local economy. These include the traditional agricultural and fishery industries and tourism as well as the newly evolving industries in aerospace, electronic components for cars and medium-tech telecommunications equipment. This is vital if these industries are to flourish in an increasingly competitive European market-place since, these sectors would help tackle the severe, region-wide problems of unemployment.

As part of this overall strategy, the Cartuja science and technology complex forms the regional focus for research and development. Regional centres complementing this role include the Malaga Technology Park, where an electronics, computer and telecommunications production complex has developed around Acatel, Siemens and Fujitsu enterprises, the Cadiz Bay Area, the Biotechnological Area in Cordoba and the Renewable Energy Complex in Almeria. The presence of scientific institutions, educational and research centres and innovative companies should place the Cartuja complex at the cutting edge of research and development. Attracting private-sector research is critical to its success, and many multinational companies have research institutes there. There is explicit consensus between the regional government, as owner of the land, and the Municipality of Seville, as the planning authority, to maintain the site as an area of the highest environmental quality and to keep out incompatible activities. At the local level, an important aspect of the Cartuja proposals is to ensure its integration into the city. The mixed-use diversity of La Cartuja should ease its assimilation into Seville. The Cartuja site will not just be a scientific-technological complex, it will incorporate parkland, sporting areas, museums and exhibition areas and cultural facilities.

Whether Cartuja 93's imaginative initiatives, and the infrastructural investments beyond, will succeed in their primary aim of stimulating region-wide economic development or make sufficient impact on Andalusia's acute unemployment is an open question. Seville clearly stands to gain from Expo 92, Cartuja 93 and the related investments. However, important questions remain concerning the social and spatial distribution of benefits and costs.

Future scenarios and issues

Seville has undergone rapid and extensive physical change inducing economic expansion and important social consequences. The massive infrastructural developments – Expo 92, the innovative plans for Cartuja in its aftermath and the heavy investment of regional, national and EC resources – all influence Seville's future and its impact on the wider regional economy. Also, its status as the regional capital is likely to ensure a continued concentration of resources and economic and political activity in the city.

If economic expansion can be sustained it should further reduce the numbers of unemployed, and the increased use of new technologies in the production process is likely to raise income levels. Nevertheless, the level of unemployment is very high and, although falling, is likely to remain far above EC averages for the foreseeable future. Moreover, experience elsewhere indicates that the distribution of the benefits of economic growth is highly selective and that the impact of any 'trickle-down' effect is, at best, only marginal. Economic growth will exclude those unable to compete effectively in an overcrowded labour market. This trend, so apparent in many cities throughout Europe, is likely to be exacerbated in Seville. Consequently, an increasingly polarised social structure may emerge within the city.

There are also distributional issues, from a spatial perspective, at the regional level. The concentration of resources in Seville, despite the intention to promote an integrated regional development strategy, may further widen intra-regional imbalances in economic growth and standards of living. For instance, in relation to the regional economic impact of Expo 92, Cruz *et al.* (1985) have argued that commercial logic dictates that business activity will concentrate in the areas with most economic advantages. In the case of Andalusia, the centre of economic gravity already lies in the western provinces, and especially in Seville. Despite initiatives to improve access to less attractive areas, physical and telecommunications infrastructural activity has concentrated in Seville. The economy of Seville is likely to receive a further boost and spatial disparities, associated with regional imbalances, will widen. It is too early, however, to predict these trends with any certainty. The regional development dimension to the Proyecto Cartuja strategy, with its emphasis on enhancing technological capacity in the existing economic structure, may prove an effective means of supporting the regional economy on a sectoral rather than a spatial axis.

Despite the distributional implications of the developments in Seville, the city has many assets which suggest it has a bright economic future. In addition to the wealth of infrastructural provision, the city's ability to link into the global telecommunications system and the unique economic impulse provided by Expo 92 and Cartuja 93, the city also possesses many inherent advantages that may give it an economic edge in the evolving European urban hierarchy. Seville's dry climate, its access to the coast and attractive countryside, the outstanding architectural quality of the city imbued with its rich history, the wealth of Sevillean culture and the Andalusian lifestyle all contribute to a quality of urban life difficult to match anywhere in Europe.

With all these tangible and intangible advantages, Seville is well placed to attract free capital seeking a location in Andalusia or, potentially, in the Iberian peninsula and beyond. Moreover, the competitive situation for indigenous enterprises will be enhanced by improved communications and a more dynamic local economy. However, it is important to temper this optimism for the future of Seville with a certain degree of caution. We have already mentioned the tendency for 'succeeding' cities to encounter problems of increasing social polarisation. Other costs of success relate to rapidly rising land and property values which can exclude local people and, if not checked, raise important questions about who economic development is for (Dawson 1991). For instance, rising land and property values can have acutely adverse effects on local businesses and the provision of affordable housing. Higher costs of production, through higher rents or inflated unit labour costs, may force less competitive but local businesses – often meeting local needs – into closure. Equally, rising land values may force existing residents out of traditionally low-cost housing areas as new generations are unable to afford to buy or as property owners wish to redevelop for profit. There are already signs of this process evolving in the historic core of Seville where property prices have risen dramatically in recent years. The attraction of international capital and high-income employment to the city will, inevitably, exacerbate this trend. Imaginative approaches are needed to protect and promote the availability of affordable housing in areas most likely to be affected by rising land and property values, speculation and property development.

It is unlikely that contemporary developments will be sufficient to satisfy the demands of an overflowing labour market, especially as many of the unemployed lack appropriate skills. In addition to prestigious and high-profile initiatives and massive infrastructural projects, there is a need for economic intervention targeted directly at those who find it most difficult to secure employment.

Seville is at a critical juncture. Despite its geographical peripherality within Europe, the city has many advantages, and current developments enhance its capacity to acquire an important role in the future European urban hierarchy. At the same time, Seville and its region have acute structural weaknesses which present fundamental challenges to policy makers. If these challenges are not met social and spatial inequalities will widen and the quality of life will deteriorate for many.

References

Cruz, J. (1986), La Poblacíon de Sevilla, Ayuntamiento de Sevilla.

Cruz, J., Lopez, A. & Bernier, E. (1985), Informe Sobre las Repercusiones a Escala Regional de la Expo 92, Junta de Andalucía.

Dawson,J. (1991), 'Seville – A Sunny Future for Some', Town and Country Planning, 60 (5), 149–51.

Gabinetede Estudios Metropolitanos (1989), Directrices para la Coordinación Urbanística del Area Metropolitana de Sevilla, Avances I y II, Junta de Andalucía.

Lasarte, J. (1989), 'El Impulso de Sevilla y la Situación Económica de Andalucía', Estudios Regionales, 24, 167–177.

Oficina de Planificación Económica (1990), Coyuntura Económica de Andalucía en 1989, Junta de Andalucía.

Román, C. (1987), Sobre el Desarrollo Económico de Andalucía, Editorial Arguval.

Sociedad Estatal Para La Exposición Universal de 1992 & Instituto de Fomento de Andalucía (1989), Proyecto Cartuja 93: A Technological Development Project in Andalusia.

Conclusion: towards the entrepreneurial European city?

Alan Harding

The chapters in this book suggest that the process of decline which affected many of Europe's major metropolitan areas in the twenty years before the mid-1980s has, in many respects, been reversed. In the case-study cities examined here, the later 1980s appeared to herald a shift in metropolitan fortunes. There were clear signs of economic renaissance, population growth or stabilisation and greater vibrancy in cities as places to live in, work in and visit. Political and administrative change, although uneven, seemed to give cities greater political weight and a potentially critical role in the development of single-market Europe.

In the same period, the debate about major European cities began to change from one which was inward-looking and problem-orientated to one which looked outward and concentrated upon the potential of cities in the regional, national and international economy. Looking ahead to the millennium, the boldest scenario suggests that major cities will become even more important to the unified Europe. This scenario would predict that, in the new Europe of the regions which many argue will result from the single market, nation states will have fewer economic levers to pull than ever before. Increasing global economic interdependence will mean that key macro-economic decisions will need to be co-ordinated at supranational level. National economic performance will therefore depend more on the performance of supranational institutions like the European Commission at one level and on the power of key urban areas in international markets on the other. The role of national governments will undergo further change as the global and local levels of decision-making become more important.

This scenario suggests that cities will compete vigorously with one another for investment and trade. Sophisticated urban development strategies are likely to become more important in determining the winners in this competition, not least because the location factors which once tied economic activities firmly to particular areas are breaking down in the face of innovations in electronic and physical communication systems. The successful cities, increasingly linked together in international network organisations, could become the key decision-making centres where the relationship between localities and the increasingly global economy is managed. In short, the years to 2000 will be an age of entrepreneurial cities.

The case-studies provide a wealth of insights as to how likely it is that this scenario will be realised. They are also valuable in suggesting the many factors which will influence the future balance of power in urban Europe and the opportunities and dilemmas that key urban decision-makers will face in the years to 2000. The remainder of this chapter addresses four sets of questions, all linked to the issue of urban entrepreneurialism, that are likely to be central to the urban debate of the 1990s.

The first asks whether the notion of the 'entrepreneurial city' is more symbolic than substantive. Does this term merely reflect the changing rhetoric of city-boosters? Or do wider economic and political changes encourage urban decision-makers to behave more competitively? Second, can the 'game' of urban entrepreneurialism be played by any participant, with any result? Or can urban decision-makers merely tinker at the margins of forces that lie far beyond their control? Third, are there particular configurations of administrative, political and cultural conditions that encourage the development of effective strategies to induce desired urban changes? And finally, does the case-study evidence suggest that the competitive quest for growth can be managed so as to provide a balance between economic, social and environmental goals? Or are the 1990s likely to see increased conflict over how cities are run and for whom?

The entrepreneurial city: myth or reality?

An entrepreneurial city can be defined as one where key interest groups in the public, private and voluntary sectors develop a commitment to realising a broadly consensual vision of urban development, devise appropriate structures for implementing this vision and mobilise both local and non-local resources to pursue it. There are obvious differences between the case-study cities in national and local institutional structures, in how clearly city visions are articulated, the key interest groups supporting development strategies and the level of consensus achieved. On all of the above criteria, Montpellier, Rotterdam and Birmingham – with Frankfurt and Lyon not far behind – would have to be classed as the most entrepreneurial.

Nonetheless the case-studies show clearly that the movement over the last decade has been in the same broad direction, towards greater entrepreneurialism, more intense inter-urban competition and the conscious promotion of place-specific development strategies and projects. This general shift in emphasis suggests that key decision-makers did not simultaneously undergo a spontaneous and unrelated conversion to competitive impulses. Rather, as suggested in the Introduction, they were reacting to common threats and opportunities.

The economic and political context in which urban decision-makers are acting in the 1990s is fundamentally different to, and in many ways harsher than, that of the 1970s. Economic recessions and the globalisation of the economy have not only affected the economic fortunes of urban areas, they have had important implications for the organisation and roles of national governmental systems too. During the 1980s, Europe's national governments came under growing pressure to respond to the economic, social and environmental consequences of the restructuring of the international economic order but found that traditional strategies were increasingly ineffectual.

At the most general level, globalisation meant that national economic fortunes were more and more dependent on international trading conditions. A dash for growth, pursued by a single government through expansionary macroeconomic policies, became increasingly difficult to achieve. National governments have increasingly recognised the limits to country-specific demand management. With varying degrees of enthusiasm they have seen one important way forward on macroeconomic policy to lie in greater cross-national co-operation, principally through the widening and strengthening of the EC.

At the same time, no national government, whatever its political philosophy, has been able to avoid making difficult decisions about the balance of priorities between economic and social welfare policies in periods of sluggish economic growth and perceived public expenditure constraints. These trends meant that cities, and particularly the least privileged groups within them, have been less cushioned than before by national governments from the effects of wider economic change. The policy vacuum has been filled, to varying but significant extents, by local decision-makers. Whilst the case-studies suggest that the route to greater urban activism varies considerably, in almost all cases responsibility for the promotion of urban change – particularly through economic development – has been shifting from national to local agencies.

A clear pointer from the case-studies that urban leaders are no longer content to leave national governments to mediate between them and the external world is provided by the rapid development of cross-national city and regional network organisations. The growth of these networks suggests a determination amongst key decision-makers in cities like Montpellier, Amsterdam, Lyon, Rotterdam and Birmingham to lead in the development of Europe-wide, inter-city relationships and to enhance the European profiles of their respective cities. Often encouraged by European Commission Directorates, these networks act as fora for the transfer of knowledge and best practice and for stimulating innovation in the development of policies and projects. They also act as catalysts in inter-urban economic co-operation, as mechanisms for lobbying at the national and EC levels and help to manage the EC's relations with cities and regions in member states.

Quite what the ultimate importance of urban networks will be in an integrated European economy is open to question. For the moment, the fact of their existence is at least as important as the effects of their actions. They give an interesting insight into the way cross-national relations might be managed in an era in which the character and roles of nation states are likely to be in a state of flux. They also present fascinating parallels with the time before the great age of nation-state-building, when independent city states tended to form themselves into trading networks for the purposes of managing economic and cultural relations. If the single market does bring about the development of a Europe of the regions, major city networking organisations are likely to have an increasingly important role.

Strategic choices and European urban change

The entrepreneurial city is a reality, albeit an often ambiguous one. And it increasingly has an European orientation. But can the strategic choices made by urban decision-makers really make much difference to the nature, pace and geographical distribution of development in the context of increasingly global economic forces? Whilst this question has constantly exercised the minds of policy-makers, the experience of the case-study cities sheds some light on this critical, complex issue.

The case that strategic choices can increasingly affect urban development patterns rests on a wider argument about the factors which influence the locational decisions of businesses. Traditionally, the areas with greatest economic potential were those which had good access to fuel supplies, raw materials, capital, a ready supply of unskilled and semi-skilled labour and large local markets. But these natural advantages, shared by established metropolitan areas in the European core, have declined with the development of new information technologies and advanced telecommunications and transportation systems. Such innovations offer greater freedom of locational choice, at least in principle, because they can help overcome the problem of distance.

The case-studies suggest that modern businesses are increasingly influenced by new locational factors more relevant to the information age. They depend on good quality higher education institutions to provide the skilled labour and the technological innovations that can feed into local economies. They seek out urban areas with a good quality of life – in residential, cultural and environmental terms – which can attract and retain skilled and potentially mobile workers and provide a magnet for visitors. They require good access to modern communications facilities such as advanced telecommunications, international airports, high-speed trains and efficient motorway networks.

The common thread running through these locational factors is that, compared to the fortune involved in the distribution of natural resources, they are heavily influenced by strategic decision-making and investment. One indication of this is the considerable lobbying that interest groups in Amsterdam, Rotterdam, Lyon, Brussels, Frankfurt and Seville, for example, have put into ensuring that the developing European high-speed train system serves their cities. The planned expansion of airport facilities in Birmingham, Lyon, Seville, Amsterdam, Frankfurt, Brussels and Milan are another, since they are designed to enhance their cities' attractiveness to producers of low-bulk, high value-added goods and their accessibility to visitors, particularly business tourists.

Does this mean that in future there will be no comparatively advantaged cities, only carefully planned and self-willed ones? The case-studies suggest not. The examples of Frankfurt, Montpellier, Lyon and Milan present clear evidence of rapid development and economic recovery beyond the traditional European core. But there is still a clear gap between the experiences of major metropolitan areas, based on location. Businesses in all the urban regions of Europe do not compete on a level playing-field. Despite the evidence of economic decentralisation and the growing importance of new locational factors in the new core of Europe, historical development trajectories remain important to the current and future potential of cities.

A comparison of the peripheral cities of Dublin and Seville with other more centrally-located cities suggests that it is a mistake to assume that the balance of power in urban Europe to 2000 can change more quickly than it has in the last decade. In Seville there has been a determined attempt by national and local public agencies and the EC to modernise the city and provide better physical and telecommunications links to the rest of Europe. Much the same has happened in Dublin, albeit on a smaller scale. The process of economic reconcentration in the cities of the European core, how-ever, has triggered far more rapid development than that achieved so far in these two peripheral cities.

The quality of urban life, educational infrastructures and commu-nications technologies have become more important. But they are bound up in complex ways with the sheer size and economic power of Europe's dominant metropolitan centres. In an increasingly com-petitive environment, the major cities of the European core retain significant advantages. At the political level, the public sectors of the richer core countries find it easier to finance the improvements needed to help cities take advantage of new locational factors. The examples from the Netherlands, where programmes for supporting the international gateway roles of Amsterdam and Rotterdam are well advanced, give a clear indication that national as well as local policies are increasingly targeting key cities as economic assets.

In comparison to the level of infrastructural investment taking place within particular countries, the support made available through the one mechanism for the redistribution of public resources across national boundaries – EC programmes – is relatively small. Peripheral cities in the poorer European countries are therefore disadvantaged when it comes to public investment. They are doubly disadvantaged in that the technological and infrastructural innovations which facilitate greater freedom of locational choice tend to be applied first and most extensively in areas where market activity is already most densely concentrated – in the expanded EC core.

This does not mean that changes will not take place in the European urban hierarchy. It is possible, for instance, that the cities discussed in this book are outstripping others within their respective countries. On a wider canvas, the development of market economies in the former Eastern Block countries is creating a potentially profitable eastern European periphery. At the very least, this will enhance competition between these countries and the current EC periphery and could ultimately lead to the economic gravity of Europe shifting further eastward.

None the less, the case-studies suggest that both political and market factors will continue to favour the strong metropolitan areas of the expanding European core. These cities are more able to improve the climate for investment and economic growth because of the relative buoyancy of national and local resources, their continued locational strengths and the sheer economic weight which they have accrued over the years. The best pointers to patterns of urban development in the medium term remain the realities of uneven development in the Europe of today. Thus cities like Brussels, Frankfurt and Amsterdam will continue to be comparatively advantaged for some time to come.

Organising for urban entrepreneurialism

Urban entrepreneurialism, not surprisingly, cannot produce miracles. Key decision-makers must work with the materials they have available. They have to acknowledge the legacy of earlier investment and development patterns and accept that the market will continue to favour some cities more than others. There are no magic solutions to urban problems, nor any foolproof strategies or policy instruments which can guarantee development. The case-studies presented a very wide range of alternative policy choices, each geared to the particular constraints and opportunities of particular cities. They ranged from infrastructural development (roads, airports, high-speed trains, light rapid transport systems, telecommunications and cable), through high-tech development (transport logistics, science parks), to tourism initiatives (including fairs, exhibition and conference centres), cultural policies (museums, galleries, festivals) and flagship physical development projects. Given the need for sensitivity to local problems and potentials, do the case-studies suggest that certain sets of political and organisational arrangements are more effective than others? This is clearly another big question for urban decision-makers. It is also difficult to answer unambiguously since it is difficult to separate the effects of conscious development policies, other public sector programmes, the legacies of urban economic history and the effects of location.

There is huge variation amongst the case-study cities in the way various agencies and interest groups have been linked to the promotion of urban development. But there are a number of considerations which appear to enhance the possibility of success. Not all of these considerations were satisfied in a single city. In various combinations, however, they have helped to develop more coherent forms of what might be called local governance; that is, the integration of the wide range of public and private bodies whose efforts are needed to promote change. Development strategies are more likely to succeed where there is a strong local administration, possessing a wide range of resources and powers and steered by a strong, stable and visionary political leadership. Also important is the pattern of relations between local administrations and the private sector. In many cases, these often led to the development of novel public-private partnership organisations. Strong local public and private-sector leadership also helped smooth access to non-local sources of public and private-sector investment.

National government resources remain important to development strategies. They appear to be more effective when channelled through local agencies than when administered directly, on a sectoral basis, by national departments. This emerged clearly from the case of Brussels, where the internationalisation of the city has largely been led by Belgium's national government to the detriment of local housing and social conditions and the city's cultural and architectural traditions. European Community resources are also becoming more important, particularly in peripheral cities that stand to gain most from EC regional policy but also in those more centrally-located cities where local administrations are well geared up to lobby for and access funds. Birmingham is a good illustration of the latter.

Also important, although much more problematic, are relations between sub-national levels of government. There were numerous examples amongst the case-studies of difficult relations between central city municipalities and their neighbouring suburbs. These were often exacerbated by local tax regimes which encouraged municipalities to compete against each other for development and by administrative boundaries that are now too narrowly drawn to make economic sense. Given this pattern of inter-municipal conflict, and the difficulties it generates for city-regional planning, regional tiers of administration appeared to be taking on added importance. The studies of Amsterdam, Rotterdam, Brussels, Frankfurt, Milan and Seville give an indication of the pressures to create appropriate city-regional decision-making structures.

A strong sense of regional culture appeared to improve the potential for consensus amongst key players. The deep south culture of Montpellier was the best example. But in Milan, Lyon and Birmingham too, a sense of rivalry with national capitals served to focus the minds of decision-makers on their cities, needs and potentials. Conversely, in Brussels, the continuing tensions between two linguistic communities and a national government which is primarily concerned with the city's international role, make it difficult to achieve a consensus about the appropriate role of the city.

Irrespective of the pattern of organisational and interest group arrangements, one key consideration emerged. There are no short cuts to success. Clearly focused and sustained investment over a long period of time is needed. Montpellier's spectacular development might owe something to chance; the arrival of IBM, new locational advantages. But it has been guided very carefully by a consistent and well-resourced package of policy initiatives developed over a fifteen-year period.

The urban agenda towards 2000

The case-studies offer ample evidence that the dominant urban agenda in the 1980s and early 1990s centred on the promotion of economic growth and competition between cities – increasingly at the European level. As the last section argued, this approach partially served the interests of many public and private agencies and interests at local, regional, national and even supra-national levels. A variety of inter-governmental and public–private coalitions for urban redevelopment emerged, sharing the assumptions that the fruits of economic growth would be diffused widely or that the economic costs of inaction would be greater than that of action.

However, it is clear that the development-at-all-costs approach was associated with an array of negative social and environmental effects. In none of the case-study cities did renewed economic development translate easily into the regeneration of local labour markets. Indeed, economic growth strategies tended to be associated with growing income polarisation, deepening social segregation, higher volumes of commuting and, in the poorer sections of cities, stubbornly high levels of long-term unemployment. This was clearly linked to the widespread trend toward dual labour markets described in the Introduction, itself driven by economic globalisation and technological change.

Amsterdam stands out as a clear example of a metropolitan area which can share a number of these contradictory characteristics: rapid employment growth in leading sectors; deepening integration into the global economy; growing levels of international investment; growing social marginalisation and segregation, particularly between city and suburb; and persistently high rates of structural unemployment, limited mainly to areas of the central city. But such trends were common and particularly acute in cities like Brussels, Frankfurt and Montpellier which had developed strong internationalisation strategies. Immigrants, and ethnic minority communities in particular, emerged as the group which gained least from the positive economic experience of the later 1980s. There were worries in many cities that unless ways could be found of integrating immigrants into the socio-economic mainstream, higher birth-rates amongst ethnic minority families would mean that this group would form a growing proportion of the urban disadvantaged.

The growing gap between rich and poor, combined with dwindling public investment in the provision of social rented housing, also had negative consequences for the housing market. The case-study cities in the Netherlands, where there was sustained investment in social rented housing during the 1970s and 1980s, are exceptional. In the rest the provision of affordable housing for low-income groups dropped dramatically, or even ceased, during the last decade. In some cases the process of inner city redevelopment had encouraged rising rents and land values and changes from residential to commercial uses, resulting in the displacement of low-income residents to social housing estates on the urban periphery. In others the poor quality, older rented housing of the inner-city remained the residential base for the bulk of the urban poor. In both cases, the concentration of those groups with the bleakest employment prospects into housing which was either sub-standard or badly served by transport and community facilities generated substantial social problems and tensions. In Lyon and Brussels, amongst others, this even resulted in outbreaks of violent social disorder.

Growing economic success also has a severe impact on the urban environment. A combination of economic development, increasing personal mobility and over-reliance on the private car had led to severe traffic congestion, most clearly in Milan, Frankfurt, Amsterdam, Birmingham and Brussels. This resulted in growing pollution levels and damage to the environment. It triggered responses which ranged from the desperate (selective traffic bans), through the environmentally dubious (provision of more road infrastructure) to the environmentally enlightened (investment in public transport to reduce traffic volumes).

The developing consciousness about the social and environmental costs of growth meant that the dominant urban agenda of the 1980s and early 1990s was already being questioned in some of the case-study cities. The development of the Dutch social renewal programme, as pioneered in Rotterdam, and the French Government's *contrat d'agglomeration* initiative indicated growing concern with the effects of contemporary development trends on marginalised social groups. There were also signs, particularly in Frankfurt, Amsterdam, Birmingham and Milan, that environmental issues were assuming greater importance. Whether social and environmental considerations will percolate through to the key groups that had supported competitive development strategies remains an open question. There is little doubt, though, that the pressure for a modified approach with a stronger social and environmental agenda will grow in the current decade.

The urban agenda of the 1990s will be heavily contested amongst different economic and social interests. The key decisions that will affect relations within and amongst Europe's major cities will be highly political. The stakes are high. Potentially severe and even explosive tensions could arise if highly internationalised, competitive development strategies fail to encourage a greater sense of urban social cohesion. The most hopeful scenario is that a wide range of interests can coalesce around the idea that improvements in the quality of urban life for all – an increasingly crucial economic as well as social consideration – can satisfy a wide range of demands and needs. The more pessimistic scenario is that a more narrow range of interests, driven by increased inter-urban competition, will continue to favour the pursuit of development at any cost. The hope of this book is that the issues raised in these two alternative scenarios become the subject of a healthy debate on the future shape and management of European cities.